LET'S STUDY
REVELATION

Conews Van Til - _Presuppontunal_ Apologetics
genre - HisToRICAL, Poetic, Prophecy, etc

7 divisions 1-3, 4-8 usl, 8:2-11, 12-14
15-16, 17-19, 20-22

AMILL position in book

In the same series:

Series Editor: SINCLAIR B. FERGUSON

Let's Study

REVELATION

Derek Thomas

THE BANNER OF TRUTH TRUST

THE BANNER OF TRUTH TRUST
3 Murrayfield Road, Edinburgh EH12 6EL, UK
P.O. Box 621, Carlisle, PA 17013, USA

*

© Derek Thomas 2003
First Published 2003
Reprinted 2008

ISBN-13: 978 0 85151 827 5

*

Typeset in 11/12.5 pt Ehrhardt MT at the
Banner of Truth Trust, Edinburgh

Printed in the U.S.A. by
Versa Press, Inc.,
East Peoria, IL

To

RALPH AND BARBARA DAVIS
WOODLAND PRESBYTERIAN CHURCH,
HATTIESBURG, MISSISSIPPI

Contents

Publisher's Preface

Let's Study Revelation is part of a series of books which explain and apply the message of Scripture. The series is designed to meet a specific and important need in the church. While not technical commentaries, the volumes comment on the text of a biblical book; and, without being merely lists of practical applications, they are concerned with the ways in which the teaching of Scripture can affect and transform our lives today. Understanding the Bible's message and applying its teaching are the aims.

Like other volumes in the series, *Let's Study Revelation* seeks to combine explanation and application. Its concern is to be helpful to ordinary Christian people by encouraging them to understand the message of the Bible and apply it to their own lives. The reader in view is not the person who is interested in all the detailed questions which fascinate the scholar, although behind the writing of each study lies an appreciation for careful and detailed scholarship. The aim is exposition of Scripture written in the language of a friend, seated alongside you with an open Bible.

Let's Study Revelation is designed to be used in various contexts. It can be used simply as an aid for individual Bible study. Some may find it helpful to use in their devotions with husband or wife, or to read in the context of the whole family.

In order to make these studies more useful, not only for individual use but also for group study in Sunday School classes and home, church or college, study guide material will be found on pp. 185–202. Sometimes we come away frustrated rather than helped by group discussions. Frequently that is because we have been encouraged to discuss a passage of Scripture which we do not understand very well in the first place. Understanding must always be the foundation for enriching discussion and for thought-ful, practical application. Thus, in addition to the exposition of Revelation, the additional material provides questions to encourage personal thought and study, or to be used as discussion starters. The Group Study Guide divides the material into thirteen sections and provides direction for leading and participating in group study and discussion.

Acknowledgements

A sked to contribute a volume to the *Let's Study* series by the Banner of Truth Trust, I must admit to some tension when I discovered that I was invited to submit the volume on Revelation! Why not a Gospel, or one of Paul's epistles? The truth is, I was then preaching my way through Revelation for the second time – on this occasion to the faithful members of First Presbyterian Church, Jackson, Mississippi, where I serve as Minister of Teaching. This occasion necessitated my taking large segments and traversing the book in 15 sermons.

There is a value in taking Revelation quickly: it keeps both preacher and listener away from the details! And it is in the details that trouble emerges! My aim in writing this volume has been to try to do something similar: move quickly and avoid trouble, thereby dispelling some of the fear that Christians often seem to have concerning this book. I have long since come to the conclusion that God does not intend his final word to the church to be intimidating. Revelation is a book for children! And there's more to that last sentence than meets the eye, for just as children relate to pictures better than to words, so Revelation is a picture book designed to *show* as much as to relate.

Various people have helped me in its production including Ruth Bennett, my long-suffering secretary at Reformed Theological Seminary where I (principally!) work, Marshall Brown, my one-time Thornwell Scholar and more recently Reformed University Ministry campus minister at the University of Alabama, John Tweeddale, my current Thornwell Scholar, Ligon Duncan, my friend and boss at First Presbyterian Church, and not least, Sinclair Ferguson who ruthlessly purged some of my tortuous sentences.

During the final stages of this volume, the seminary kindly gave me a sabbatical in order to help facilitate its completion. I am truly thankful to the Executive Board of the seminary and its current president, Dr Ric Cannada, for granting me this leave of absence.

The final pages of this book were written in the recently-vacated office of my friend and former colleague, Dr Ralph Davis. I know of no one I would sooner hear preach the Old Testament than Ralph, and the fact that I now occupy his former office is testimony, in part, to the hope that somehow I might acquire an ounce of his skill and wisdom!

Though we differ in our eschatological convictions, I regard Ralph and his wife Barbara as among the treasures that the Lord has passed my way. It is to them that I dedicate this book.

DEREK THOMAS
February 2003

Introduction

The book of Revelation is unlike almost anything else in the Bible. Almost – because there are a few precursors to the kind of thing we find in this final book of Scripture. Readers who have gone to the book of Daniel, for example, assured of uncovering some cracking good stories of faith and courage, find themselves (in the second half) adrift in a sea of visions that challenge the most ardent enthusiast!

Revelation is a *different kind of literature* from almost anything else that we find in Scripture. It is an 'apocalypse' – as the very first verse indicates (the Greek word *apokalupsis* means 'revelation') – an unveiling by God of things he wants the church to know in language and forms that quite simply dazzle and shock. In an age given to the primacy of the visual (films rather than books), this has a surprisingly contemporary feel about it. G. K. Chesterton once wrote in a child's picture book:

> *Stand up, and keep your childishness,*
> *Read all the pedant's creeds and strictures*
> *But don't believe in anything*
> *That can't be told in coloured pictures!*

Revelation is a book with pictures!

It begins harmlessly enough, with seven letters to seven churches. Harsh and encouraging things are said in the context of warnings – warnings of impending difficulty and hardship. This provides the introduction for the series of visions – by turns fantastic, horrific, grotesque and exquisitely beautiful – that make up the rest of the book. It is about the future – yes! But, it is also about the present – our present. Things unfold that describe for us (often employing Old Testament language) what we can expect when we live boldly for Christ in a world in which Satan is 'the prince of the power of the air'.

In the end, the goal is worship: of God, of Christ, by the church here on earth as well as in heaven. Praise songs bind the visions together, rejoicing as they do in God's sovereignty over every hostile and evil force.

WHEN WAS REVELATION WRITTEN?

Is this question really important? More than we might think! A date *after* the destruction of the temple in Jerusalem (70 AD), for example, will render it impossible to interpret its prophecies as predictive of this event, since it had already occurred.

The consensus of opinion amongst those who study these things has been, and continues to be, for a date in the mid-nineties of the first century, during the reign of the Emperor Domitian. However, devotees of a much earlier date – during the reign of Emperor Nero (c. 65 AD) – abound insisting, amongst other things, that Revelation 11:1–2 seem to indicate that the temple is still standing! Counter arguments are made which call attention to the fact that this temple is not Herod's temple, but the visionary temple described in the closing chapters of Ezekiel.

The view adopted in this book favours the majority opinion – a date in the last decade of the first century. In part, we adopt this view because many passages in Revelation seem to imply emperor worship. This suits Domitian's reign better than it does that of Nero. Letters exist, written some 15–20 years after Domitian's rule, suggesting that such was indeed the case (though the authenticity of these letters has also been questioned!).

Whether early or late, persecution is the context of this book – present and future – and, in part, Revelation is designed to strengthen those tempted to either despair or compromise. John, exiled on the island of Patmos, speaks of himself as being a '*brother and partner in the tribulation*' in the opening chapter (1:9).

WHICH VIEW OF REVELATION DOES THIS BOOK TAKE?

Does my view of the future (that is, whether I am '*premill*,' '*amill*,' or '*postmill*' to suggest but three possibilities—yes, others do exist!) prejudice the way I read Revelation? I use the word 'prejudice' because that is precisely what it does. It tells me, *in advance* what a passage *can* and *cannot* mean. We all have these prejudices and they govern the way we approach *everything*, not just the book of Revelation. The answer to this question, then, is 'Yes!'

To tell you, then, here in the Introduction, that I hold to one or other of these millennial views (and I do hold tenaciously to one of these views!) might well prejudice you from the start – a bit like knowing the score on a pre-recorded football match! Discovering that I hold to a premillenial understanding of the return of Jesus Christ (which I do not!) might lead some of you to close the book and read no further. Though it sounds naïve (and in some ways it is) I want the text itself to uncover this for you.

However, a part of me thinks that this information is necessary here. There is an inevitability that a grid of some kind will be employed as you read Revelation.

Hopefully, the exegesis of the text informs and reshapes this grid, but it is impossible to begin reading Revelation with a blank slate – that, in any case, would be a recipe for disaster.

PRE-, POST-, AND AMILLENIALISM: THE MAZE OF PROPHETIC THOUGHT

Without getting into cumbersome technicalities, I will outline some of the paradigms employed in the interpretation of Revelation.

The *first* issue to note concerns the scope of the prophecies of Revelation. Some interpreters (*preterists*) insist that most (if not all) the prophecies of this book relate to the events surrounding the destruction of the temple in 70 AD. This is an important issue and affects considerably how Revelation is understood. Its advantage lies in its ability to dismiss the weird and bizarre interpretations (of which there are many) in a single stroke. None of these prophecies relate to actual events in the future, apart from those specifically relating to Christ's return and the final judgment that follows it (though, there are some who even deny that Revelation speaks of this). Dating the book of Revelation *after* 70 AD makes this view problematic.

The *second* issue can be put like this: are we to expect, in some form or another, a span of history *on earth* following the return of Christ? Various viewpoints of varying complexity have answered this in the affirmative. Some (*historic premillennialists*) insist that following Christ's return, believers who have died will rise to meet Christ in the air, whilst believers who are alive at the time of Christ's coming will be transformed and glorified. Together, they will live *on earth* establishing a 'millennial' reign of Christ. Some insist that it will be exactly one thousand years in duration. Towards the end of this period, and before history culminates in the judgment of the Great White Throne, Satan will be released to deceive the nations and gather them together for the Battle of Gog and Magog.

Others (*Dispensationalists*, whether of the older or newer variety) divide this period into two segments, involving an initial (*secret*) 'rapture' of the saints from this earth for a period of seven years (during which time several prophetic fulfilments take place, including a period of tribulation), and a *consequent* 'coming' of Christ to begin his reign on earth.

The details of this last view can differ widely, but the principal point – that there will be some kind of existence on earth *following* Jesus' return – enables us to consider them as a group. The exegetical warrant for either a 'secret' rapture of the saints or a two-fold coming of Christ is non-existent. Besides which, it is questionable whether the New Testament envisions any existence on earth *following* his return.

The *third* issue relates to the quality of life, *Christian* life in particular, in the period immediately preceding Christ's return. Some (*postmillennialists*) see in Scripture, a time of unprecedented blessing and revival for the church just prior to Christ's return. The problem with this view is that Scripture appears to have a consistent testimony as to the presence of blessing *and evil* in the world until the end. In order to *downplay* the effect of such issues as the appearance of a personal Antichrist and the Battle of Armageddon – both of which in some form or other appear to describe particular manifestations of evil in the time immediately prior to the second coming, postmillennialists have tended to be drawn by the view that most of the prophecies of Revelation were fulfilled in 70 AD.

The *fourth* issue has to do with how we understand the individual prophecies to relate to each other. Some (*historicists*) understand them as stairs, each one building upon the previous one but distinct from it, thereby describing the course of history from the first century to the end. What we have in Revelation is, more or less, a chronological diary of future events, from which certain predictions can now be made as to what may happen in the future. Others (*futurists*) understand the prophecies as, in the main, predicting events that focus largely on the end and are therefore still future. Some, as we have already said, understand most (if not all) of the prophecies to have already occurred (*preterists*). Still others (*idealists*) regard the prophecies as descriptive of spiritual realities that are to be found in every age including our own.

You may already be suspicious as to where I come down (I have inserted negative remarks about some of these views already), but allow me to reveal my own grid as we unfold the text of Revelation together.

THE SHAPE OF THE BOOK OF REVELATION

Just think of the number seven and allow it to shape the way you see the book of Revelation. Inside the bookends of an introduction and conclusion, seven visions unfold. Think of it as repeating the same message (as 'flashbacks' might do in a film), but from different perspectives and with different goals. Thus:

VISION 1: The Church in Asia Minor. Actually, seven (!) churches, probably meant as typical of all churches everywhere at all times (Chapters 1–3).

VISION 2: Seven Seals. It begins with a vision of the throne of God. Each seal grows in intensity and clearly, at the seventh seal, we are at the day of judgment itself. (Chapters 4–7, including the opening of Chapter 8).

VISION 3: Seven Trumpets. As with the seven seals, there is an interlude between the sixth and seventh in which further visions are given (Chapters 8–11).

VISION 4: The Battle against Satan. A further pattern of seven unfolds. This is perhaps the key to the whole book of Revelation. It describes the real battle between God and Satan (Chapters 12–14).

VISION 5: Seven Bowls. Growing more intense in its description, the vision describes bowls of wrath poured upon the earth (Chapters 15–16).

VISION 6: The Downfall of Babylon. A section in which Christ systematically gains victory over every foe (Chapters 17–19).

VISION 7: The New Heaven and New Earth (Chapters 20–22); or, in table form:

VISION	CHAPTERS	CONTENT
1	1 – 3	Seven Churches
2	4 – 8:1	Seven Seals
3	8:2 – 11	Seven Trumpets
4	12 – 14	Battle against Satan
5	15 – 16	Seven Bowls
6	17 – 19	Downfall of Babylon
7	20 – 22	New Heaven and New Earth

Make a note of this page and return to it whenever the details of the visions get a little confusing.

And in case you need something to hold on to as you study this amazing book of Revelation, remember that at any point in the book, the message is about a *Great Throne*, a *Lamb* who is actually a Lion, and a fearsome *foe* who always threatens more than he can deliver and whose doom is certain. Keeping those three things in mind will keep you on track.

I

The Revelation of Jesus Christ

*T*he revelation of Jesus Christ, which God gave him to show to his servants the things that must soon take place. He made it known by sending his angel to his servant John, *²who bore witness to the word of God and to the testimony of Jesus Christ, even to all that he saw. ³ Blessed is the one who reads aloud the words of this prophecy, and blessed are those who hear, and who keep what is written in it, for the time is near.*

⁴ John to the seven churches that are in Asia:
Grace to you and peace from him who is and who was and who is to come, and from the seven spirits who are before his throne, ⁵ and from Jesus Christ the faithful witness, the firstborn of the dead, and the ruler of kings on earth.
To him who loves us and has freed us from our sins by his blood
⁶ and made us a kingdom, priests to his God and Father, to him be glory and dominion forever and ever. Amen. ⁷ Behold, he is coming with the clouds, and every eye will see him, even those who pierced him, and all tribes of the earth will wail on account of him. Even so. Amen.

⁸ "I am the Alpha and the Omega," says the Lord God, "who is and who was and who is to come, the Almighty."

⁹ I, John, your brother and partner in the tribulation and the kingdom and the patient endurance that are in Jesus, was on the island called Patmos on account of the word of God and the testimony of Jesus. ¹⁰ I was in the Spirit on the Lord's day, and I heard behind me a loud voice like a trumpet

¹¹ saying, "Write what you see in a book and send it to the seven churches, to Ephesus and to Smyrna and to Pergamum and to Thyatira and to Sardis and to Philadelphia and to Laodicea."

¹² Then I turned to see the voice that was speaking to me, and on turning I saw seven golden lampstands, ¹³ and in the midst of the lampstands one like a son of man, clothed with a long robe and with a golden sash around his chest. ¹⁴ The hairs of his head were white like wool, as white as snow. His eyes were like a flame of fire, ¹⁵ his feet were like burnished bronze, refined in a furnace, and his voice was like the roar of many waters. ¹⁶ In his right hand he held seven stars, from his mouth came a sharp two-edged sword, and his face was like the sun shining in full strength.

¹⁷ When I saw him, I fell at his feet as though dead. But he laid his right hand on me, saying, "Fear not, I am the first and the last, ¹⁸ and the living one. I died, and behold I am alive forevermore, and I have the keys of Death and Hades. ¹⁹ Write therefore the things that you have seen, those that are and those that are to take place after this. ²⁰ As for the mystery of the seven stars that you saw in my right hand, and the seven golden lampstands, the seven stars are the angels of the seven churches, and the seven lampstands are the seven churches' (Rev. 1: 1–20).

Many Christians find the book of Revelation intimidating. For some, it is the most difficult book in the Bible. The reasons lie in the later chapters rather than these opening ones. The first chapter of Revelation contains a vision of the sovereignty of God. More precisely, it is a vision of the majesty of Jesus Christ, '*The revelation of Jesus Christ, which God gave*' (1:1). It is God's last word to us about his Son. It is important to keep this focus clear: Revelation is about Jesus Christ. He is the key that unlocks its mysteries. What the Gospels give in spoken form, Revelation gives in pictorial form.

In some ways, Revelation is the outworking of what Jesus told Peter, 'On this rock I will build my church, and the gates of hell shall not prevail against it' (*Matt.* 16:18). If these words from Matthew comprise the still photograph, the Book of Revelation is the

Luke 1:44
Matt 19:14

movie. In a day when the visual and cinematic take precedence over the written word, the genre of Revelation seems particularly suitable.

Revelation is a book of pictures designed to appeal to the visual senses. As we turn over its pages, we are meant to be overwhelmed by its descriptions of the Saviour. Noting that the prevailing command in the book is not 'Listen!' but 'Look!' we are being introduced to the idea that Revelation is about *pictures* as well as about *words*.

The book of Revelation is meant to humble us by a vision of the absolute sovereignty of God over history: past, present, *and* future. There is nothing outside of God's control. Every power, every evil-power is subject to the rule of God. 'There is not a single inch of the whole terrain of our human existence', wrote Abraham Kuyper, 'over which Christ . . . does not proclaim, "Mine!"' This is the perspective of the last book of the Bible.

PROLOGUE

Just as the Bible begins with God (*Gen.* 1:1), so it ends with God (*Rev.* 1:1; 22:21). The focus is theological. It is a view of God that we are meant to reap from these closing pages. To a church facing persecution and death, the message they most needed to hear was one that assured them of a Helmsman, a Governor, a Transformer who would keep his people, no matter what. The prologue is meant to convey just that message.

The key word with which this book begins is *apokalupsis*! What we are about to study is in the nature of an apocalypse, that is to say, an unveiling, a revelation. The curtains are about to be pulled back to disclose sights and sounds almost too strange to relate. We are going to be transported to a different kind of literature from, say, the Gospels, or Paul's letters. But more of this later. For now, it is important to grasp that God is showing us something he wants his 'servants' (verse 1) to know.

Five things follow in quick succession in the opening three verses which give meaning to this revelation, or apocalypse:

i. As to its *source*, ultimately it is from God the Father. 'The revelation . . . which God gave' (1:1). These strange visions, with their gorgeous colours and vivid descriptive power, are not the product of a deranged, hallucinating mind. These are 'visions from God' (see *Ezek.* 1:1, margin). At the same time, the revelation comes from Jesus Christ. The opening verse wants us to appreciate the role Jesus always plays as a mediator between God and men. It is from God through Jesus Christ to John (and eventually God's servants) that this revelation emerges.

It is possible that the phrase, '*the revelation of Jesus Christ*', means that the revelation is *about* Christ – the *book* of Revelation is certainly about Jesus Christ! But, the words 'gave him' would seem to imply that the revelation is through Jesus. One way, or another, Christ is central. The Greek is very emphatic, putting the name *Jesus Christ* immediately after the word *apokalupsis*. Everything about this unfolding revelation has Christ in it. He will be the focus of our attention. Like two bookends, it is his name that straddles this last book of the Bible, but in the opening five verses, the more intimate name 'Jesus' is heightened to the full, dignified, 'Jesus Christ' three times. We are not to be in doubt as to the focus of this study. We are going to be told about Jesus.

Furthermore, these visions are mediated through an 'angel'. There are two ways of understanding what is meant by, '*He made it known by sending his angel to his servant John.*' Taking the angel as Jesus himself, it could mean that God made it known to John by Jesus, repeating the opening phrase; or, more likely, that Jesus made it known to John through an angel – the angel mentioned in the closing chapter (22:16). John is so struck by the majesty of this angel that he falsely offers worship and is immediately rebuked (22:8–9). The ministry of angels is very important in the book of Revelation (for example, 5:2; 7:2; 10:1–2; 14:19).

ii. As to the *recipients* of the revelation, there are two: John and 'his servants'. A scribe in the fourth century seems to have added the words, *tou theologou*, 'the theologian', to the text at this point. It is thus attributed to 'St. John the Divine' in the Authorized Version. This is John: the son of Zebedee (*Matt.* 4:21), brother of James (*Mark* 1:19, the apostle who died in 44 AD). He is thought by some to have been Jesus' first cousin (through Salome, assumed to be Mary's sister, *Mark* 15:40; 16:1–2), a fisherman (*Mark* 1:19),

one of the inner circle of three (with Peter and James, *Luke* 9:28).
He was also the 'disciple whom Jesus loved' (*John* 13:23), who
became the pastor (bishop) of Ephesus and now a prisoner on
Patmos (1:9).
The reference to 'servants' helps us to understand the nature
of the Christian life: the recipients of this apocalypse are 'slaves',
willing slaves of Christ. All Christians are bond-slaves of Jesus. To
believers facing what appears to be a troubled future (compare 1:9),
the knowledge that we are in the service of our Master keeps us
going. The idea that we are *useful* provides motivation to persevere
whenever the going gets difficult.

iii. As to the *content* of the revelation, two things are said about
it: John bears witness to the word of God, attested as it is by Jesus
Christ (1:2), and then writes it down in the form of '*words*' (1:3).
He is to '*write in a book*' what he sees (1:11). The prologue appears
to have been written after the main part of the book in much the
same way as an author would do today. It attests to the divine
origin and self-authenticating character of Revelation as Scripture.
It is inerrant because its author cannot lie and invaluable because
the Shepherd of our souls corroborates its truthfulness. Though
we are introduced here to visions of great splendour and complexity, they are still given in '*words*', needing to be read and studied.

iv. There is a great blessing promised to those who read
and study the book of Revelation! That should be all the encouragement we need to continue. But, as the Bible is never tired of repeating, *mere* study is not enough; we have to 'take to heart' (literally '*keep*') what is written (1:3). This is first of seven beatitudes in
the book (14:13; 16:15; 19:9; 20:6; 22:7, 14). Blessing comes in the
way of *obedience* (see Deuteronomy 5:1; 33:29). Reading Scripture
ought to change us; when it does not, and we still insist that we are
holy, great harm is done to the cause of Christ.

v. There is a sense of *urgency* about this book of Revelation: '*the
time is near*' (1:3). Does this mean that the predicted events of this
final book of the Bible are to take place within the span of John's
lifetime, or that of his readers?

How we answer that question will radically affect the way we understand the book. Some interpret Revelation this way, assigning much of its contents to a description of the downfall of Jerusalem at the hands of the Roman Empire in the time of Nero in 70 AD. This means, of course, that the book was written *before* this date. Others have observed that 'near' (or 'suddenly') is a relative term and could mean that when the time comes, the predicted events will take place in a relatively brief time-span. This allows for a later dating of the book, and the more traditional view that the persecutions took place during the reign of Emperor Domitian, c. 96 AD. This was the view attested by Irenaeus (c.130 – c.200 AD). Resolving this issue is a matter we will have to face in the course of our study. For now, it is sufficient to note that, either way, there is a sense of urgency: the time for the fulfilment of these things has arrived. A decisive moment in time has been reached.

Behind this phrase lies the idea that a sovereign hand is in charge of the future: that history is His-story. What happens to God's servants is not chance, but decree. God orders and fulfils his plan for his people, even in the face of terrible and terrifying events. No matter how bad it may seem, God never abdicates his rule.

GREETINGS

Unusual as this book is, it is still a letter with the customary three-fold opening: (i) the name of the writer, '*John*'; (ii) the name of the recipients, '*the seven churches . . . in Asia*'; and, (iii) the greeting: '*grace to you and peace*' (1:4).

Since there were more than seven churches in the province of Asia at the time John wrote, '*the seven churches . . . in Asia*', identified in verse 11, seem to have been chosen for symbolic significance, seven being a number the Bible associates with wholeness and perfection (think of the Sabbath, the Sabbatical Year and the Year of Jubilee which followed the seven sabbatical years).

Grace is God's undeserved love for sinners, disclosed in the coming of Jesus and his self-giving on the cross (cf. 1:5–6); *peace* is the first of many Old Testament allusions in Revelation, being a rendering in Greek of the Hebrew *shalom*, connoting spiritual and physical well-being.

All three persons of the Trinity are mentioned as givers of the 'greeting'. The Father is expressed in terms that remind us of the revelation of the divine name as 'I AM WHO I AM' in Exodus 3:14–15. He is the One '*who is, and who was, and who is to come*'. In the face of changing circumstances, God remains the same; he continues in being as the self-existent, self-sustaining, unchanging Lord. The '*seven spirits*' (1:4) probably refers to the Holy Spirit (seven being the number of fullness or perfection). It reminds us of one of Zecharaiah's visions (*Zech.* 4:2–10). The Spirit is depicted as '*before his throne*', waiting to do the will of the Father. His ministry is one of service, highlighting the work of the Father and of the Son.

Of Jesus Christ, three things are said: that he is a '*faithful witness*' (1:5, compare 2:13; 3:14), in the sense that he is a *Prophet* who accurately relates his Father's character and plans. Secondly, *Kingly* allusions lie behind the term '*firstborn of the dead*', a description also found in Colossians 1:18. Its background lies in the Greek translation of the Old Testament (known as the Septuagint), and signifies, not that Jesus was the first person to be raised from the dead, but the status and dignity he had as a consequence. Thus, Moses was to tell Pharaoh that Israel as a nation is the Lord's 'firstborn' (*Exod* 4:22), and God promises to appoint David 'the firstborn, the highest of the kings of the earth' (*Psa.* 89:27). To Christ belongs the unique honour and rank of the firstborn; of those who have died and will rise, he is the chief. To this is added yet another allusion to Psalm 89:27: he is '*highest of the kings of the earth*'. To Christians facing tyrannical Roman Emperors, some of whom bordered on the irrational and megalomaniac, this was comforting news.

Thirdly, mention of Jesus causes John to overflow with references to his work as our *Priest*. Not surprisingly, John, '*the apostle of love*', mentions Jesus' love for sinners. Greater love cannot be envisaged than the love expressed at Calvary. What was it all about? The liberation of sinners from bondage to sin by sacrificial blood-shedding, '*To him who loves us and has freed us from our sins by his blood*' (1:5).

Citing and alluding to the Old Testament as much as he does, John now explains that Christians, redeemed by Christ's death and resurrection, are the true Israel of God. In Christ we become '*a kingdom*' and '*priests*' (1:6) to God, the Father of our Lord Jesus Christ. This is an allusion, perhaps, to Exodus 19:6 (see also 1 Peter 2:5,9), and an evidence for the doctrine of the priesthood of all believers, so valued at the Reformation.

The climax of this multi-faceted reference to Jesus and his saving work is a doxology: '*to him be glory and dominion forever and ever. Amen.*' A sight of Jesus' greatness ought to elicit worship. True worship is a focus on Christ: his Person and his finished work. Perhaps John was encouraging this pilgrim church of the first century to give more praise to Christ. We can never praise him too much.

KEEPING THE FOCUS ON JESUS

Revelation looks forward to the second coming of Christ. The details need not concern us yet, just the fact of it. John could see it in his mind's eye. His words, '*Behold, he is coming with the clouds*' sound like the words of Jesus in the Olivet discourse (1:7, compare *Mark 13:26; Matt.* 24:30; 26:64; *Luke* 21:27). The story of God's purposes is still unfolding. The Bible's story has been about this from the start. It leads unerringly to Calvary, but also to 'the day of the Lord'. This day is '*soon*' (1:1), and '*near*' (1:3), and will bring to an end the unfolding time-line as we now know it. God is bringing history to its culmination; he who is the Lord of time gathers it together. Jesus comes with the '*clouds*' (1:7), where God's presence had so often been realized (*Exod.* 13:21; 16:10; *Matt.* 17:5; *Acts* 1:9).

Again, two Old Testament images are woven into the present scene: one in Daniel, where the prophet saw one like a son of man coming '*with the clouds of heaven*' (*Dan.* 7:13), and another, from Zechariah, where the prophet depicts Jerusalem looking on '*him whom they have pierced*' and who '*mourn for him*' (*Zech.* 12:10). But the mourning in view in Revelation is not that of repentance, but of remorse. When Jesus comes, it will not be possible to repent; the time for turning will be past. All that is left now is the grief of rejection: those who have rejected Christ will be themselves rejected.

Difficult as this is, we are encouraged to agree with the divine judgment and say, '*Amen*.' The reason is not difficult to grasp: the verdict is pronounced by the One who calls himself, '*the Alpha and the Omega*' (1:8). *Alpha* is the first letter of the Greek alphabet, *Omega* the last. By inserting these Greek characters John intends us to understand that all that lies between, the completed revelation of God, comes from him. It is an affirmation of his sovereignty. He is '*the Almighty*', an expression which will be repeated eight more times before we finish our study of this book (4:8; 11:17; 15:3; 16:7,14; 19:6,15; 21:22).

John adds that all of this is true *eternally*. Jesus is the One '*who is and who was and is to come*' (1:4, 8). Reflecting, as this phrase does, Exodus 3:14 and the section in which the divine name of God is revealed, the identification of Jesus as the God of the Old Testament becomes clear. The whole sequence of time is under Jesus' control. What better news can Christians have in the face of impending trials, then or now?

This is a lesson in piety and Christian growth: the harsher the difficulties, the sweeter is God's sovereignty. 'He gives power to the faint and to him who has no might he increases strength' (*Isa.* 40:29). God can do whatever he wills to do. It was the refuge Job came to rest in: 'I know that you can do all things and that no purpose of yours can be thwarted' (*Job* 42:2). Knowledge of God's greatness produces great faith and great praise.

THE CHURCH IN TROUBLE

Commenting upon a passage in 1 Peter, Calvin once wrote: 'The church of Christ has been so divinely constituted from the beginning that the Cross has been the way to victory, death the way to life.'

The shadow of the cross fell in deeply-etched lines on the first followers of Jesus. John talks about '*the tribulation*' (1:9), knowing that his readers knew full well what he meant by it. Using the same word, Jesus, in the tense stillness of the Upper Room, had forewarned his disciples: 'In the world you will have *tribulation*' (*John* 16:33). And, using the same word again, the apostles testified to an early lesson learned following the first missionary journey:

'Through many *tribulations* we must enter the kingdom of God' (*Acts* 14:22).

According to Jerome, the Apostle John, following the years of ministry in Jerusalem (see Galatians 2:9, where Paul describes him as a 'pillar' of the Jerusalem church), engaged in a lengthy ministry in Ephesus, where he died at an advanced age. At some point, he was banished to '*Patmos*' for a few months in the year 95 AD, '*on account of the Word of God and the testimony of Jesus*' (1:9).

Patmos is a small island, some 30 miles south-west of Ephesus. It was a rugged prison island with craggy volcanic hills, about eight miles long and four miles wide. Here John wrote the Apocalypse. According to the testimony of Eusebius (265–340 AD), John was released by the Emperor Nerva, somewhere between 96 and 98 AD. John was no stranger to trials.

'Losses and crosses' are part of what we should expect in following Jesus Christ. The testimony of the last book of the Bible confirms that given by the previous sixty-five books: the closer we follow Jesus, the more likely we are to draw the enemy's fire. In this sense, John is a '*brother and partner*' with many others in the '*tribulation*' and '*kingdom*' (1:9). All this requires '*patient endurance*'. All three of these ideas: suffering – kingdom – patient endurance, will find echoes throughout this book. They are key ideas.

A key thought needs explaining before we go further: '*patient endurance*' (ESV) is an attempt to get at the heart of one word. The Authorized (King James) Version renders it 'patience', which may suggest to some readers a passivity which this word does not intend. In fact it conveys both a passive idea (*patience*) and an active (*perseverance*): standing firm under pressure, maintaining a trust in God and a desire to maintain spiritual disciplines. 'Stickability' may get to the core of what we mean, and it is a major reason why this book was written.

When the temptation abounds to cut and run, to crumple and collapse, the Apocalypse encourages backbone and bravery. How brave? '*Be faithful unto death, and I will give you the crown of life*' (2:10). *That* brave!

John's exile brought him more blessing than his freedom might have done. Exiled from his friends and companions in worship, and without the letters of Paul that might have comforted him, he discovers that his worship is but a faint echo of the worship of heaven. On the Lord's Day, he hears the voice of God speaking to him. And then (1:10), he hears a loud voice like a trumpet that instructs him to write down what he sees and hears.

THE LORD'S DAY

John is '*on . . . Patmos*' (1:9), and, at the same time, '*in the Spirit*' (1:10), thus attesting to the truth that one can be in two realities at the same time. Surrounding him were the earthly realities of a volcanic prison island; concurrently, he was experiencing the spiritual blessings of a day which had now begun to have special significance, '*the Lord's day*'.

i. For a time, the early Christians seemed to observe two holy days – the Jewish Sabbath (since at first the church was made up of Jews) and the Lord's Day. As time went by, the observance of the former was dropped, but not the latter. Commemorating as it did the resurrection of Christ, and with it the dissolving of the Old Covenant and the dawning of the New Covenant administration, the Lord's Day continues the principle enacted within the fourth commandment of the Decalogue: that of one-day-in-seven, different from the rest. On this first day of the week, Christians would meet together for worship. This is the only reference to the 'Lord's Day' in the New Testament, but it is clear that it refers to the first day of the week. Clement of Alexandria (*c*.150 – *c*.215), wrote, 'A true Christian, according to the commands of the Gospel, observes the Lord's day by casting out all bad thoughts, and cherishing all goodness, honouring the resurrection of the Lord, which took place on that day.'

ii. There is a sense in which every Christian knows the Spirit's ministry on the Lord's Day, but John implies more by '*in the Spirit*' than that. He is perhaps referring to an experience like Peter's in Acts 10:10. John's experience is accompanied by '*a loud voice like a trumpet*' which urges him to '*write what you see in a book*' (1:11), and distribute it to seven different churches in Asia Minor. This experience was part of a revelatory process whereby God made his will known to the church, a process which culminated in written words which edify those who read them (see 1:1–3). There is something unique in this process, unique to the apostles of the New Testament. This is what marks them out as apostles (2 Cor. 12:12). So unique is this process that a fearful curse hangs on those who attempt to add to it (22:18–19; see also Deuteronomy 4:2; 12:32; Numbers 11:25). Anyone who modifies this revelation is condemned. We are not to tamper with the Word of God to suit our own desires and whims.

iii. Evidently John had been so faithful to the '*word of God and the testimony of Jesus*' (1:9) as to warrant exclusion from Ephesus. There had been sufficient evidence in the eyes of the authorities to label him dangerous! There is a lesson there for us that may not sit well: evidence, sufficient enough to convict, is too often lacking in our testimony. John is on Patmos, not as a short-term missionary, but as a prisoner. John's Christ-centred preaching had caused a major problem.

THE EXALTED CHRIST

Turning around in the direction of the voice, John sees '*seven golden lampstands*' (1:12). These are symbolic of the seven churches of Ephesus, Smyrna, Pergamum, Thyatira, Sardis, Philadelphia and Laodicea (1:20, see 1:11). The church is meant to be a source of light in a dark world (*Matt.* 5:14–15). Whenever it fails to shine, God threatens judgment (see 2:5).

It is not the lampstands that attract John's attention so much as the vision of Christ. Recalling an expression in the book of Daniel, John sees someone '*like a son of man*' (1:13; see Daniel 7:13), whose appearance he goes on to describe in vivid detail.

No expression was more important to Jesus than the title he most frequently used about himself, 'the Son of Man.' What does this mean? A common answer is to suggest that it refers to Jesus' humanity, his solidarity with our human existence, his incarnation. Most of the early church Fathers understood it this way. But, strange as it may sound, its meaning is virtually the opposite! In the book of Daniel, for example, the expression is used of one worthy to receive 'dominion and glory and a kingdom, that all peoples, nations, and languages should serve him; his dominion is an everlasting dominion' (*Dan.* 7:14). Equally interesting is the question put to Peter at Caesarea Philippi, often regarded as a turning point in the ministry of Jesus: 'Who do people say that the Son of Man is?' (*Matt.* 16:13). The answer Peter gave did not draw attention to his humanity so much as his deity! 'You are the Christ, the Son of the living God', Peter said (*Matt.* 16:16). The Bible uses the title, 'Son of Man' to reflect Jesus' transcendent majesty.

What did John see? There are several features worth noting:

i. There was one '*clothed with a long robe and with a golden sash around his chest*' (1:13). This is High Priestly apparel (see Exodus 28:4; 29:5). His head and hair are both described as '*white like wool*', again similar to the vision of the 'Ancient of days' in Daniel (*Dan.* 7:9). This depicts great age and therefore, great wisdom and dignity. His eyes are said to be '*like a flame of fire*' (1:14; see 2:18; 19:12), an image of purity and purification, and his feet '*like burnished bronze, refined in a furnace*' (1:15; see also 2:18). And when he speaks, it is like the sound of '*rushing waters*' (1:15; see also 14:2; 19:6; Ezekiel 43:2). These descriptions further enhance the magnificence of the One John sees. This is Someone to be reckoned with. It is meant, at once, to strike us with a sense of awe and wonder. In a very real sense, Jesus is altogether different from us. This is how God wants us to think about him. (see 1:1).

ii. Kept safely in his right hand are '*seven stars*' (1:16), further described as '*the angels of the seven churches*' (1:20). 'Angels' are mentioned over sixty times in Revelation. It is tempting to think that here we have an allusion to angelic creatures whose business it is to look after the needs and concerns of individual churches. This would seem to be the most natural reading. Certainly the ministry of angels is something that the church has either neglected or distorted.

Others have noted that the Greek word for 'angel' can mean simply 'minister', and suggested that the reference is to the leaders or elders of the individual churches. Some have seen a more general reference – something like the *prevailing spirit*, or 'mood', or 'temperature' of the churches. It is also tempting to think that in view here are the individual leaders of each church. What a helpful image that would be for a church leader or elder! God has his people in the palms of his hands for safe keeping (see John 10:28). Perhaps John was homesick for his own congregation, which he now sees held safely in Jesus' hand.

iii. Out of Jesus' mouth appears '*a sharp double-edged sword*' (1:16; see also 2:12, 16; 6:8; 19:15, 21). The allusion is to the long Thracian sword, an instrument of judgment. The word of God divides and dissects us (see Hebrews 4:12). In the second of the four Servant Songs in Isaiah, the Messiah is depicted in this way (see Isaiah 49:2). What Jesus has to say to us is not always a comforting word. Sometimes he comes to rebuke and chastise. Sometimes he comes to judge. Already in our study, the picture of a 'gentle Jesus, meek and mild' is retreating into the background. This is the One who '*holds the keys of Death and Hades*' (1:18). He has the power to vivify and to destroy.

iv. As if to summarize the transcendence of the One whom John sees, the face of Jesus is now described as '*like the sun shining in full strength*' (1:16). Of course, the point is clear: we cannot look directly at the sun without risking permanent blindness; its rays are too strong for the naked eye. Similarly, the resplendent majesty of Christ is a thing too dazzling to see. This majesty was hidden, or veiled, in Christ's incarnation, only to be glimpsed in his works (*John* 2:11), and, once, in the transfiguration (*Matt.* 17:2; *Mark* 9:3). God accommodates his majesty to us by clothing himself in human flesh (*John* 1:14).

THE FEAR OF GOD

Just as the description of Jesus' majesty is of interest, so is the response of John. He '*fell at his feet as though dead*' (1:17). Twice in this book, John collapses under the strain of a glimpse of another world. In 19:10 he inappropriately falls and offers worship to an angel, and is swiftly reproved. Here, the response is quintessentially correct; the Christ before whom he falls is the Sovereign Lord of heaven and earth. Christ, to cite a C. S. Lewis-ism, is good; but he is certainly not *safe*!

What John has seen is from another world. His response is similar to that of Abraham (*Gen.* 17.3), Isaiah (*Isa.* 6:5), Ezekiel (*Ezek.*

1:29), and Peter (*Luke* 5:8). It is the appropriate sense of awe in the presence of One wholly other than ourselves. It is what Calvin refers to as 'that dread and wonder with which Scripture commonly represents the saints as stricken and overcome whenever they felt the presence of God'. Not until we have compared ourselves to God's majesty are we sufficiently aware of our lowly state.

One of the things that the book of Revelation teaches us is that there are many appropriate ways of responding to Christ, but if the fear of God is not one of them, we have never fully responded to him. It was not inappropriate for John to fall before Jesus as though he were dead, yet Jesus says to John, '*Fear not*' (1:17). These two things go together. We fall down before his exalted majesty, and we feel the reassurance of his hand upon our shoulder encouraging us not to be afraid. There is no other Jesus and there can be no other adequate response. We are awed by his majesty and drawn by his grace.

It is not difficult to see why this vision should occur here, at the very start of the book. John is being prepared for something greater. The Christ who appears here will disclose himself as the 'KING OF KINGS AND LORD OF LORDS' at the close of the book (19:16). Just as Paul was humbled before receiving the glimpses of heaven he could not later describe (*2 Cor.* 12:1–9), so John is humbled here. We are at best only 'jars of clay' (*2 Cor.* 4:7) in which God is pleased to deposit his glory. John could well have said with Jacob, 'How awesome is this place!' (*Gen.* 28:17).

How terrifying the initial realization of a hand touching him must have been (1:17)! But, the God of majesty is also a God of mercy and compassion. The same hand which keeps safe the ministers of the church now reassures and strengthens this prostrate servant. '*Fear not*,' he says. Is it ever right to be afraid of God? Of course it is, when there is every reason to be afraid. Notes Calvin again, wisely: 'All wickedness flows from a disregard of God . . . Since the fear of God is the bridle by which our wickedness is held in check, its removal frees us to indulge in every kind of licentious conduct.' But John is to be spoken to with words of grace. Three things are now said to identify the one who speaks:

i.   Using an expression used by Isaiah of God, Jesus identifies himself: '*I am the first and the last*' (1:17; see also *Rev.* 2:8; 22:13; *Isa.* 44:6; 48:12).

ii.   Alluding to his death and resurrection, he describes himself as '*the living one*' (1:18). His existence is '*forevermore*'. The language of death to One so majestic and powerful is paradoxical. He 'who, though he was in the form of God . . . humbled himself by becoming obedient to the point of death' (*Phil.* 2:6,8).

iii.   He holds '*the keys of Death and Hades*'. To those facing imminent death, many by brutal means, the knowledge that Christ holds the key to what lies beyond must have been of overwhelming significance to John's first readers.

We are back where we began: John is being shown '*the things that must soon take place*' (1:1), '*those that are and those are to take place after this*' (1:19). But, before we begin to unfold this glimpse of the future, it is Christ who holds centre stage. As Alpha and Omega (1:8), First and Last (1:17), everything comes to focus on him. This is what the Old Testament, the Gospels, and the Epistles have prepared us for: a glimpse of the majesty and glory of Christ who holds the church and the world in his hands.

2

Letters from Jesus (Part 1)

*T*o *the angel of the church in Ephesus write: 'The words of*
him who holds the seven stars in his right hand, who walks
among the seven golden lampstands.

²"'I know your works, your toil and your patient endurance,
and how you cannot bear with those who are evil, but have tested
those who call themselves apostles and are not, and found them to
be false. ³I know you are enduring patiently and bearing up for
my name's sake, and you have not grown weary. ⁴But I have
this against you, that you have abandoned the love you had at
first. ⁵Remember therefore from where you have fallen; repent,
and do the works you did at first. If not, I will come to you and
remove your lampstand from its place, unless you repent. ⁶Yet
this you have: you hate the works of the Nicolaitans, which I
also hate. ⁷He who has an ear, let him hear what the Spirit
says to the churches. To the one who conquers I will grant to eat
of the tree of life, which is in the paradise of God.'

⁸"And to the angel of the church in Smyrna write: 'The words
of the first and the last, who died and came to life.

⁹"'I know your tribulation and your poverty (but you are
rich) and the slander of those who say that they are Jews and
are not, but are a synagogue of Satan. ¹⁰Do not fear what you
are about to suffer. Behold, the devil is about to throw some of
you into prison, that you may be tested, and for ten days you
will have tribulation. Be faithful unto death, and I will give
you the crown of life. ¹¹He who has an ear, let him hear what
the Spirit says to the churches. The one who conquers will not
be hurt by the second death.'

¹² "And to the angel of the church in Pergamum write: 'The words of him who has the sharp two-edged sword.
¹³ " 'I know where you dwell, where Satan's throne is. Yet you hold fast my name, and you did not deny my faith even in the days of Antipas my faithful witness, who was killed among you, where Satan dwells. ¹⁴ But I have a few things against you: you have some there who hold the teaching of Balaam, who taught Balak to put a stumbling block before the sons of Israel, so that they might eat food sacrificed to idols and practice sexual immorality.
¹⁵ So also you have some who hold the teaching of the Nicolaitans. ¹⁶ Therefore repent. If not, I will come to you soon and war against them with the sword of my mouth. ¹⁷ He who has an ear, let him hear what the Spirit says to the churches. To the one who conquers I will give some of the hidden manna, and I will give him a white stone, with a new name written on the stone that no one knows except the one who receives it' (Rev. 2:1–17).

The book of Revelation is a word from the Lord to the church. At the outset, he sends letters to *'seven churches that are in Asia'* (1:4). Specifically, these churches are at *'Ephesus, Smyrna, Pergamum, Thyatira, Sardis, Philadelphia and Laodicea'* (1:11). 'Asia' here means the ancient province of Asia, or, roughly, what we would now call Turkey. On a map, the churches are listed *clockwise*, beginning with the location nearest Patmos (where John was in exile), Ephesus.

These churches are all facing trouble. The persecutions of Emperor Domitian are raging. The hostility is fierce and some are giving their lives for the cause of the gospel. But trouble comes from within as well as from outside the church. The temptations of the flesh and mind impinge upon her health. False doctrine as well as immorality call for the King of the church to issue warnings. As A. W. Tozer once said, the trouble is not that the church is in the world; rather the trouble comes from the fact that the world is in the church.

Letters from Jesus (Part 1)

What does Jesus think of the church? Since the church is his, only he has the right to say, 'My church' (see *Matt.* 16:18); only he has the right to scrutinize and complain. He 'knows' the church more intimately than anyone else: '*I know your works*' (2:2, 9; 3:1, 8, 15), '*I know your tribulation*' (2:9), '*I know where you dwell*' (2:13). He has the data by which to make a right assessment. The letters are, in a sense, another vision; a vision of the chief Pastor-Shepherd supervising his flock.

The description of the churches as '*lampstands*' is drawn from the visionary symbols of the first chapter (2:1; see also 1:12, 13, 20), and before that, the vision of Zechariah 4:2–6 and the earlier description of the tabernacle lampstands in Numbers 8 and Exodus 25. From these passages comes the idea that the lampstands are meant to emit the light of God, the Holy Spirit. Zechariah's message is: 'Not by might nor by power, but by my Spirit,' says the LORD of hosts' (*Zech.* 4:6). The church is meant to be a community in which the presence of God shines (note the way the lampstand is mentioned directly after the 'bread of presence' in Exodus 25:30–31).

Jesus is now identified as the one who '*holds the seven stars in his right hand*' (2:1; see also 1:16, 20). The stars are the 'angels of the seven churches' (1:20) best understood as the angels or guardians whose function it is to watch over the church and protect it. Perhaps it is our worldliness that prevents us from accepting this interpretation. Why should it be difficult for us to think of angels protecting the church in a corporate sense, just as they do individual Christians (see *Heb.* 1:14)? In the midst of these lampstands, Jesus now walks. Some shine more clearly than others. And there are some whose light is fading. In response, Jesus comes with a word from the Lord: '*The words of him . . .*' (2:1, 8, 12, 18; 3:1, 7, 14, literally, 'Thus says', a typical Old Testament formula of divine speech and authority). When the Lord speaks, we are meant to listen.

All these letters have a similar pattern. Each one contains,

- an analysis of the spiritual condition of the church;
- an exhortation to be faithful, or to repent, or both;
- a promise that Jesus Christ gives.

Ephesus

Good news and bad news form the content of the first letter (2:1–7). The background seems crucial to an understanding of the form of the letter. Augustus, who reigned from 27 BC to 6 AD, had allowed Ephesus to build two temples in his honour, while Domitian had called Ephesus the 'guardian of the Imperial cult'. At the Olympic games, shortly before this letter was written, Ephesus had given particular honour to Domitian. We know from Acts that other forms of religion included the worship of Artemis and the practice of magic (*Acts* 19:8–9, 23–40).

The commendation begins with the assertion, '*I know your works*' (2:2). Three features are noted:

i.   '*Toil*' (*2:2*). The word used here is a specific one that includes the idea of diligence and effort (see also *1 Thess.* 2:9).

ii.   '*Patient endurance*' (*2:2*). In the face of opposition, these Christians had continued in their witness to Jesus Christ. They had not yielded to the pressures to conform. They had stood firm, enduring the cross that came in the wake of their bold testimony. '*I know you are enduring patiently and bearing up for my name's sake, and you have not grown weary*' (2:3).

iii.   *Orthodoxy*. Hatred of the Nicolaitans (2:6) had earned them the commendation of the Saviour, for he also bore a similar '*hate*'. All kinds of theories persist as to the identity and character of the Nicolaitans. Some, from the identification given by Irenaeus in the second century, have equated their leader with the Nicolas mentioned in Acts 6:5. Others have seen here a reference to the Gnosticism of the first century. It is not necessary to be certain here. Paul had warned of false teachers ('wolves' is what he called them) in his farewell address to the Ephesians (*Acts* 20:29). In response the Ephesians had 'test(ed) everything' and held fast to what was 'good' (*1 Thess.* 5:21).

But there is a complaint which Jesus has 'against' them: '*You have abandoned the love you had at first*' (2:4). It is not clear whether it is a loss of love for God or for each other that is in view; commentators have taken both opinions, and modern commentators favour the latter. Probably both are in view, for a lack of love to God will invariably be accompanied by a lack of love for one another (see Hebrews 6:10).

Keeping the flame of love glowing brightly is something we have to work at in marriage; and in our love-relationship with Jesus Christ, things are no different. It is all too possible for us to grow cool, accepting grace with indifference. It is to this that Hosea witnesses. Israel had 'cooled' towards her Saviour-Lord and he in turn goes to woo her back.

> 'Therefore, behold, I will allure her;
> And bring into the wilderness, and speak tenderly to her . . .
> And there she shall answer as in the days of her youth,
> > as at the time when she came out of the land of Egypt.'
> 'And in that day,' declares the LORD,
> 'you will call me "my husband" . . .
> And I will betroth you to me forever.
> I will betroth you to me in righteousness and in justice,
> > in steadfast love and in mercy.
> I will betroth you to me in faithfulness,
> And you shall know the LORD.'
>
> > > > (*Hos.* 2:14–16, 19-20)

This letter is a warning to those who can detect false doctrine a mile away, but whose hearts do not beat in tune with the love of God shown in the gospel. The danger is formalism. The cure is to '*repent*' (2:5). Turning away from sin and turning towards God is the direction to which Christ calls this church. Re-learn the joy of love to God and to one another, as the 'royal law' (*James* 2:8) and the 'greatest' fruit of the Spirit's work in our hearts (*1 Cor.* 13:13). Only then can we be assured of partaking of '*the tree of life*', the symbol of eternal life (2:7; see also Genesis 2:9; Revelation 22:2, 14, 19). Failure to repent is catastrophic: Jesus threatens to remove the lampstand! Licence leads to apostasy, which in turn leads to death.

Each letter ends with a formula, '*He who has an ear, let him hear what the Spirit says to the churches*' (2:7, 11, 17, 29; 3:6, 13, 22). In this case it is followed by a promise: '*To the one who conquers I will grant to eat of the tree of life, which is in the paradise of God*' (2:7). The allusion is to Genesis. Faithful Christian living promises a restoration to, and enjoyment of, Eden (paradise). God intends through his Son, Jesus Christ, to bring his people to circumstances more blissful than can ever be imagined. This is the Bible's way of expressing the inexpressible. Those who ridicule such a hope by saying they do not want 'to spend eternity playing harps', or in this case, eating fruit from a tree, cannot understand (as C. S. Lewis put it) 'books written for grown-ups'. The allusion is to the bliss of heaven and the life of the new creation.

SMYRNA

The second letter is brief and recalls the suffering of the early church (2:8-11). *'I know your tribulation'* (2:9). Suffering is a mark of the New Testament church.

Situated some thirty-five miles north of Ephesus, Smyrna was the next most important city in Asia. Its status within the Empire was established two centuries earlier when, in 195 BC, a temple was built for *Dea Roma* (Rome personified as a goddess). During the last days of Jesus, Smyrna was the city chosen to erect a temple in honour of Tiberius.

Christians in this city would have a difficult time of it, particularly since the Jewish community was large and on good terms with Rome – hence the reference to the Jews in verse 9. It was in the interest of the Jews to be dissociated from Christians. Later, in the second century, the godly Polycarp, after following Christ for eighty-six years, was cruelly put to death, aided by the antagonism of the Jews in Smyrna.

Nothing is said in the New Testament about the church at Smyrna, or when it was founded. It is enough to know that it existed, and that it suffered greatly for its faithfulness. Following a suffering Saviour will inevitably bring its share of trouble. It is in this way, Paul suggests, we make up 'what is lacking in Christ's afflictions' (*Col.* 1:24).

Paul could warn the Philippians that 'it has been granted to you that for the sake of Christ you should not only believe in him, but also suffer for his sake' (*Phil.* 1:29). The Christians at Smyrna evidently knew all about this. 'Suffering', wrote Dietrich Bonhoeffer (himself executed by the Nazis in 1945), 'is the badge of the true Christian.'

The source of suffering here is malevolent: the Jewish synagogue – source of tension and opposition – is Satanic (2:9). Furthermore, the devil is also involved in putting some of the believers 'into prison' (2:10). As the story of Job's suffering portrays, Satan is always involved in the persecution and testing of Christians. Although nothing happens without God's ultimate involvement, it is the devil that is singled out here for blame.

What was the nature of their suffering? Four elements are highlighted.

i.   *Poverty* (*2:9*). Perhaps because the Jews were refusing to do business with them, or because the Christians were drawn from the needier sections of society, they were poor.

ii.   *Slander* (*2:9*). The Jews were insulting Christians. 'The words of a whisperer are like delicious morsels; they go down into the inner parts of the body' (*Prov.* 26:22).

iii. *Prison* (*2:10*). Something more ominous now comes to which Jesus adds: 'Do not fear what you are about to suffer' (2:10). He warns of imprisonment and persecution 'for ten days'. The relatively short duration of confinement, though symbolic of course, is meant as encouragement. In any event, it is a 'test.' God is moulding his own into the shape he wants them to be.

iv.   *Death*. 'Be faithful unto death, and I will give you the crown of life' (2:10). Polycarp, according to Irenaeus and Tertullian, was consecrated as bishop of Smyrna by the apostle John himself. He would, then, have read this warning of Jesus to Smyrna. There can be no doubt that when he was executed in 154 AD he was encouraged by the thought that all things happen according to a divine plan and purpose, and lead to the crowning of believers.

What comfort would Christians have drawn from this? Three things: that the one who speaks is '*the first and the last*' (2:8), and whose identity therefore is divine; that Jesus also suffered, but '*came to life*' (2:8) and is therefore able to 'bring with him' those who sleep in Jesus (*1 Thess.* 4:14); and that he knows their trouble (2:9), which reassures in the darkest hour that we are never alone. This sovereignty assures '*the crown of life*' to the faithful (2:10). They will have no fear of the Day of Judgment, or '*the second death*' (2:11).

At Smyrna there were Christians who were evidently heroic. They *endured* with patience. Jesus exhorts to further examples of stamina: *'Be faithful, even to the point of death . . .'* They were to die with the assurance that Jesus would not forsake them in their hour of need. This is authentic Christianity, the real thing, the genuine article.

Pergamum

Jesus knows not only what we do (2:2), and the extent of our suffering (2:9), but he also knows where we are (2:13). The letter to the church at Pergamum (2:12–17) was written to a city some fifty-five miles from Smyrna. Like Ephesus and Smyrna, it too had its temples and altars. Like Smyrna's temple to Tiberius, Pergamum had been granted permission to erect one to Augustus.

A concern for the truth is what emerges first. Jesus commends them: *'You hold fast my name, and you did not deny my faith even in the days of Antipas my faithful witness, who was killed among you, where Satan lives'* (2:13). But there is also criticism: *'But I have a few things against you: you have some there who hold the teaching of Balaam . . .' (2:14).* There was a fidelity of sorts, but not uniformly so. Some had evidently succumbed to error.

Doctrine is important. Certain truths are of 'first importance' (*1 Cor.* 15:3). They are undeniable. Without them, we cannot be saved. Other truths are secondary. Over them Christians may disagree but still be assured of their salvation. But truths such as those Paul enumerates in the opening verses of 1 Corinthians 15, such as Jesus' death, burial and resurrection, are essential to what a Christian is. Without these, the entire faith is lost. There needs to be, in the words of Rupert Meldenius, 'In essential things, unity; in non-essential things, liberty; in all things, charity.'

What essential truth is Jesus thinking of here, when he says, *'You hold fast my name, and you did not deny my faith'* (2:13)? It is those truths directly concerned with who Jesus is and what he had come to do. The person and work of Jesus are among the essential truths of the gospel. They are non-negotiable. The Christians at Pergamum, like Athanasius standing *contra mundum* ('against the world'), had stood firm against any attempts to deny these truths.

One had already been so faithful that he had been prepared, like Polycarp later in Smyrna, to die for his faith. His name was Antipas. Perhaps he had refused to say those words demanded by imperial Rome, *Kurios Kaisar* (Caesar is Lord). Perhaps, for two words, he had been prepared to lay down his life.

The particular false teaching making the rounds in Pergamum was '*the teaching of Balaam*' (2:14) and '*the teaching of the Nicolaitans*' (2:15). A single error is meant by these two descriptions. What it was can be ascertained by recalling the story of Balaam in the Old Testament (Numbers 22–24). Balak, the King of Moab, summoned Balaam to come and curse the tribes of Israel who were about to cross the river Jordan and enter the promised land. But Balaam found that every time he opened his mouth, words of blessing rather than cursing emerged. Greed (according to 2 Peter 2:15) caused Balaam to devise another plan, suggesting that Moabite girls should seduce the Israelite men by inviting them to take part in idolatrous feasts. Perhaps this is a reference to the ease with which sexual sins can destroy a church. Perhaps, too, it is yet another example of how the church can so easily fall into the sin of presumption when it considers its relationship with God. The message, as before, is '*repent*' (2:16; compare 2:5).

Once again Satan lies behind the trouble. He had his throne there in Pergamum (2:13). It is part of the message of Revelation to point out to us that Satan's power is limited and ultimately doomed. But that does not mean he has no power at all! He is very much alive and active, even though the fatal wound has already been given to him. In defence of the church at Pergamum, Christ comes with a '*sharp two-edged sword*' (2:12; compare 1:16). The King of Kings comes into the battle to destroy his ancient foe. God's way of destroying error is by proclaiming the truth. Some of the early church Fathers believed that the two edges of the sword represented the Old and New Testaments.

To those who overcome, Jesus promises '*the hidden manna*' and '*a white stone, with a new name written on the stone*' (2:17). The manna reminds us of God's provision in the days of the Exodus, sufficient for each new day. In the new exodus and the journey towards the new Canaan, God promises to provide our daily bread (*Matt.* 6:11).

The white stone has been given a variety of interpretations, but the one which seems to make the most sense is the one that alludes to a practice in ancient courtrooms. Jurors often voted for acquittal with a white stone and conviction with a black stone. Since the populace of Pergamum had voted for their conviction, Jesus promises to give them the white stone of acquittal – an assurance of eternal life. On this stone God promises to write a '*new name*' (2:17). This is an allusion to Isaiah: 'You shall be called by a new name that the mouth of the LORD will give. You shall be a crown of beauty in the hand of the LORD, and a royal diadem in the hand of your God' (*Isa.* 62:2–3).

3

Letters from Jesus (Part 2)

*A*nd to the angel of the church in Thyatira write: 'The words
A of the Son of God, who has eyes like a flame of fire, and
whose feet are like burnished bronze.

19 " 'I know your works, your love and faith and service and
patient endurance, and that your latter works exceed the first.
20 But I have this against you, that you tolerate that woman
Jezebel, who calls herself a prophetess and is teaching and seduc-
ing my servants to practice sexual immorality and to eat food
sacrificed to idols. *21* I gave her time to repent, but she refuses
to repent of her sexual immorality. *22* Behold, I will throw her
onto a sickbed, and those who commit adultery with her I will
throw into great tribulation, unless they repent of her works,
23 and I will strike her children dead. And all the churches will
know that I am he who searches mind and heart, and I will
give to each of you as your works deserve. *24* But to the rest of
you in Thyatira, who do not hold this teaching, who have not
learned what some call the deep things of Satan, to you I say,
I do not lay on you any other burden. *25* Only hold fast what
you have until I come. *26* The one who conquers and who keeps
my works until the end, to him I will give authority over the
nations, *27* and he will rule them with a rod of iron, as when
earthen pots are broken in pieces, even as I myself have received
authority from my Father. *28* And I will give him the morning
star. *29* He who has an ear, let him hear what the Spirit says
to the churches.'

3:1 "And to the angel of the church in Sardis write: 'The words
of him who has the seven spirits of God and the seven stars.

" *'I know your works. You have the reputation of being alive, but you are dead. ² Wake up, and strengthen what remains and is about to die, for I have not found your works complete in the sight of my God. ³ Remember, then, what you received and heard. Keep it, and repent. If you will not wake up, I will come like a thief, and you will not know at what hour I will come against you. ⁴ Yet you have still a few names in Sardis, people who have not soiled their garments, and they will walk with me in white, for they are worthy. ⁵ The one who conquers will be clothed thus in white garments, and I will never blot his name out of the book of life. I will confess his name before my Father and before his angels. ⁶ He who has an ear, let him hear what the Spirit says to the churches.'*

⁷ *"And to the angel of the church in Philadelphia write: 'The words of the holy one, the true one, who has the key of David, who opens and no one will shut, who shuts and no one opens.*

⁸ *" 'I know your works. Behold, I have set before you an open door, which no one is able to shut. I know that you have but little power, and yet you have kept my word and have not denied my name. ⁹ Behold, I will make those of the synagogue of Satan who say that they are Jews and are not, but lie—behold, I will make them come and bow down before your feet and they will learn that I have loved you. ¹⁰ Because you have kept my word about patient endurance, I will keep you from the hour of trial that is coming on the whole world, to try those who dwell on the earth. ¹¹ I am coming soon. Hold fast what you have, so that no one may seize your crown. ¹² The one who conquers, I will make him a pillar in the temple of my God. Never shall he go out of it, and I will write on him the name of my God, and the name of the city of my God, the new Jerusalem, which comes down from my God out of heaven, and my own new name. ¹³ He who has an ear, let him hear what the Spirit says to the churches.'*

¹⁴ *"And to the angel of the church in Laodicea write: 'The words of the Amen, the faithful and true witness, the beginning of God's creation.*

¹⁵ *" 'I know your works: you are neither cold nor hot. Would that you were either cold or hot! ¹⁶ So, because you are luke-*

warm, and neither hot nor cold, I will spit you out of my mouth.
[17] For you say, I am rich, I have prospered, and I need nothing,
not realizing that you are wretched, pitiable, poor, blind, and
naked. [18] I counsel you to buy from me gold refined by fire, so
that you may be rich, and white garments so that you may clothe
yourself and the shame of your nakedness may not be seen, and
salve to anoint your eyes, so that you may see. [19] Those whom
I love, I reprove and discipline, so be zealous and repent. [20]
Behold, I stand at the door and knock. If anyone hears my voice
and opens the door, I will come in to him and eat with him, and
he with me. [21] The one who conquers, I will grant him to sit
with me on my throne, as I also conquered and sat down with my
Father on his throne. [22] He who has an ear, let him hear what
the Spirit says to the churches' " (Rev. 2:18–3:22).

THYATIRA

The fourth letter is written to the church at Thyatira (2:18–29). It
is, according to some, the least important of the seven cities, and
yet it receives the longest letter! But it is not the city to which the
letter is written, but the church. Whatever the relative size and
influence of the city, the church is far more important. Thyatira
lay some forty miles south east of the previous city mentioned,
Pergamum. Archaeological work has uncovered the fact that the
city was noted for its many trades, including clothiers, bakers,
bronze-workers, cobblers, weavers, tanners, dyers and potters.

Readers of the New Testament will recall that Lydia, 'a seller
of purple goods' (*Acts* 16:14), came from Thyatira. In God's
providence, she became important in the planting of the church at
Philippi. Had she returned to Thyatira, and been instrumental in
the establishment of a church there, too? By the time Revelation
is written, the church seems to be flourishing: '*I know your works,
your love and faith and service and patient endurance . . .*' (2:19). Four
essential qualities are singled out: love, faith, service and perseverance. In many ways, there could hardly be a better commendation
of any church than to note these characteristics. Three of them,
faith, hope and love, are highlighted by Paul as constituting the

very essence of spiritual maturity (*1 Cor.* 13:13). Not only that, but they were *increasing* in virtue. Christians are meant to grow, and the Thyatiran Christians had done just that: '*Your latter works exceed the first*' (2:19).

Yet, despite the commendations, the church at Thyatira was tolerating '*Jezebel*' in its midst (2:20). Possibly an individual (female) teacher is in view, but this is unlikely to have been the case. It is more likely that the feminine reference here is to the entire church. The later expression '*her children*' (2:23), brings to mind something that John says elsewhere using the expression 'the elect lady and her children' in which he has in mind the church rather than particular individuals (*2 John* 1).

Jezebel was the one who incited her husband, King Ahab, to compromise Israel by encouraging the worship of Baal (*1 Kings* 16:31). Her father, Ethbaal, priest of Astarte, became king of Sidon by murdering his predecessor. Astarte (or Ashtoreth) was the Phoenician equivalent of the Greek Aphrodite, or the Roman Venus. All three encouraged licentiousness beneath a cloak of morality.

Jezebel had been responsible for the spiritual adultery of the Old Testament church. The Jezebel in view here may be a similar spirit of compromise that existed within the church that tolerated idolatry and licence. Perhaps this included attending various guilds at which offerings were given to pagan deities and ended in licentious riot – '*sexual immorality*' and eating '*food sacrificed to idols*' (2:20).

Interestingly, what is probably an oft-used expression of the Jezebel cult appears at the end of the letter: they loved to speak of the '*deep things*' (2:24). An elitist claim to special knowledge and revelation, known only to the select few, has been a feature of many religions, including Christianity. To some extent, the epistle to the Colossians deals with this very issue: the claim to special experiences that gave insight into the hidden secrets of God. Those who claimed such experiences were often bound together in fraternal relationships and sworn to secrecy. Gnosticism is perhaps the best known example of such a fraternity.

Whatever claims they were making to knowing the '*deep things*', Jesus' words are forthright: they are '*the deep things of Satan*' (2:24). Within this church that demonstrated such love, faith, service and perseverance, Satan was busy at work! Like the Nicolaitans and Balaamites in the churches at Ephesus and Pergamum respectively, Jezebel had the potential of undoing the church at Thyatira.

The key word which seems to highlight the spirit of the church at Thyatira is *toleration*: '*You tolerate that woman Jezebel . . .*' (2:20). This was in contrast to the church at Ephesus who did not '*bear with those who are evil*' (2:2). Perhaps this suggests a spirit of indifference to sin. It is not that they were eagerly embracing it; they were apathetic to its influence. There was an unwillingness to root it out from their midst. They had no desire to engage in the messy business of church discipline. So long as good things existed, things worthy of commendation and note, these things, they thought, would outshine any shortcomings in their midst. After all, no church is perfect. A *laissez-faire* attitude to sin can be the ruination of a church, as we see in what Jesus goes on to say.

Jesus introduces himself in terms which exalt the holiness of his character: '*These are the words of the Son of God, who has eyes like a flame of fire*' (2:18). With such eyes he '*searches mind and heart*' (2:23). John had given testimony to this in his Gospel, saying of Jesus that 'he himself knew what was in a man' (*John* 2:25). He knows each church, and each individual, intimately. Interestingly, holiness is not something for which this church is commended!

Like the church at Ephesus and Pergamum, repentance is what Jesus desires of Thyatira (2:5, 16, 21, 22). Evidently, he had been patient with them and had given time to repent already, but they had failed to do so (2:21). And the consequence can only be judgment. The response of Christ's holiness to sin which has not been repented of is certain judgment, either immediate or on the Day of accountability. '*Behold I will throw her on to a sickbed, and those who commit adultery with her I will throw into great tribulation . . .*' (2:22). Such punishment is 'what you deserve' (2:23, *New Living Translation*).

Any thought of harshness in the punishment is removed: the judgments of God are according to his justice. It is the realization of what sin deserves, no more and no less. The equity of God is paramount. Beds of sin will become beds of sickness. The pleasures of sin will yield pain and tribulation. Perhaps, even more startling, are the words: '*I will strike her children dead*' (2:23).

Such words bring home the utter seriousness of God's judgments and the folly of trifling with sin. This should bring a spirit of seriousness into the church and its oversight. The Corinthian church had experienced the reality of these threats: 'That is why many of you are weak and ill, and some have died' (*1 Cor.* 11:30).

To those in the church who had maintained a good testimony despite the presence of Jezebel, Jesus urges perseverance. They are to '*hold fast*' (2:25). Interestingly he adds: '*I do not lay on you any other burden*' (2:24). Perhaps the instinctive reaction of the pious at Thyatira was to retreat into a legalistic and ascetic view of life. Not wishing to be tolerant of Jezebel's licentiousness, the temptation to ensure godliness by imposing a system of rules over and above that which the Bible had given was considerable. But no such '*burden*' is to be imposed. They are to live by the standards of the revealed Word of God and no more. As John said elsewhere: 'His commandments are not burdensome' (*1 John* 5:3).

To such conquerors he promises '*the morning star*' (2:28). Revelation 22:16 describes Jesus as '*the bright morning star*', and the assurance would then be that rejecting Jezebel will ensure the possession of Jesus Christ. That would be their greatest possession.

The promise is given to Thyatira that successful opposition to the false teaching of Jezebel will ensure that they will share with Jesus in his reign over the nations (see 5:10). They will reign *with him*. The citation of Psalm 2 says a great deal about how important this psalm became in the early church. Through this portrayal of Christ triumphant over all the forces of darkness, the church at Thyatira is being assured of complete and final victory:

'He will rule them with a rod of iron, as when earthen pots are broken in pieces' (*Rev.* 2:27; *Psa.* 2:9).

Despite the animosity and fury of the opposition arrayed against the anointed Messiah, Psalm 2 declares Messiah's total victory. And the staggering thing is that Christians will share in that victory. They, too, will reign, for ever and ever (22:5).

SARDIS

The next church is Sardis, some thirty miles south-east of Thyatira. As with Thyatira, nothing is known of the origins of this city. The letter to this church is brief, but stinging (3:1–6). Situated at the base of Mount Tmolus and the valley of the River Hermus, Sardis became a focal point of much traffic. It was the capital of the kingdom of Lydia, where Croesus reigned until Cyrus of Persia eventually toppled him in the sixth century BC. Later, both Alexander the Great and Antiochus the Great captured this city.

There is hardly anything complimentary said of the church at Sardis. In words that must have come as deeply shocking, Jesus says to them: '*You have the reputation of being alive, but you are dead*' (3:1). It is hard to imagine what their reaction must have been upon hearing these words. There were '*works*' in evidence (3:1) but they were not '*complete*' (3:2). That is, they were imperfect, deficient in some way. They had no divine approval. The work they did was not in accord with anything that God requires. Industry in itself is of no value.

Despite their acquisition of a '*reputation*', it was all a pretence. Hypocrisy was written all over the walls of the church; it was all a sham. Nominal Christianity prevailed. Like those in Isaiah's day, these people 'draw near with their mouth and honour me with their lips, while their hearts are far from me' (*Isa.* 29:13). Like the Pharisees, of whom Jesus uses these same words, they were 'whitewashed tombs' (*Matt.* 23:27).

There are two main things the Sardis church is to do: first, there are those, even in this dead church, who are alive, '*who have not soiled their garments*' (3:4), and are able to heed a word of warning to '*wake up!*' and '*strengthen what remains*' (3:2). Here is the doctrine of the holy remnant, which crops up in Scripture again and again to bring encouragement in the midst of what looks like doom and gloom (*Gen.* 6:5–18; *1 Kings* 19:18; *Isa.* 1:9; 6:13; 7:3; 10:20-22; *2 Pet.* 2:7). These '*few names*' (3:4) are the ones who keep hope alive in a sepulchre. But, even these have succumbed to a torpid slumber. They, too, need to '*wake up*', having yielded to the soporific, mesmerizing vapours of the dead all around. Sardis had, in fact, twice fallen to surprise attacks: once, to Cyrus and yet again to Antiochus the Great. Failure to keep watch had been their undoing.

They were, in particular, to '*strengthen*' what remained (3:2). The term here is often used of nurturing in the New Testament (*Luke 9:51; 16:26; 22:32; Rom.* 1:11; 16:25; *1 Thess. 3*:2; 3:13; *2 Thess.* 2:17; 3:3; *James* 5:8; *1 Pet.* 5:10; *2 Pet.* 1:12). Christians needed support and encouragement, by providing motivation and reinforcement.

Failure to heed Christ's exhortation may result in their discovering that he has come in judgment against them, '*like a thief*', not knowing '*at what hour I will come against you*' (3:3). They could find their lampstand removed entirely and not even a 'few people' left.

Second, they are to remember what it is they have received (3:3). Recollecting past blessings is at the heart of covenant life. Before Israel found themselves in the promised land, they were given a similar exhortation to 'remember' (*Deut.* 8:2). The power of advance would be hampered by a faulty memory of the Lord's blessings to them.

To those who comply, repenting of failure (3:3), soiled clothes will be replaced by '*white*' ones (3:5). 'Blessed are those who wash their robes, so that they may have the right to the tree of life and that they may enter the city by the gates' (22:14; see also 7:14).

Additionally, in what at first looks like an encouragement, Jesus adds: '*I will never blot his name out of the book of life. I will confess his name before my Father and before his angels*' (3:5). But the encouragement contains a veiled threat, too. Failure to repent would incur such obliteration. Of course, there is no actual erasing of names from the Book of Life. The number of the elect is sealed (*John* 13:18; *2 Tim.* 2:19). God stoops to our weakness and accommodates himself to our way of thinking in order to reinforce the point that what he desires is our compliance and obedience.

PHILADELPHIA

The sixth letter comes to a town less than thirty miles south-east of Sardis (3:7–13). Like Sardis, Philadelphia, 'the city of brotherly-love', was known for its earthquakes, one of which (in 17 AD) had almost destroyed the city and severely damaged Sardis. Again, we have little idea as to how the church began in this city. But one thing is sure: it was a fine church, for unlike the previous letter, this letter contains mostly commendation and praise.

Evidently, following some local persecution, the church at Philadelphia had kept the faith: '*You have kept my word and have not denied my name*' (3:8). They exhibited '*patient endurance*' (3:10; compare 1:9). Jesus has noted their trouble and approves of their continuing love for him.

Three things stand out in this letter:

First, the words, '*I have placed before you an open door which no one is able to shut*' (3:8). Other uses of this expression in the New Testament suggest that what Jesus has in mind here is their service. Paul could say to the Corinthians, 'a wide door for effective work has opened to me' (*1 Cor.* 16:9). Similarly, he could solicit the prayers of the Colossians that 'God may open to us a door for the word, to declare the mystery of Christ' (*Col.* 4:3).

Is the thought the same here? Had the Philadelphian Christians been given liberty to witness because of the *pax Romana* which permitted the church, for a while, to enjoy the same privileges as the Jews? We know from the history of this period that secular Philadelphia had great ambitions to become the most important city in the region. Perhaps the church had been fired with similar ambitions for the kingdom.

Despite these opportunities, they were pathetically weak: '*I know that you have but little power*' (3:8). Perhaps, they were few in number; perhaps they lack gifted men able to proclaim the gospel with any power. Whatever the exact reason, the Jews took advantage of their weakness. Jesus calls these Jews a '*synagogue of Satan*' (3:9). God has a way of turning the tables on those who oppress and harass. Those who persecute will be brought to confess the integrity of the persecuted: '*I will make them come and bow down before your feet and they will learn that I have loved you*' (3:9). Centuries before, Isaiah had prophesied that 'the sons of those who afflicted you shall come bending low to you, and all who despised you shall bow down at your feet; they shall call you the City of the LORD, the Zion of the Holy One of Israel' (*Isa.* 60:14).

Tribulation was not far away for the church at Philadelphia and, as we read in this letter of '*the hour of trial that is coming*' (3:10), it sounds as though it might come at any moment. How will they cope? '*I will keep you*', Jesus promises (3:10).

Second, we read of Christ and the key of David: '*The words of the holy one, the true one, who has the key of David*' (3:7). The language is taken from Isaiah 22 where it is used of Eliakim. One of three chosen to negotiate with Rabshakeh the Assyrian, Eliakim was given 'the key of David', that is, the authority to speak and negotiate on David's behalf: 'I will place on his shoulder the key to the house of David. He shall open, and none shall shut; and he shall shut, and none shall open' (*Isa.* 22:22). Jesus has the key to the royal palace. When he opens no one can shut the door; when he closes, no one can open it. His word is supreme and powerful. By extension he gives the keys into the hands of Peter and the other disciples, and, through the proclamation of the gospel, doors are opened and closed (see *Matt.* 16:19). Disobedience to Jesus Christ has fatal consequences. He is the One who is '*the holy one, the true one*' (3:7).

Third, Jesus exhorts the Church at Philadelphia to '*hold fast what you have,*' in the knowledge that '*I am coming soon*' (3:11). Adding, '*the one who conquers I will make a pillar in the temple of my God. Never shall he go out of it, and I will write on him the name of my God, and the name of the city of my God, the new Jerusalem, which comes down from my God out of heaven, and my own new name*' (3:12). By becoming pilgrims in this life, Jesus promises that we shall be pillars in the next. The promise concerns our becoming something immoveable and sturdy, part of the very fabric of the city of God.

LAODICEA

The final letter of Jesus is addressed to the church at Laodicea (3:14–22). Situated yet another forty miles south-east of Philadelphia, in the Lycus Valley, near the New Testament city of Colosse, the church at Laodicea was probably founded by Epaphras.

Unlike any of the letters that have gone before, this one contains no items of praise at all. The letter to Sardis had been deeply troubling, but at least the church there did contain 'a few names' who had kept the faith. In Laodicea, there was nothing, not even a remnant in which to find some consolation.

The trouble comes from neither persecutors nor heretics. The trouble is *lukewarm hearts*: '*You are neither cold nor hot. Would that you were either cold or hot!'* (3:15). 'Laodicean' is now a word we use to describe those who are lukewarm.

Near to Laodicea were the famous hot springs of Hierapolis. Possibly this forms a background to the metaphor of lukewarm water. Hezekiah could plead to the Lord that he had been wholehearted (*Isa.* 38:3). Paul could say, 'Do not be slothful in zeal, be fervent in spirit, serve the Lord' (*Rom.* 12:11). Titus was said to be 'very earnest' as he came to Corinth (*2 Cor.* 8:17). The Laodiceans, by contrast, were none of these things. No warmth glowed in their hearts for the gospel. They had grown indifferent to its message.

Further diagnosis follows. Three claims – boasts – of the Laodiceans are picked up: their claims to being *rich, prosperous* and *full*. '*I am rich, I have prospered, and I need nothing*', they said (3:17). Living in a prosperous city, the Laodicean Christians had no doubt fallen prey to the materialistic philosophy that gripped so many and held them as prisoners to avarice. Seeing this world as more important, they set their sight on the acquisition of things, forgetting that none of these are of value in the world to come. '*You are not realizing that you are wretched, pitiful, poor, blind, and naked*', Jesus says to them.

Poor, blind and naked! Laodicea was famous for its banking industry, medical schools (with a concentration on ophthalmology), and garment industry. Jesus' words seem designed to cut through their boasting at every level. Pride had redirected their focus away from eternal issues and their hearts had grown indifferent to spiritual realities. 'We do not need a thing' was their own assessment, but it was sadly misguided. They were in desperate need. It is all too possible to be in need without knowing it.

What does Jesus say to nominal Christianity? '*I will spit you out of my mouth*' (3:16). He is nauseated by their complacency. A visit to the regions of Laodicea today will reveal no evidence of the church. However, with such warnings comes the offer of mercy: '*I counsel you to buy from me gold refined by fire, so that you may be rich, and white garments so that you may clothe yourself and the shame of your nakedness may not be seen, and salve to anoint your eyes, so that you may see*' (3:18). He invites them to have dealings with him concerning the free offer of mercy that he gives!

Again, for this to be possible, repentance must take place. They must '*be zealous and repent*' (3:19). Repentance has been a key feature of these letters from the start (2:5, 16, 21, 22; 3:3, 19).

Jesus desires a repentant church. Faith and repentance belong together.

'*Behold, I stand at the door and knock. If anyone hears my voice and opens the door, I will come in to him and eat with him, and he with me*' (3:20). Although these words have often been interpreted evangelistically and personally, the mention of eating and drinking might suggest that what is in view here is something different. These are letters to churches. The mode of expression has been corporate rather than individual. Is Jesus thinking here of his spiritual (Spiritual!) presence at the Lord's Table? Could it be that their nominalism had driven him away from the sacrament of the Supper? Perhaps. The Lord's Supper is, after all, an anticipation of the 'marriage supper' of the Lamb (19:9, 17). Feasting without Jesus is a meaningless activity.

Jesus stands outside the door. It is not so much a picture of weakness and inability as of accusation and contempt. He will only come on invitation. Only warm hearts can bring him in. Coldness – even lukewarmness – drives him outside.

A promise is offered to the conqueror. A place on the throne! That is what he offers: '*The one who conquers, I will grant him to sit with me on my throne, as I also conquered and sat down with my Father on his throne*' (3:21).

Can anything be more wonderful or unexpected?

SUMMARY

There is a pattern in each of these seven letters. Jesus makes a spiritual assessment of these churches based on two fundamental issues:

i.   Each letter tells us something that Jesus 'knows' about the church. Five of them spell it out as, 'I know your works' (2:2, 19; 3:1, 8, 15). His assessment is based not simply on their knowledge of the gospel, but on what they *do* with that knowledge. 'What have you done with the gospel?' is the measure by which the church is judged. Faith is expressed in terms of *faithfulness*.

ii.   A willingness to suffer for the gospel is one of the principal ways of measuring spiritual faithfulness (2:3, 13, 19; 3:8). The cross has to be more than a symbol of what Jesus did in the past; it must also represent the way the church suffers *for Jesus' sake*! From the very beginning, the cross is the way to life, and death the way to victory. Suffering for the sake of righteousness and spiritual maturity are always married together. The church walks in the footsteps of a crucified Saviour.

How do the churches fare? Only two churches avoid criticism, Smyrna and Philadelphia. The rest receive stinging rebukes. In summary, we can say that Jesus is concerned about three things:

i.   Many of the churches emerge as *compromised* rather than *committed*. There is praise, too. But there are serious areas of concern. Sexual immorality and idolatry are the chief problems in at least two of the churches (Pergamum, Thyatira). In both, false teaching had led to false behaviour, as it always does.

ii.   Two of the churches have developed a concern for *reputation* (Sardis, Laodicea). When the church thinks more of how the world perceives her rather than how Jesus perceives her, she is on the verge of apostasy. Size, numbers, financial balances, these are statistics that can damn the church.

iii.   Ephesus, together with Laodicea had become content with mediocrity. They had 'forsaken their first love' (2:4). The Laodicean church was typical of this, in that it was 'neither cold nor hot'. These churches had abandoned the zeal that had insisted on nothing but the best for Jesus. Their approach to discipleship had become minimalist. 'How little can I get away with?', rather than, 'What more can I do?'

What are we to do to ensure glory? 'Overcome.' Seven times Jesus says, '*To him who conquers. . .* ' (2:7, 11, 17, 26; 3:5, 12, 21). What is he talking about? *Overcoming*!

The same word comes again at the end of the book of Revelation: 'The one who conquers will have this heritage, and I will be his God and he will be my son' (21:7). The thought is that of perseverance in the face of massive obstacles and opposition. What

North Americans call 'stick-to-it-iveness', or keeping going when things get tough. 'Where there's life there's hope', folk say, but the real truth is, 'Where there's hope, there's life!' It is the prevailing message of the book of Hebrews, especially chapter 12. Keep on running the race that is set before you and don't look back! Keep on looking to Jesus to the very end. That is the only way to live for Jesus Christ.

What are the consequences of failure for the church? These letters reflect Jesus' commitment to his covenant. And covenant entails both blessings *and* curses. To those who overcome, he promises his presence and guidance. To those who do not, he threatens extinction. He removes the lampstand from those who fail to walk in his ways. Can anything be more sobering than that?

Whilst these letters have been about the state of the churches, there is a sense in which they have also been about Christ. The descriptions given of him are rich indeed:

- He holds the seven stars in his right hand (2:1; see also 3:1)
- He is the first and the last, who died and came to life again (2:8)
- He has the sharp two-edged sword (2:12)
- His eyes are like blazing fire, his feet like burnished bronze (2:18)
- He is holy and true and holds the key of David (3:7)
- He is the 'Amen', the faithful and true witness, the ruler of God's creation (3:14)

A study of these appellations would in itself be richly rewarding. It is the power and glory of Jesus that emerges here, in contrast to the weak and compromised church. Our problem is an unwillingness to hear what Jesus is saying to us in his Word (see 2:7, 11, 17, 29; 3:6, 13, 22).

Spiritual deafness is a fatal condition.

4

Heaven's Throne

[handwritten: Chpt 4 Scripture Revelation]

[handwritten: 4.1] *A*fter this I looked, and behold, a door standing open in heaven! And the first voice, which I had heard speaking to me like a trumpet, said, "Come up here, and I will show you what must take place after this." ² At once I was in the Spirit, and behold, a throne stood in heaven, with one seated on the throne. ³ And he who sat there had the appearance of jasper and carnelian, and around the throne was a rainbow that had the appearance of an emerald. ⁴ Around the throne were twenty-four thrones, and seated on the thrones were twenty-four elders, clothed in white garments, with golden crowns on their heads. ⁵ From the throne came flashes of lightning, and rumblings and peals of thunder, and before the throne were burning seven torches of fire, which are the seven spirits of God, ⁶ and before the throne there was as it were a sea of glass, like crystal.

And around the throne, on each side of the throne, are four living creatures, full of eyes in front and behind: ⁷ the first living creature like a lion, the second living creature like an ox, the third living creature with the face of a man, and the fourth living creature like an eagle in flight. ⁸ And the four living creatures, each of them with six wings, are full of eyes all around and within, and day and night they never cease to say,

"Holy, holy, holy, is the Lord God Almighty,
who was and is and is to come!"

⁹ *And whenever the living creatures give glory and honour and thanks to him who is seated on the throne, who lives forever and ever,* ¹⁰ *the twenty-four elders fall down before him who is seated on the throne and worship him who lives forever and ever. They cast their crowns before the throne, saying,*

¹¹ *"Worthy are you, our Lord and God,*
to receive glory and honour and power,
for you created all things,
and by your will they existed and were created."

⁵:¹ *Then I saw in the right hand of him who was seated on the throne a scroll written within and on the back, sealed with seven seals.* ² *And I saw a strong angel proclaiming with a loud voice, "Who is worthy to open the scroll and break its seals?"* ³ *And no one in heaven or on earth or under the earth was able to open the scroll or to look into it,* ⁴ *and I began to weep loudly because no one was found worthy to open the scroll or to look into it.* ⁵ *And one of the elders said to me, "Weep no more; behold, the Lion of the tribe of Judah, the Root of David, has conquered, so that he can open the scroll and its seven seals."*

⁶ *And between the throne and the four living creatures and among the elders I saw a Lamb standing, as though it had been slain, with seven horns and with seven eyes, which are the seven spirits of God sent out into all the earth.* ⁷ *And he went and took the scroll from the right hand of him who was seated on the throne.* ⁸ *And when he had taken the scroll, the four living creatures and the twenty-four elders fell down before the Lamb, each holding a harp, and golden bowls full of incense, which are the prayers of the saints.* ⁹ *And they sang a new song, saying,*

"Worthy are you to take the scroll
and to open its seals,
for you were slain, and by your blood you ransomed people for God from every tribe and language and people and nation,
¹⁰ *and you have made them a kingdom and priests to our God,*
and they shall reign on the earth."

¹¹ Then I looked, and I heard around the throne and the living creatures and the elders the voice of many angels, numbering myriads of myriads and thousands of thousands, ¹² saying with a loud voice, "Worthy is the Lamb who was slain, to receive power and wealth and wisdom and might and honour and glory and blessing!" ¹³ And I heard every creature in heaven and on earth and under the earth and in the sea, and all that is in them, saying, "To him who sits on the throne and to the Lamb be blessing and honour and glory and might forever and ever!" ¹⁴ And the four living creatures said, "Amen!" and the elders fell down and worshipped (Rev. 4:1–5:14).

A new section begins. After the letters to the seven churches comes a section where seven seals are opened (4:1–8:1).

'*After this I looked . . .* ' (4:1) is a phrase sometimes rendered, '*After this I saw . . .* '. We will see it again as we study this book (7:1, 9; 15:5; 18:1; 19:1).

It is important for us to realize that John is not indicating a particular chronology of the future by this statement, as though what happens next will be *subsequent* to whatever happened in the previous section or chapter. Rather, John is telling us the order in which *he received these visions.*

Since the messages of the visions are repeated in different forms, a failure to appreciate this point will lead us astray. Having *heard* in the letters of chapters 2 and 3 that Jesus reigns over the church, John is now given a *sight* of Jesus reigning in glorious triumph. The sight he sees is accompanied by music and words which have become the source of the church's praise ever since.

> *Holy, holy, holy, Lord God Almighty!*
> Early in the morning our song shall rise to Thee;
> Holy, holy, holy, merciful and mighty!
> *God in Three Persons, blessed Trinity!*

Reginald Heber's hymn still evokes what is central to our understanding of God. Full of biblical allusions to Isaiah 6 and Revelation
4 as it is, it reminds us that the praise we offer to God is filled with
a sense of awe and wonder at the majesty of his holy character.

The scene has changed from the closed door in Laodicea to an
open door that leads to heaven; the mention of a 'throne' (3:21)
now leads to a glimpse of one. From the poverty-stricken state of
the church below, John's gaze is taken upwards to things as they
truly are. The upward glance is often the signal of a new perspective on things. John is being reminded that God is in control. The
church may be languishing; Satan may be doing his worst; but God
is reigning on high. Two issues change the perspective: location
and time.

As for location, we are taken up to *'heaven'* (4:1), not the life
hereafter so much as the life here and now, but from a different perspective. As Paul reminded the Ephesians that they are
'blessed' and 'seated' with Christ 'in the heavenly realms' (*Eph.*
1:3; 2:6), so John is reminded of a greater reality than that which
can be seen and touched. The opening of heaven is a characteristic
apocalyptic phenomenon, preparing us for the giving of new (or
perhaps forgotten) revelation. How much the church needs to heed
it! There is a reality which transcends that which we can see with
our physical eyes.

As for time, John is shown *'what must take place after this'* (4:1),
a reference which appears to include within it the whole of history
from John's time to ours and beyond. Since John has already used
this phrase in 1:19, it is reasonable to conclude that its repetition
here indicates a parallel vision: what we see in chapter 4 is true at
the same time as what is seen in the previous chapters.

Jesus is reigning and surrounded by the praise of angels and
departed souls as he writes to the seven churches. Encapsulated in
a single vision is a glimpse of the church and the world. God has
the whole world in his hands! More particularly, he has the church
and her future in his hands! As Jeremiah put it: 'A glorious throne
set on high from the beginning, is the place of our sanctuary' (*Jer.*
17:12).

Chapters 4 and 5 belong together for they establish the same truth,
or *truths*: that God is sovereign, and that he is to be worshipped. Both

of these truths are, of course, complementary; they belong together, but fallen mankind has neglected both, and the church has often failed to see the connection between the two. 'If God is not sovereign, then God is not God', the saying goes; and how right it is! From the very beginning, God showed himself as Creator, sovereignly making all things out of nothing, bringing everything that has existence into being by the Word of his mouth.

The story of the Bible is the story of mankind ignoring his kingship, coveting other lords to rule over them, gods that could be manipulated and cajoled to do whatever man desired. Worship, consequently, has been misplaced: man has worshipped 'the creature rather than the Creator' (*Rom.* 1:25). The mind of fallen man, as Calvin put it, is a perpetual factory of idols.

In a single vision, Revelation now brings into focus the One who truly rules the world. '*A throne stood in heaven, with one seated on the throne*' (4:2). It is not the first of its kind in the Bible. It shows some similarities to the vision of God in Ezekiel 1, with its depiction of a throne. Here in Revelation 4, God's dazzling light is bedecked with precious jewels. Several images come together, including that of a rainbow whose beauty is a sign of God's covenant mercy to a fallen world (4:3; *Gen.* 9:13), and stones (jasper, carnelian, and emerald; 4:3) anticipating an entire list of precious stones in chapter 21 (verses 19–20).

God's throne is surrounded by twenty-four thrones on which sit twenty-four elders (4:4). The number twenty-four symbolizes the twelve tribes of Israel and the twelve apostles of the New Testament era – who together represent the church of all ages. What is being shown is of great significance. The saints of the Old Testament period, together with those who have died thus far in the New, are not only alive; they are reigning! To saints concerned about loved ones who have been martyred – many of the first readers of Revelation were concerned about their friends and relatives who had died in this way – this vision must have come as wonderful news.

The '*flashes of lightning, and rumblings and peals of thunder*' (4:5; see also 8:5; 11:19; 16:18) are reminiscent of Sinai and the giving of the Law (*Exod.* 19:16). Before the throne are seven lamps (compare *Zech.* 4:2–3, 10) which are said to be '*the seven spirits of God*' (4:5; see *Zech.* 4:6). In the next chapter, a further explanation is given describing these seven spirits as the '*seven horns and seven eyes*' of the slain Lamb standing '*between the throne and the four living creatures*' (5:6). The Zechariah passages help us understand that what is in view here is that the Lamb (Jesus) sees and knows what is taking place on earth (eyes) and is able to do something about it (horns = strength). By the 'seven spirits' (that is, the Holy Spirit – 'my Spirit', *Zech.* 4:6), God exercises his sovereignty in the earth. The Holy Spirit carries out God's plan and purpose.

The '*sea of glass*' (4:6, note that it '*was as it were*' a sea of glass, John is having difficulty describing everything that he saw) brings back memories of the laver of water in the temple used for ceremonial washings, a symbol that continues in New Testament times in baptism. The heaven portrayed in Revelation is the true temple of God (of which the earthly temple was a copy – 7:15; 11:19; 14:15, 17; 15:5–16:1; 16:17), and here we are being given a symbolic portrait of its 'cleansed' inhabitants. 'Nothing unclean will ever enter it . . .' (21:27). Some have seen in the 'sea of glass' an allusion to the Red Sea, and the power of God that calmed it and brought it into submission; an allusion to cosmic power.

In the centre, around the throne, were four living creatures (4:6). It is not the *church's* worship that is first alluded to, but that of the *entire creation*. The four '*living creatures*' are a lion (the noblest), an ox (the strongest), a man (the wisest) and an eagle (the swiftest). Early Christian writers thought these creatures represented the four Gospel writers. However, what is more likely is that they signify the Bible's anticipation of the redemption of the creation itself (*Rom.* 8:21); there will be a new heaven and a new *earth* (*2 Pet.* 3:13). In the background are similar (though not identical) passages in the Old Testament (Isaiah 6 and Ezekiel 1).

The entire creation is worshipping God! Heaven is a place of worship.

HOLINESS

It is interesting that the focus of heavenly worship is the *holiness* of God. The stress upon God's holiness reminds us of the seraphim in Isaiah 6 who sing a similar song emphasizing the same attribute of God. God's holiness implies that he is different, 'separated' from his creation.

The importance of this word 'holy' is seen in an interesting fact: in the Bible, where God's 'name' is mentioned, it is qualified by the adjective *holy* more often than it is by all the other qualifiers put together. The first and the last songs of the Bible exalt God's holiness. Moses, thinking of what God had done in the crossing of the Red Sea and the deliverance of Israel, sang: 'Who is like you, O LORD, among the gods? Who is like you, *majestic in holiness*, awesome in glorious deeds, doing wonders?' (*Exod.* 15:11). And we shall find in Revelation 15 that those who had been victorious over the beast sang a similar song: 'Who will not fear you, O Lord, and glorify your name? For *you alone are holy*' (15:4).

Taking the worship offered by the four creatures and by the twenty-four elders together, several attributes seem to surface in the worship of the heavenly host which give further expression to God's holiness:

i.   *God is Almighty*. He is the '*Lord God Almighty*' (4:8). His power and majesty are beyond human grasp. He is the Creator of everything that has existence; by the Word of his power he brought what is into being. This truth encourages as much as it intimidates. For languishing churches such as these depicted in Asia Minor, facing the onslaughts of Satan, struggling in a wicked and hostile world, the knowledge that God is sovereign is invigorating in a way that nothing else is. God's sovereignty is the guarantee of providence. 'The LORD reigns' (*Psa.* 93:1). He is the Creator of all that is: '*For you created all things, and by your will they existed and were created*' (4:11).

ii.   *God is great, in the sense that he is exalted*. When the twenty-four elders join in the worship of God later in the chapter (4:10), they fall down before him, expressing awe and submissiveness. God is incomprehensible. His ways are not our ways; his thoughts are not our thoughts (*Isa.* 55:8). There is a mystery about the nature of God that should make us fear him in a spirit of reverence and humility. Genuine worshippers wish to blot themselves out of the picture so that God may become everything.

The four living creatures are said to have six wings, as though ready to fly in whatever direction God commands: worship must always lead to service (4:8). It was Paul's conclusion to his systematic treatment of the application of redemption: 'I appeal to you there-fore, brothers, by the mercies of God, to present your bodies as a living sacrifice, holy and acceptable to God, which is your spiritual worship' (*Rom.* 12:1).

iii.   *God is glorious.* The Bible word '*glory*' (4:11) has its root meaning in the idea of 'weight', and thus significance. There is a consideration to be given to God that exceeds that which we give to anyone or anything else. No-one is of greater significance than God. God's glory is his nature and power *shown forth* (see *John* 2:11). When God is said to *receive* glory, it indicates God being worshipped *as* God; he is being given the honour that is due to him. Worship is our response to God as revealed to us.

iv.   *God is eternal.* God '*was and is and is to come*' (4:8; compare 1:8). In contrast to ourselves, the four creatures exalt the eternity of God's existence. Unlike the creation, there is neither beginning nor end to the existence of God.

Worship is all about our response to God. It is giving him the praise and adoration that is due to his name. The more we know of God, the more childlike our faith ought to become. We cannot know too much, nor can this truth ever be over-emphasized. Even John was to get it wrong, mistakenly worshipping an angel rather than God. 'Worship God!' the angel said to him (19:10).

An important feature of the creatures' worship is the allusion to God as '*the Lord God Almighty, who was and is and is to come*' (4:8). There are echoes here of God's revealed name as the 'I AM WHO I AM' given to Moses (*Exod.* 3:14). It is also capable of being rendered 'I WILL BE WHO I WILL BE'. The name is further identified as 'LORD' (*Exod.* 3:15, and capitalized in our English translations). This is God's covenant name.

The worship of heaven is the worship of Israel's Covenant LORD. He will be identified as Jesus in chapter 5, as he has been already (1:8). This is the staggering claim of New Testament revelation: 'Jesus Christ is Lord' (*Phil.* 2:11). He is given glory (4:9), and worshipped (4:10).

'*Worthy are you, our Lord and God, to receive glory and honour and power, for you created all things, and by your will they existed and were created*' (4:11). The words remind us of Daniel 4:35:

All the inhabitants of the earth are regarded as nothing.
And he does according to his will
    among the host of heaven
And among the inhabitants of the earth.
And none can stay his hand
    Or say to him, 'What have you done?'

God's creative and upholding sovereignty is the basis for worship. The will of God is ultimate: not man's will, not the church's will, but the will of God alone. He creates and upholds to fulfil his own purpose. Appreciating this reduces us to size. 'To God alone be the glory' was one watchword of the sixteenth-century Reformation, and that because they had understood that God is sovereign. Heaven will eternally reflect this and earthly worship ought to seek to conform to it.

Jesus Is Lord

The identity of the One who sits on the throne deserves further attention. Who is he?

Clearly, in chapter 5, we are introduced to a parallel truth: Christ, too, sits enthroned in heaven. Worship is afforded him also. The focus on God in chapter 4 now narrows to Jesus Christ.

The sovereignty of God we see depicted in chapter 4 begs the question, How can God show mercy and remain faithful to his sovereign justice? The answer is that God has in himself – *in Christ!* – resolved the problem that sin has caused. God has become the Saviour of sinners!

Such is the problem depicted in the opening of the fifth chapter. A '*scroll written within and on the back, sealed with seven seals*' (5:1) is viewed, suggesting a comprehensive knowledge of things. The ESV adoption of 'scroll' rather than 'book' may be right: scrolls written on both sides and sealed in such a way that their contents were successively revealed as each separate seal was broken are known to have existed in the first century. Some have noted the similarity to wills or testaments, the contents of which were preserved against alteration by seals. The fact that John uses the verb 'to open' rather than 'unroll' (5:2) may suggest a book, rather than a scroll, but most commentators believe it is a scroll. But what does the scroll contain?

An angel proclaims the predicament: Is there anyone in all of heaven and earth who can break open the seals and peep inside? Isaiah had depicted a similar scenario (*Isa.* 29:11–12). The allusion is almost certainly to Ezekiel 2:10 where the prophet is shown a scroll, on both sides of which were words 'of lament and mourning and woe'.

This would seem to indicate that the scroll contains the purposes of God in judgment and salvation, rather than, say, the names of the elect (as some have suggested). The fact that as yet these judgments (revealed by the breaking of the seals) have not been revealed (from John's perspective) argues against the idea that these judgments portray a history that has already happened.

Is anyone able to open these seals? The point of this vision is to tell us that the one who is able to break the seals is Jesus Christ, our Mediator. He is *able* to do so because he stands '*between the throne and the four living creatures*' (5:6). The sovereignty of God is the sovereignty of Christ.

At the very point where we have seen the Father in chapter 4, we see the Son in chapter 5. Christ is the focus of all attention, the one with whom every other is enthralled. The paeans of praise rise to him as they do to God himself, for there is no distinction: the church, the angels, the whole of creation sing his praise and offer him worship.

And why? Because a kingdom has been given to him. The Lamb is worthy to open the scroll because he has purchased men by his blood. In appearance he looks as though he has been slain (5:6, 9). Through his passion he has '*ransomed people for God*,' establishing them as '*a kingdom and priests to our God*' (5:9–10). Several things seem to come to the surface:

i.   The very existence of a Mediator is a cause for celebration. The natural reaction to the sight of a sealed scroll was to weep (5:4). But God has found a way both to be just and the Justifier of the one who believes in Jesus (*Rom.* 3:26).

ii.   The Mediator is both a Lion (5:5) and a Lamb (5:6); he stands in the very centre of the throne (5:6) and appears slain

(5:6,9,12). He is both God and man. To him belongs sovereignty and dependence. He is both invincible and mortal.

iii.   The kingdom (5:10) which he makes from 'every tribe and language and people and nation' (5:9) is one given to him as the Mediator. He reigns in the interests of this kingdom which he has won on the basis of the redemption which he has purchased. One day, he will surrender this kingdom to the Father (*1 Cor.* 15:28).

iv.   The imagery is suggestive of the fact that Christ, in his exalted condition, still bears the marks of his suffering (5:6). The pre-ascension body of Jesus was in a temporary, transitional state and this explains in part the inability of the disciples to recognize him – Mary, for one, thought him to be the gardener (*John* 20:15)! Whatever changes mark his ascension, whatever Paul may mean when he describes the resurrected body as 'glorious' (*Phil.* 3:21), it does not mean that he has lost the marks of his humanity, and certainly not those marks which identify his role as the suffering Servant.

SONGS OF LOUDEST PRAISE

The worship described in the closing verses of chapter 5 is that of the ransomed church. Its praise is mixed with that of angels, 'numbering thousands of thousands' (5:11). Angels, though unfallen and not themselves part of the redeemed community mentioned in 5:9–10, nevertheless join in the acclamation of Christ.

Heaven is preoccupied with the worship of God and of the Lamb (5:13). Three features are worth noting.

First, the corporate '*Amen*' (5:14). There is something affirming about the 'Amen'. It is an audible response to the truthfulness of all that has been said. According to Justin Martyr, describing mid-second-century worship, the 'Amens' punctuated the worship. (*Epeuphémei* he called them, 'shouts in applause'). 'The Amen' is the title already given to Jesus (3:14; see also *Isa.* 65:16). The church tried using other words, including the Greek word for 'truth', and even the Greek for 'Amen' but eventually reverted to using the Hebrew 'Amen', as the Jewish saints did.

Secondly, praying (5:9). No gathering for worship can avoid the suppliants' cry to God. Prayers are like '*incense*', delighting God's senses as a sweet smelling aroma (see 5:8).

Thirdly, singing (5:9, 12, 13). Worship *sings*. When Jesus is viewed in his majestic glory, and his work comprehended in its regal splendour, songs are irrepressible. There are five songs in these two chapters, the first two to God the Creator, the third and fourth to the Redeemer, and the last one to both Creator and Redeemer together (4:8, 11; 5:9–10, 12, 13).

5

The Opening of the Seals

*N*ow *I watched when the Lamb opened one of the seven seals, and I heard one of the four living creatures say with a voice like thunder, "Come!"* ² *And I looked, and behold, a white horse! And its rider had a bow, and a crown was given to him, and he came out conquering, and to conquer.*

³ *When he opened the second seal, I heard the second living creature say, "Come!"* ⁴ *And out came another horse, bright red. Its rider was permitted to take peace from the earth, so that men should slay one another, and he was given a great sword.*

⁵ *When he opened the third seal, I heard the third living creature say, "Come!" And I looked, and behold, a black horse! And its rider had a pair of scales in his hand.* ⁶ *And I heard what seemed to be a voice in the midst of the four living creatures, saying, "A quart of wheat for a denarius, and three quarts of barley for a denarius, and do not harm the oil and wine!"*

⁷ *When he opened the fourth seal, I heard the voice of the fourth living creature say, "Come!"* ⁸ *And I looked, and behold, a pale horse! And its rider's name was Death, and Hades followed him. And they were given authority over a fourth of the earth, to kill with sword and with famine and with pestilence and by wild beasts of the earth.*

⁹ *When he opened the fifth seal, I saw under the altar the souls of those who had been slain for the word of God and for the witness they had borne.* ¹⁰ *They cried out with a loud voice, "O Sovereign Lord, holy and true, how long before you will judge and avenge our blood on those who dwell on the earth?"*

[11] Then they were each given a white robe and told to rest a little longer, until the number of their fellow servants and their brothers should be complete, who were to be killed as they themselves had been.

[12] When he opened the sixth seal, I looked, and behold, there was a great earthquake, and the sun became black as sackcloth, the full moon became like blood, [13] and the stars of the sky fell to the earth as the fig tree sheds its winter fruit when shaken by a gale. [14] The sky vanished like a scroll that is being rolled up, and every mountain and island was removed from its place. [15] Then the kings of the earth and the great ones and the generals and the rich and the powerful, and everyone, slave and free, hid themselves in the caves and among the rocks of the mountains, [16] calling to the mountains and rocks, "Fall on us and hide us from the face of him who is seated on the throne, and from the wrath of the Lamb, [17] for the great day of their wrath has come, and who can stand?" (Rev. 6:1–17).

Just as chapters 4 and 5 belong together, so, in some senses at least, do chapters 6 and 7. Chapter 5:1 introduced us to a scroll (or 'book') sealed with seven seals. Chapter 6 now relates the opening of the first six of these seals (the seventh is opened at 8:1).

We may already be asking, What is this scroll? One way to answer that is to allow the seals to be opened and let the text tell us what is inside!

And what is inside? Trouble and more trouble! But it is not as simple as that. In some sense at least, we do not need Jesus to tell us that the world is going to be full of troubles. What we need, and what we find here, is an *interpretation* of trouble. Providence, however dark, is always purposive. Revelation 6 gives us a way to look at the troubles of this world and give them an explanation from a Christian and theocentric, or God-centred, point of view.

For John's readers, the Christian life was costly. For some it involved imprisonment, for others, death. Jesus, so it seemed, had not taken all their troubles away. Ownership of Jesus' name seemed to involve a costliness that was beyond the ability of many to understand. Faith itself was under attack as the cost of discipleship rose. The book of Revelation is a glimpse of the future in order to steel the nerves of the faithful. But it is also a glimpse of the present (*their* present) in order to reassure the faithful that God had not abandoned them.

If Christ is establishing his kingdom, as chapter 5 has suggested, then why is it that so many Christians are being put to death? This was an intensely personal issue for the church in John's day, and it remains problematic for Christians today in many parts of the world. The book of Revelation gives us an answer that is designed to instil in us the greatest confidence in the unfolding providence of God. It has prepared us for the worst. After examining chapter 6 we will be all the more grateful for chapters 4 and 5. Only to the extent that we know Christ's rule shall we appreciate how he conquers every foe.

THE FOUR HORSEMEN OF THE APOCALYPSE

There is no real break following the end of chapter 5. John had seen and heard the worship of heaven. Then, '*I watched when the Lamb opened one of the seven seals*' (6:1). It is not as though the worship has ended and something else has begun. The Lamb is reigning in heaven and *at the same time* there is chaos and disorder on earth. The Lamb is being presented to John as the interpreter of history, as the Lord over chaos and evil.

A seven point sermon follows, as each seal, in turn, is unlocked. The first four seals are broken to reveal four horses. Strange? Of course! But only because we no longer associate horses with war as John's readers no doubt did (see *Job* 39:25; *Psa.* 76:6; *Prov.* 21:31; *Ezek.* 26:10).

What these un-sealings prepare us for is warfare. Tribulation is part of the believer's lot. The problem of evil is a problem for the atheist! For the believer, evil is going to be conquered; it has, in one sense, been conquered in Christ's death and resurrection, and what we now see of evil's machinations are the death throes of a defeated enemy who cannot bring himself to believe that it is all over.

The first unsealing gives us a glimpse of a man riding a *white horse* (6:2). Who is this rider on a white horse? Commentators have been sharply divided: some suggesting that it is Christ and others suggesting that it is Antichrist!

It is not difficult to see why some have thought this white horse-
man is Christ. Revelation 19:11–16 portrays Christ riding on a
white horse. There we are given a vivid picture of how Jesus makes
sense of history in a fallen world. He is working out his Father's
purpose, so that one day he may present him with a kingdom (see
1 Cor. 15:24).

However, it would be unusual for Christ to open the seal which
contains a revelation of himself. Other considerations suggest that
the white horse and its rider belong, in fact, to the same grouping
as the other three: together they form a quartet of evil aimed against
the world. Satan often mimics Christ. What we have here is parody!
The figure riding forth conquering and to conquer is not Christ,
but Christ's enemy!

The next three unsealings provide us with glimpses of the *red horse*
of war (6:4), the *black horse* of famine (6:5–6), and the *pale horse* of
death and Hades (6:8). This evil quartet wreaks havoc in every sphere
of human life: social, ecological and biological. Wherever Adam's
fall has penetrated, death's sting has reached. There is no escaping
its clutches. History, no matter what century, is a story of assaults
on life, land, and body. History, from John's time until now, has
been about war, famine and death. The twentieth century was the
bloodiest in the history of mankind. John's prophecy is being fulfilled
before our very eyes. All four riders are called to battle, '*Come!*'
(6:1,3,5,7). Jesus is calling the evil horsemen to wage war! How can
this be? It is the same problem that emerges when Satan harasses
Job. He does so at the suggestion of God himself (*Job* 1:8; 2:3).

God's sovereignty means that, in an ultimate sense, nothing
happens outside of his will or decree. *Nothing!* And yet, theologians
have always been eager to add that God is not the author of sin.
Sin is under his control, and here the mayhem that these horsemen
and their riders exert is under his control, too. They cannot move
a muscle without the permission of God.

What the four horsemen of the apocalypse reveal is that which Jesus
had predicted in the Olivet Discourse: 'When you hear of wars and
rumours of wars, do not be alarmed. This must take place, but the
end is not yet. But nation will rise against nation, and kingdom against
kingdom. There will be earthquakes in various places; there will be
famines. These are but the beginning of birth pains' (*Mark* 13:7–8).

MARTYRED SOULS IN HEAVEN

There is a narrower dimension of evil in the unsealing of the fifth seal (6:9–11). This is a depiction of religious persecution in its most vicious form. John sees the *'souls'* of martyred saints before the throne of God. His first readers would have understood this well. They, after all, had lost loved ones to successive waves of Roman persecution and were about to experience some of its fiercest expressions.

The word *'soul'* here signifies that part of our existence which survives the death of the body (for a similar use of the word, see Matthew 10:28). This must have been encouraging to John's readers. Those who died so brutally were in heaven! The vision will return again towards the close of the book of Revelation. In chapter 20, in the notoriously problematic passage which refers to the 'thousand years', John sees 'the souls of those who had been beheaded' (20:4; compare this with *'slain'* in 6:9).

Although the souls are said to be before the throne of God, their specific location is described as *'under the altar'* (6:9). The altar was where sacrificial blood was poured under the Old Covenant administration and where 'life' resulted for the offending party (*Lev.* 17:11). The souls John sees have life, but only because atonement by blood-shedding has been provided for them.

It is difficult to imagine anything of greater help to John's readers than to know that loved ones and friends who had been cruelly killed for their testimony to Christ are now alive and *with* Christ. To the question, 'Why does God allow such terrible things to happen to God's people?', comes a two-fold reply. First, they are given white robes – a symbol of victory. Second, they are told to rest for a while until the number of their fellow servants who are killed is complete (6:11).

Suffering is to be understood as something that happens in this world. It lasts only *until* the course of this world is *'complete'*. This provides for us the basic *eschatological* thrust of the New Testament view of life: we live in expectation of the end when God shall wrap everything up. It is a reminder that he is in control of history. Until then, they are to wait *'a little longer'* (6:11).

But it is their cry that proves interesting, and it will prove so throughout the rest of the book. Their cry is haunting: *'O*

Sovereign Lord, holy and true, how long before you will judge and avenge our blood on those who dwell on the earth?' (6:10). Christians who do not appreciate the role justice plays in the works of God, who think that all Christians do is forgive, find themselves puzzled by this cry. But it is not at all puzzling. It is simply the cry of those who long that the justice of God (as well as his mercy) prevail. They are not encouraging vengeance on the part of their surviving relatives. No! They are asking for God to vindicate his own name and honour. The Day of Judgment will be God's answer to this prayer.

Verse 11 becomes important, interpretatively, for the entire book of Revelation. It assumes that the persecution that befalls Christians has come to an end, their number is 'completed' (6:11). Whatever happens next (6:12–17) – the opening of the sixth seal – belongs to something at the very close of history, when, in fact, history has run its course. What follows is a description of the judgment of unbelievers on the Day of Judgment itself.

THE DAY OF JUDGMENT

The language of this final judgment is taken from a compilation of Old Testament passages from the prophets, including Isaiah 34:4: 'All the host of heaven will rot away, and the sky roll up like a scroll. All their host shall fall, as leaves fall from the vine, like leaves falling from the fig tree.' It is a vivid and figurative depiction of the Last Judgment and the language employed will occur again (for example, 11:13; 16:18).

When God's wrath falls, it is terrifying. Those who experience it desire to hide themselves from its fierceness. The regions of Asia Minor (present-day Turkey) to which this letter was addressed were known for caves in which shelter from passing storms could be sought. Despite their cries for somewhere to hide from God's wrath, they will not find it (6:16). No one will be able to '*stand*' on the Day of his wrath (6:17).

It is perhaps most revealing of all that the wrath from which they seek to hide is that of a Lamb! The Lamb will be the judge on the Last Day. 'God judges the secrets of men by Jesus Christ', says Paul (*Rom.* 2:16). Jesus himself taught this! Speaking of the 'Son of Man' (his favourite self-designation), he said, 'The Father . . .

has given him authority to execute judgment' (*John* 5:27; see also *Matt.* 7:21; 25:31–33; *Acts* 10:42; 17:31; *2 Cor.* 5:10; *2 Thess.* 1:7–8; *2 Tim.* 4:1).

Why is this significant? Because we can never say that God does not know what we have to endure. In Christ he has been tempted. He has suffered. He knows our human condition. On that basis he will judge (*Rom.* 2:16).

The chapter ends with this great question: 'For the great day of their wrath has come, and who can stand?' (6:17).

Who can stand? That is the question which chapter 7 will answer for us. The question is not, 'Will I survive the trouble that lies in this world?', but, 'Will I survive the judgment of the Lamb?' And there is only one sure way to answer that question. We must believe the message of the gospel that says that faith in Jesus Christ delivers us from the wrath which is to come. The great answer of chapter 7 is that every single soul that Jesus seals in this world, will withstand the judgment of the world to come. Every single one!

That is a truth worth knowing and making our own.

6

The Glorified Spirits in Heaven

*A*fter this I saw four angels standing at the four corners of the earth, holding back the four winds of the earth, that no wind might blow on earth or sea or against any tree. ² Then I saw another angel ascending from the rising of the sun, with the seal of the living God, and he called with a loud voice to the four angels who had been given power to harm earth and sea, ³ saying, "Do not harm the earth or the sea or the trees, until we have sealed the servants of our God on their foreheads." ⁴ And I heard the number of the sealed, 144,000, sealed from every tribe of the sons of Israel:

⁵ 12,000 from the tribe of Judah were sealed,
  12,000 from the tribe of Reuben,
  12,000 from the tribe of Gad,
  ⁶ 12,000 from the tribe of Asher,
  12,000 from the tribe of Naphtali,
  12,000 from the tribe of Manasseh,
  ⁷ 12,000 from the tribe of Simeon,
  12,000 from the tribe of Levi,
  12,000 from the tribe of Issachar,
  ⁸ 12,000 from the tribe of Zebulun,
  12,000 from the tribe of Joseph,
  12,000 from the tribe of Benjamin were sealed.

⁹ After this I looked, and behold, a great multitude that no one could number, from every nation, from all tribes and peoples

and languages, standing before the throne and before the Lamb, clothed in white robes, with palm branches in their hands, [10] *and crying out with a loud voice, "Salvation belongs to our God who sits on the throne, and to the Lamb!"* [11] *And all the angels were standing around the throne and around the elders and the four living creatures, and they fell on their faces before the throne and worshipped God,* [12] *saying, "Amen! Blessing and glory and wisdom and thanksgiving and honour and power and might be to our God forever and ever! Amen."*

[13] *Then one of the elders addressed me, saying, "Who are these, clothed in white robes, and from where have they come?"* [14] *I said to him, "Sir, you know." And he said to me, "These are the ones coming out of the great tribulation. They have washed their robes and made them white in the blood of the Lamb.*

[15] *"Therefore they are before the throne of God,*
and serve him day and night in his temple;
and he who sits on the throne will shelter them with
his presence.
[16] *They shall hunger no more, neither thirst anymore;*
the sun shall not strike them,
nor any scorching heat.
[17] *For the Lamb in the midst of the throne will be*
their shepherd,
and he will guide them to springs of living water,
and God will wipe away every tear from their eyes."

[8:1] *When the Lamb opened the seventh seal, there was silence in heaven for about half an hour.* [2] *Then I saw the seven angels who stand before God, and seven trumpets were given to them.* [3] *And another angel came and stood at the altar with a golden censer, and he was given much incense to offer with the prayers of all the saints on the golden altar before the throne,* [4] *and the smoke of the incense, with the prayers of the saints, rose before God from the hand of the angel.* [5] *Then the angel took the censer and filled it with fire from the altar and threw it on the earth, and there were peals of thunder, rumblings, flashes of lightning, and an earthquake* (Rev. 7:1–8:5).

Revelation 7 functions as an interval between the opening of the sixth seal (6:12–17) and the seventh seal (8:1). It is an answer to the question posed at the end of chapter 6: '*The great day of their wrath has come, and who can stand?*' (6:17). It depicts a company of the redeemed who emerge triumphant by the grace of God in Jesus Christ through 'the tribulation'. There are close parallels with chapter 14:1–4.

We have seen how this question was posed as a response to the opening of the sixth seal, one in a series of seven, each one allowing us to glimpse a part of the unfolding of history. To a war-torn church, the present looked difficult enough; but what about the future? Seals 2–6 had unveiled trouble of immense proportions, a glimpse of things to come, and the sixth seal had brought us to the end: the judgment at the end of the age. 'If the foundations are destroyed, what can the righteous do?' (*Psa.* 11:3).

So where does chapter 7 belong in the chronology of things? '*After this*' (7:1) might seem at first to imply that the events of chapter 7 belong *chronologically* after chapter 6, but this hardly seems to be the case. At 7:3 it is clear that the earth has not yet been harmed and it is difficult to see how this can follow what has already been described in 6:12–14 where the earth is breaking apart under the weight of judgment.

We might have expected following the description of the opening of the sixth seal a depiction of the Day of Judgment itself. Instead, chapter 7 begins by saying that John sees four angels, '*standing at the four corners of the earth, holding back the four winds*' (7:1).

This gives us a clue as to how we should read the book of Revelation. The chronology that John gives us is not the order in which events take place in history, but the chronology of the order of the events *as he saw them*. John is being given a vision of the same events from a different perspective. Chapter 7 is providing for us a picture of an order of reality that exists *simultaneously* with the depiction of the judgments described in the first six seals.

What we have, then, in chapter 7 runs parallel with the sixth chapter, repeated in a slightly different way in order to bring out an important truth not mentioned in the preceding chapter. Chapter 6 had opened with the destruction brought about by the 'four horsemen of the apocalypse'. Nothing has been said about the ultimate security of God's people. Will they survive the ravages of war and destruction? Will they persevere?

Who Can Stand?

Chapter 7, in retelling the story of things to come, tells the same story, but uses a different image – *'winds'* instead of 'horsemen.' In this way, the imagery echoes the vision of Zechariah 6 where four chariots are said to represent the four 'winds'. The angels of chapter 7 are given power to restrain the 'winds' of destruction. No wind is to blow *'on the earth or sea or against any tree'* (7:1). The kind of power attributed to instruments of evil in chapter 6 is now attributed to angels in chapter 7. God is the ultimate sovereign over all events. Even Satan does his bidding in the end.

The question remains, 'Who can stand?' It is a question which this seventh chapter seeks to answer in a way that gives the greatest relief to the people of God. First, the repetition of the verb 'to stand' at the end of chapter 6 and the beginning of chapter 7 (6:17; 7:1) tells us immediately that the angels of heaven are unaffected by the turmoil described. They are safe and secure. They are standing firm (7:1,11). Evil, in all its machinations, does not unsettle them from their God-given positions. Throughout the turmoil, they continue to serve and worship (7:11). Heaven is a *safe* place, and worship continues unhindered even when hell itself breaks loose to destroy the world below. In addition, *'a great multitude that no one could number'* (7:9) are standing, too. John sees *'another angel'* having *'the seal of the living God'* (7:2) who is restraining the other angels from doing their work *'until we have sealed the servants of our God on their foreheads'* (7:3). The judgments are not to take place until the servants of God are identified and secured.

Two questions emerge: 'What is this seal?' And, 'Who are ones who are sealed?' The answer to both (as is often the case in Revelation) lies in the Old Testament.

The Sealing of 144,000

Even though the seventh seal is not opened until chapter 8, a seal is mentioned in this chapter. *'Then I saw another angel ascending from the rising of the sun with the seal of the living God'* (7:2). If the un-sealings of chapter 6 had shown history in all its terrifying prospects, the seal spoken of here has a different connotation. In chapter 6, seals 2–6 had unleashed evil; here the seal speaks of peace, protection and promise. '*We have sealed the servants of our God on their foreheads*' (7:3).

The book of Ezekiel describes a similar event whereby an angel is given responsibility to identify and seal the people of God, thereby reassuring them of their security amidst the judgment that follows (*Ezek.* 9:1–4). God identifies and thereby keeps and protects those that belong to him for ever. As disasters come upon the earth God reassures his people of their eternal security within the covenant of grace.

Seals are meant to be reassuring. Recovered from the biblical site of Megiddo was a jasper seal bearing the figure of a roaring lion. An inscription reads, 'Belonging to Shema, servant of Jeroboam.' It was once the property of an official of Jeroboam II, king of Israel, 785–743 BC (*2 Kings* 14:23–29). Shema no doubt used it each day to press upon documents the seal and authority of his king.

God's seals have a similar significance. We speak of the sacraments as signs and *seals*. In baptism God seals us by giving us his name; in the Lord's Supper we are promised his presence. God's seal is more than an emblem to be pressed on paper; it is his own presence promised to his people. The Holy Spirit is the seal: Having 'believed in him, [you] were sealed with the promised Holy Spirit, who is the guarantee of our inheritance until we acquire possession of it, to the praise of his glory' (*Eph.* 1:13–14; see also *Eph.* 4:30).

Two complementary truths come into focus: first, God's seal is his claim upon us. 'It is he who made us, and we are his' (*Psa.* 100:3). 'The LORD's portion is his people' (*Deut.* 32:9). Second, God's seal gives us a claim on him. The Spirit certifies his pledge to us. The Holy Spirit is God's down-payment guaranteeing full and final salvation. It is interesting that Paul combines the ideas of standing and sealing in 2 Corinthians 1:21–22: 'And it is God who establishes us with you in Christ, and has anointed us, and who has also put his seal on us and given us his Spirit in our hearts as a guarantee.'

Who are ones who are sealed? The next section identifies them as the 144,000 made up of the twelve tribes of Israel (7:4–8). John sees the people of God assembled around the throne in heaven in much the same way as the tribes assembled around the tabernacle are described in Numbers 2. They are symbolic of the church triumphant in heaven, those who have come to realize the value of redeeming grace (7:10). The Reformation distinctives of *sola gratia* (grace alone), and *soli Christo* (Christ alone) accompany their worship. They are eager to magnify the sovereignty of God in grace; salvation belongs to God as the author and accomplisher of redemption.

But why 144,000? The reference in verse 4 to seeing '*144,000*' is almost certainly parallel with verse 9, where John sees, '*a great multitude that no one could number*'. Verse 9 is introduced by the expression, '*after this*' in the same way as verse 1, but we have already noted this does not necessarily imply chronological sequence, but merely the order in which the visions came to John. The number 144,000, then, is almost certainly a figurative way of expressing a very large number which is complete or fixed. Multiplying the numbers 144 (12 times 12, representing all of the tribes of Israel, an allusion which ties in with verses 5–8, or more likely, the twelve tribes and twelve apostles representing the Old and New Testament church, see 21:9-10) and 1000 (a number of completeness) produces a quantity representing vastness.

Those who are sealed are '*a great multitude that no one could number, from every nation, from all tribes and peoples and languages*'. A seal is applied to every member of the kingdom, *before* any harm comes to the earth (7:3). It is the security described by the Psalmist when he assures us that 'no evil shall be allowed to befall you, no plague come near your tent' (*Psa.* 91:10), and 'the LORD will keep you from all evil; he will keep your life' (*Psa.* 121:7).

If, as we have been suggesting, the 144,000 of verse 4, and the '*great multitude that no one could number*' of verse 9, are one and the same, why is it that detailed reference is given to the twelve tribes in verse 5–8? One possible answer would be that Revelation is mimicking what the book of Numbers does whenever it records a census of fighting men (see *Num.* 1:21, 23). Revelation 7 is therefore recording in symbolic manner an army of men who will fight for the Lamb and emerge victorious from the battle (7:14). These Christian soldiers emerge *out of* the battle – there is no indication of a Rapture away from it. In this way, the promise given to

Abraham, that he would be the father of *many nations* (*Gen.* 17:4–6) is fulfilled. God's covenant of grace has now unfolded in all its multi-faceted dimensions. The beauty of the work of redemption has been disclosed.

In John's time, the church was small and, in the world's estimation, insignificant. In many ages since, the church has appeared a dwindling community of no great significance. But in reality, what the Bible wants us to think is the reality that the church is bigger than we can estimate, '*a great multitude that no one could number*' (7:9). This takes us sweeping back through the Old Testament to the inaugural covenant with Abraham, when God beckoned him to count the stars, adding, 'So shall your offspring be' (*Gen.* 15:5).

Their variety is underlined by the expression, '*from every nation, from all tribes and peoples and languages*' (7:9; see also 5:9; 11:9; 13:7; 14:6; 17:15). The gospel is to go into all the world. Jesus' last words on earth echoed it: 'You will be my witnesses in Jerusalem and in all Judea and Samaria, and to the end of the earth' (*Acts* 1:8), a prophecy dramatically realized on the Day of Pentecost when men and women were gathered from all over the known world: 'Parthians and Medes and Elamites and residents of Mesopotamia, Judea and Cappadocia, Pontus and Asia, Phrygia and Pamphylia, Egypt and the parts of Libya and belonging to Cyrene and visitors from Rome . . . Cretans and Arabs' (*Acts* 2:9–11).

There is both a unity and diversity to the people of God. They come from *every* tribe: the mountain dwellers of the northern tribes, the farmers of the great plains, to the coastal dwellers and fishermen that occupied the coastal cities of the Mediterranean – all are represented, and interestingly, in equal numbers! They are all '*servants of our God*' (7:3), dressed in white (7:9; see *Isa.* 1:18; 64:6; *Zech.* 3:3–5), and singing the same song of redemption (7:10).

What we have here is not a picture of heaven as it will be, but a picture of heaven *now*!

> *More happy, but not more secure,*
> *The glorified spirits in heaven.*
> Augustus M. Toplady

In heaven, where angels and the redeemed understand these things so much better, there is the unforgettable response of praise 'to the Lamb' (7:10; see also 5:12). The songs of earth have tried to mimic these sentiments:

> *Bearing shame and scoffing rude*
> *In my place condemned He stood;*
> *Sealed my pardon with His blood:*
> *Hallelujah! What a Saviour!*
>
> Philipp P. Bliss

> *Turn then, my soul, unto thy rest;*
> *The merits of thy great High Priest*
> *Have bought thy liberty*
> *Trust in His efficacious blood,*
> *Nor fear thy banishment from God,*
> *Since Jesus died for thee!*
>
> Augustus M. Toplady

THE GREAT TRIBULATION

Something interesting happens in verse 13. John, who has so far been an observer, now finds himself there in heaven! One of the elders asks him a question. It is the question, no doubt, John had been asking himself! '*Who are these, clothed in white robes, and from where have they come?*' The answer? '*These are the ones coming out of the great tribulation*' (7:14).

What is the *great tribulation*?

The great tribulation is upon us already and the way to be rescued from it is to wash our robes white through the blood of the Lamb (7:14). John began his letter by identifying himself as a fellow combatant in the 'tribulation' (1:9). The church at Thyatira is warned of its imminent arrival (2:22). Peter and Paul gave similar warnings (*1 Pet.* 4:1–7, 12–13; *Col.* 1:24).

What John seems to depict here is the story of the church, emerging throughout history from one tribulation after another. It has always been so, and it ever will be until Jesus Christ brings it to a close by his coming.

Samuel Rutherford once wrote: 'I find it most true, that the greatest temptation out of hell is to live without temptations. If my waters should stand, they would rot. Faith is the better of the free air, and of the sharp winter storm in its face. Grace withereth without adversity. The devil is but God's master fencer, to teach us to handle our weapons.'

John had begun the chapter as an observer but closes it as a participant. He feels himself to be among those who are the sealed of God, praising his name, shepherded by Christ, drinking of the life-giving waters (7:15–17). His voice now mingles with theirs in praise of Jesus. He, with them, is in pain-free peace, singing and serving, secure in the knowledge that God '*will shelter them with his presence*' (7:15; see also *Lev.* 26:11–13).

THE SEVENTH SEAL

As the sixth seal depicted what is true of this world *now*, so the seventh takes us to the future, to the Day of Judgment itself. It is depicted in language which reminds us of Exodus 19 and the description of God's arrival on Mount Sinai.

Before it is revealed, there is silence in heaven for about half an hour (8:1). Two Old Testament passages seem to be in the background, Habakkuk 2:20, 'But the LORD is in his holy temple; let all the earth keep silence before him' and Zechariah 2:13, 'Be silent, all flesh, before the LORD, for he has roused himself from his holy dwelling.' Both of these passages depict the Lord 'in his temple' in heaven executing judgment, the result of which produces a sense of profound awe at the revelation of God's holy majesty. The angels fall silent at the dissolution of all things. The day of the great earthquake has come when a new heavens and new earth are formed.

The *chemistry* God uses to right wrongs is a combination of his own power and the prayers of the saints (8:4). It is an extraordinary scene. The silence is marked, not by inactivity, but by the elders who carry in their hands the bowls which contain the prayers of the saints. Then the final dissolving earthquake comes.

The Glorified Spirits in Heaven

The prayers of the saints (6:10, and now here in 8:3–4) are described as ascending to God, helped in the process by the addition of incense from the angel who stands at the altar (8:3).

Incense is associated with sacrifice (for example, on the Day of Atonement, *Lev.* 16:11–19) and suggests its acceptability and its sweetness to God. Cleansed and sweetened, these prayers really do come into God's 'nostrils'. If the idea of the scent of incense rising (see *Lev.* 16:12–13, *Psa.* 141:1–2) is strange to us, it would not have been to these first readers of Revelation. For Jewish worshippers of the Old Testament, incense demonstrated what fragrance counters in shopping malls do to us – the powerful way in which smells can evoke a response. It is a picture of the way our prayers rise before God and are accepted by him as something pleasant and sweet.

Angels assist in the presentation of our prayers before God. Our prayers rise with the Spirit's power, the Son's mediation, and the assistance of the angels in heaven.

Our prayers may make little impact to those who hear them in this world, but when they reach heaven, they are sent back, in George Herbert's phrase, as 'reversed thunder'. The power of prayer is truly immense!

7

Self-Destructive Forces of Evil

Rev 8:7– 9:21

*N*ow the seven angels who had the seven trumpets prepared to blow them.

⁷ The first angel blew his trumpet, and there followed hail and fire, mixed with blood, and these were thrown upon the earth. And a third of the earth was burned up, and a third of the trees were burned up, and all green grass was burned up.

⁸ The second angel blew his trumpet, and something like a great mountain, burning with fire, was thrown into the sea, and a third of the sea became blood. ⁹ A third of the living creatures in the sea died, and a third of the ships were destroyed.

¹⁰ The third angel blew his trumpet, and a great star fell from heaven, blazing like a torch, and it fell on a third of the rivers and on the springs of water. ¹¹ The name of the star is Wormwood. A third of the waters became wormwood, and many people died from the water, because it had been made bitter.

¹² The fourth angel blew his trumpet, and a third of the sun was struck, and a third of the moon, and a third of the stars, so that a third of their light might be darkened, and a third of the day might be kept from shining, and likewise a third of the night.

¹³ Then I looked, and I heard an eagle crying with a loud voice as it flew directly overhead, "Woe, woe, woe to those who dwell on the earth, at the blasts of the other trumpets that the three angels are about to blow!"

⁹:¹ And the fifth angel blew his trumpet, and I saw a star fallen from heaven to earth, and he was given the key to the shaft of the bottomless pit. ² He opened the shaft of the bottomless pit, and from the shaft rose smoke like the smoke of a great furnace, and the sun and the air were darkened with the smoke from the shaft. ³ Then from the smoke came locusts on the earth, and they were given power like the power of scorpions of the earth. ⁴ They were told not to harm the grass of the earth or any green plant or any tree, but only those people who do not have the seal of God on their foreheads. ⁵ They were allowed to torment them for five months, but not to kill them, and their torment was like the torment of a scorpion when it stings someone. ⁶ And in those days people will seek death and will not find it. They will long to die, but death will flee from them.

⁷ In appearance the locusts were like horses prepared for battle: on their heads were what looked like crowns of gold; their faces were like human faces, ⁸ their hair like women's hair, and their teeth like lions' teeth; ⁹ they had breastplates like breastplates of iron, and the noise of their wings was like the noise of many chariots with horses rushing into battle. ¹⁰ They have tails and stings like scorpions, and their power to hurt people for five months is in their tails. ¹¹ They have as king over them the angel of the bottomless pit. His name in Hebrew is Abaddon, and in Greek he is called Apollyon.

¹² The first woe has passed; behold, two woes are still to come.

¹³ Then the sixth angel blew his trumpet, and I heard a voice from the four horns of the golden altar before God, ¹⁴ saying to the sixth angel who had the trumpet, "Release the four angels who are bound at the great river Euphrates." ¹⁵ So the four angels, who had been prepared for the hour, the day, the month, and the year, were released to kill a third of mankind. ¹⁶ The number of mounted troops was twice ten thousand times ten thousand; I heard their number. ¹⁷ And this is how I saw the horses in my vision and those who rode them: they wore breastplates the colour of fire and of sapphire and of sulphur, and the heads of the horses were like lions' heads, and fire and smoke and sulphur came out of their mouths. ¹⁸ By these three plagues a third of mankind was killed, by the fire and smoke and sulphur coming out of their mouths. ¹⁹ For the power of the horses is in their mouths and in their tails, for their tails are like serpents with heads, and by means of them they wound.

[20] *The rest of mankind, who were not killed by these plagues, did not repent of the works of their hands nor give up worshipping demons and idols of gold and silver and bronze and stone and wood, which cannot see or hear or walk,* [21] *nor did they repent of their murders or their sorceries or their sexual immorality or their thefts* (Rev. 8:6–9:21).

This section begins the third in the cycle of seven visions (see p. xviii). This can be regarded as beginning at 8:2, but for convenience we considered 8:2–5 at the end of the last chapter. In some ways, it is the most difficult section of the book of Revelation. So far the visions have been fairly self-explanatory, but now the scenes become more complex and their identification more puzzling. Following seven seals we now have sevens trumpets; each one will disclose an element of God's judgment.

Revelation is not a book of history written in advance, written in such a way that we might readily identify fulfilments of its 'prophecies' at various points in the historical time-line. One of the ways we see this is in the use that is made within the book of the number seven. We have noted it before in the *seven letters* written to *seven churches*, followed by a vision of Christ opening *seven seals* of a scroll. Now, in this section, we are introduced to *seven trumpets*. Later we shall read of *seven thunders*, followed by *seven bowls* of wrath. Finally seven aspects of God's final victory bring the book of Revelation to its close.

This repetitive nature of the number seven offers us a clue as to how Revelation is to be read. Revelation gives us several glimpses of the same picture from different perspectives. There is a *cyclical* nature to the book that offers us recurring glimpses of the work of Christ in the unfolding of his providential purposes. It shows us how the reigning Lord Jesus Christ brings the purposes of God to fulfilment in salvation and judgment from several different angles. The story is told several times, and on each occasion the camera seems to focus on something different.

SEALS AND TRUMPETS

There are some structural similarities in the opening of the seven seals (6:1–8:5) and the sounding of the seven trumpets (8:6–11:19).

Just as the four opening seals, or the four horsemen of the apocalypse were grouped together (6:1–8), so are the first four trumpets (8:6–13). The opening of the fifth seal gave us a glimpse of heaven, where we saw the saints secure beneath the altar of God, crying for justice (6:9–11). Likewise, the fifth trumpet views the same scene, this time from the perspective of heaven rather than from the perspective of earth. Instead of seeing the saints secure beneath the altar, we are looking down on the earth, seeing the doom and despair of those who dwell on the earth (9:1–11). The sixth seal was followed by terrible judgments (6:12–16), just as the sixth trumpet will be (9:13–21). Before the seventh seal and seventh trumpet (8:1–5; 11:15–19), there is an interlude (7:1–17; 10:1–11:14).

The opening of the seals and the sounding of the trumpets point us to the same great reality but from different perspectives. The seals view the unfolding of the redemptive purposes of God from the point of view of the Lord's own people, those who are sealed; the trumpets view this same reality from the point of view of the unsealed, those who are *not* the people of God. The opening of the seals brings great consolation to the people of God. The sounding of the trumpets brings great woes upon those who are not the people of God. The seals are comforting; the trumpets are warnings.

In the Old Testament, trumpets announced an alarm, indicating that holy judgment was to be unleashed against Israel's enemy, or against Israel as God's enemy. Thus it was with Joshua against Jericho (*Josh.* 6), or Gideon against the Midianites (*Judg.* 7), or the Babylonians against Israel (*Jer.* 4).

The Joshua/Jericho pattern is particularly interesting because in that story it was the seventh sounding of the trumpets that brought upon Jericho the final cataclysmic destruction of the city walls. Trumpets were also used in the wilderness period as signals for marching, battles and festivals (*Num.* 10:1–2). Perhaps the most prominent use of trumpets was to announce the beginning of Rosh-Hashanah, or New Year's Day (*Num.* 29:1–6). Trumpets also announced the year of Jubilee (*Lev.* 25:8–9).

But the New Testament also refers to the Second Coming as accompanied by the sound of a trumpet, thus adding to the significance of the trumpets in Revelation 8 and 9. 'For the Lord himself will descend from heaven with a cry of command, with the voice of an archangel, and with the sound of the trumpet of God. And the dead in Christ will rise first' (*1 Thess.* 4:16; see also *Matt.* 24:31; *Isa.* 27:13).

Together these images create expectations of war, a new beginning, of final release from captivity and of cleansing from sin and its consequences. The trumpets signal the dawning of the kingdom of God in all its finality and fullness. Just as we have seen in the case of the seven seals, the seven trumpets comprise six trumpets depicting a series of happenings or calamities that will repeatedly occur throughout the history of the world (8:6–9:21), followed by a seventh depicting the Day of Judgment itself (11:15–19). There are three aspects to the unfolding of this vision, particularly as regards the sounding of the first six trumpets.

'NATURE' – RED IN TOOTH AND CLAW

In the first major section, John is given a pictorial vision of *the suffering of the created order* (8:6–12). The seven angels who are given the seven trumpets prepare to sound them. In the first four blasts, suffering is let loose. The aim is not total destruction (only a 'third' is affected – note the word occurs fourteen times); there is something partial about the proportions of these judgments.

The earth, sea and sky (8:7, 8, 10) are mentioned, showing that the judgments affect the totality of the created order. But the judgments are not total. They are only a precursor of the final judgment of God.

The judgments are reminiscent of the plagues that came upon Egypt, and the description of them bears a close resemblance to passages in Exodus which describe the plagues (*Exod.* 7:15–25; 9:22–25; 10:12–15, 21–23).

There is a reason for using the Egyptian plagues to describe what God is doing here in Revelation 8. Each of the plagues challenged the ascendancy of an Egyptian (cosmic) deity. The God of Israel conquered each one. Nothing can ultimately stand in his way. The book of Exodus portrays the covenant God of Israel as the only true God; the Egyptian gods are powerless before him. So in the final book of the Bible, the reign of God is portrayed in equally cosmic and victorious dimensions.

Are we, then, to interpret these events *literally*? That is, are we to expect these kinds of physical calamities in our own time? In part, this does seem to be the intent. It certainly fits in with what the Bible, and especially the New Testament, leads us to expect for this world order. Creation itself is judged and there are many parts of the world, now and in the past, that testify to events of this magnitude.

The description may also be *symbolic*. Mountains, for example (the second trumpet, 8:8) are often used to describe kingdoms in the Bible (*Isa.* 41:15; 42:15; *Ezek.* 35:2–7; *Zech. 4:7*). Jewish readers familiar with these biblical images, of a blazing mountain being hurled into the sea, for example, would readily understand the literary allusion to the triumph of God over all the hostile kingdoms of the world.

We are not simply to look for historical accounts of volcanoes or the like as fulfilments of this prophecy. We are also to anticipate far greater works of destruction in the collapse of every hostile force arrayed against God.

Similarly, the '*great star*' of verse 10 may well allude to Isaiah 14:12–15, where the fall of Satan is thought to be depicted, under the figure of the 'morning star'. Here he is called '*Wormwood*' because of the bitterness he brings to all living water (the exact opposite of the cleansing of the bitter waters at Marah in Exodus 15:25). It is a figure of speech used before, in such passages as Deuteronomy 29:17–18, where the allusion is to idolatry (see also *Prov.* 5:4; *Lam.* 3:15, 19; *Amos* 5:7; 6:12).

Whatever the symbolic allusions may be, the main focus is on the judgment that creation itself experiences. Something has gone radically wrong with the created order. John is telling us that in the natural order of things there is a curse at work that twists and misshapes.

Since the Fall, creation has within it a principle of hostility. The Garden became for Adam a graveyard (*Gen.* 3:17–19). Thorns despoil man's expectation of fruitfulness in labour. Creation (or Nature, to cite Tennyson) is 'red in tooth and claw'. There is at work in creation, according to Paul, a 'bondage-to- decay' principle from which it longs to be liberated. Creation currently groans under the weight of this decay, waiting for its rebirth (*Rom.* 8:21–22).

AN ARMY OF OPPOSITION

A second feature of chapter 9 is *the judgment of the un-sealed*. It is the result of the blowing of the fifth trumpet. A prelude appears in 8:13 with its reference to an eagle flying in mid-air, crying, '*Woe, woe, woe to those who dwell on the earth*' (other versions have 'angel' here, not 'eagle'). The three-fold repetition of the woe is Hebraic, signalling that we are to sit up and take notice. Something involving enormous anguish is to unfold in what follows, for which we need to prepare ourselves.

The punishment of covenant disobedience had been predicted in the Old Testament in terms of the coming of the Assyrians and Babylonians, whose language the Jews would not understand. The judgment was announced using the picture of an eagle (*Deut.* 28:49). Prophets who lived through this judgment, like Jeremiah, picked up the metaphor: 'For thus says the LORD: "Behold, one shall fly swiftly like an eagle . . ."' (*Jer.* 48:40).

When the fifth *seal* was opened, our eyes were lifted up to heaven so that we could behold the saints of God praying before the altar of God (6:9–11). At the fifth trumpet, our gaze is fixed on those who may be described as the great un-sealed. The picture that follows is graphic: a star is given a key to the Abyss, the realm of the demonic. From it rises smoke like a giant furnace. Out of it come locusts who are given a specific command not to harm the vegetation of the earth (the natural order, 9:4), but rather the focus of their devastation is humanity. They are to harm those '*who did not have the seal of God on their foreheads*' (9:4). They are not allowed to kill, but only to torture, and that, for five months (the approximate life of a locust, 9:5). Their victims will long to die, '*but death will flee from them*' (9:6).

It is impossible (even for literalists) not to interpret this figuratively (note the use of '*looked like*' in 9:7). Whilst some interpreters see in 9:11 a reference to a 'good' (unfallen) angel, regarding 10:1 as a parallel picture, it is hard not to see an allusion to what Jesus said concerning the disciples' mission: 'I saw Satan fall like lightning from heaven' (*Luke* 10:18). The entire picture sounds like 12:9, where we read: 'The great dragon was thrown down, that ancient serpent, who is called the devil and Satan, the deceiver of the whole world – he was thrown down to the earth, and his angels were thrown down with him.' In that case, the picture here is certainly of a fallen angel. This is confirmed by the name given to him, the angel of the Abyss, '*Apollyon*' or 'Destroyer' (9:11; note the repetition of 'bottomless pit' in 9:1 and 9:11).

The picture helps us understand the spiritual dynamics at work in the world. We are not to look for an army of two hundred million tramping across the earth from the River Euphrates (9:14). The description of the locusts defies any natural order with which we are familiar (9:7–10). These are not literal locusts!

John is being given a pictorial representation of a far greater reality: that we wrestle not against flesh and blood, but against spiritual forces of far greater magnitude and potential threat (*Eph.* 6:12). There are forces at work in this world that bring men and women into the most terrible bondage. They work among those who have not been sealed to bring about utter futility. As John puts it elsewhere, 'We know that we are the children of God, and that the whole world lies in the power of the evil one' (*1 John* 5:19). In far less dramatic terms, John uses a word that conveys the idea of a mother rocking her baby to sleep; the devil cradles the world in his arms. Incomprehensible demonic powers are released into human history that are at one and the same time attractive and repulsive. John's description is curiously appealing, yet hideous: human faces, crowns of gold, women's hair are contrasted with lion's teeth and scorpion's tails.

The book of Revelation is teaching us to see that the world in which men and women live is both beguiling and brutal at the same time. The brutality is often masked, but it is nonetheless vicious and ultimately devastating. The whole world is in the grip of the evil one.

This surrealist picture is of an evil being (Apollyon) put in charge of an army of insects. Locusts wearing iron breastplates will ascend from the pit of hell. These seemingly insignificant creatures will swell in size so that they look like horses dressed for battle. The whirr of their wings will sound like the thundering of horses' hooves. They bare teeth that look like those of the lion, and in their tail is the sting of the scorpion. This hellish mass is directed by Satan himself.

The entire picture is reminiscent of Joel 2, including the references to the darkening of the sun by the smoke that rises from the Abyss (9:2; *Joel* 2:10), but the primary allusion is again to the plague of locusts which also darkened the land prior to the Exodus (*Exod.* 10:5, 15). Covenant disobedience had been threatened with a re-visitation of the plague of locusts (*Deut.* 28:38–39, 42). The fact that this smoke and the locusts emerge from the Abyss seems to indicate that the judgment of God upon the demonic realm is now being extended to include those who worship Apollyon.

The creatures are forbidden to destroy the vegetation (9:4, in contrast to the Egyptian plague, *Exod.* 10:15). They are to harm only unbelievers, '*those people who do not have the seal of God on their foreheads*' (9:4; cf. 7:3). Whatever the precise nature of the fifth plague, those who bear the seal of God are entirely safe from its effects, in much the same way as the Israelites were protected from the Egyptian plagues (*Exod.* 8:22; 9:4,26; 10:23; 11:7).

The star '*was given*' the key to the shaft of the Abyss (9:1). The locusts were told the extent to which they could wreak their havoc ('*they were told . . .* ', 9:4; '*they were allowed to torment . . . but not to kill*', 9:5; see also the command to the sixth angel to release those 'bound' by the Euphrates River in 9:14–15 at a time that is fixed down to the very hour, day, month and year). God is sovereign over the totality of existence, including sin and Satan.

The duration is to be '*five months*' (9:5, corresponding to the life-cycle of the locust, Spring to late Summer). Just as Satan is limited in his power over Job and cannot do anything except by God's express authority (*Job* 1:12; 2:6), so here the Lord is in total control.

It is vitally important to grasp the role Satan plays in this judgment. It is a mistake to focus our attention completely upon Satan. The One in control of all things is not Satan, but God. Satan's powers are curtailed. He holds no power independently of God. Satan is 'God's tool' – though he never has nor will admit it. In allowing Satan some rope, God uses him to execute judgment on a fallen world in much the same way as a man might make use of a savage dog which hates him to drive unwelcome visitors off his estate.

But where is the judgment? If we glance at this world with its God-defiant audaciousness, where are the judgments of which these passages speak? Where is the fire and brimstone? Although it would be all too possible to discover answers to this question in the physical calamities that befall the earth, we seriously misunderstand the nature of the judgment if we think solely this way. Paul's answer to this very question is: these expressions of defiance *are* the judgments! God gives men over to shameful lusts. This is his answer (*Rom. 1:26*). The very expressions of ungodliness in the world are the evidence of the curse. Those who deny the existence of God's judgments in this world are experiencing it! God has abandoned them to their folly. God does not destroy man, even in hell. Hell will be a confirmation of man's choice: to live with the consequences of his own choice.

JUDGMENT BUT NO REPENTANCE

The third feature of this section is the blowing of the sixth trumpet. It alludes to the *impenitence of the un-sealed*.

This section builds on something that was a common fear in the latter part of the first century: that the Roman Empire would be attacked by the Parthians from beyond the Euphrates (9:13–21, especially verse 14). The mention of the altar (9:13) reminds us of the context of these trumpets. They are the answers to the prayers of the saints for retribution and justice (6:10). Those prayers rise to the altar of God (8:3–5).

Allusions to the plagues of Egypt remind us how 'Egypt' becomes synonymous with all that is evil in much the same way that 'Babylon' also does. It is not surprising, therefore, that the sixth trumpet should now depict in Old Testament language a vision of the judgment that will come upon '*Egypt*'. The Old Testament passage in question is Jeremiah 46 where an army of horsemen from the north (Babylon) is described in terms of serpent-like locusts, wearing breastplates and standing by the Euphrates River (*Jer.* 46:2, 22–23). This same picture will be taken up again in the depiction of the sixth bowl (16:12).

The number of troops under the command of these four angels is two hundred million (9:16), a general number indicating a vast quantity. Since 10,000 is a biblical way of expressing a vast number (for example, *Lev.* 26:8; *Num.* 10:35; *Deut.* 32:30; 33:2, 17), this number may be a way of expressing 2 x 10,000 x 10,000. As just mentioned, the allusion is certainly to Jeremiah 46 where the troops are said to be innumerable (*Jer.* 46:23). The monstrosity of the picture is added to by mixing metaphors, describing them as like horses, lions and snakes (9:17–19). Plagues of fire, smoke and sulphur come out of their mouths (9:18). This time, in contrast to the fifth trumpet, death is brought upon '*a third of mankind*' (9:15; see 9:6).

The cause of the judgments is now expressed, the sins of murder, magical arts, sexual immorality and theft (which can be summarized as idolatry, 9:20–21). The list is strikingly similar to Jeremiah 7:5–11. God will not be silent about our sins.

The rest of mankind did not repent (9:20–21). The rest, here, are the rest of the ones who were not marked with a seal and who did not die. Despite the expectation that judgment might lead to reformation, these do *not* repent. This provides the basis for seeing that there is such a thing as retributive judgment in which the purpose is not to convert, but to condemn. Even in the face of the most terrible judgments, there is no repentance. There is a preference for darkness rather than light. It is not that they do not know; it is that knowing their sinfulness they refuse to acknowledge it, and turn to idolatry instead. Man's idols are his greatest crimes against God. False worship is the ultimate expression of man's rebellion.

One of the consequences of these visions of seals and trumpets is the manifestation of evil that this world can expect. In one sense, the progressive nature of these seals and trumpets would seem to indicate an increasing presence of evil and hostility in the world. Those interpreters who expect the latter days of this New Testament era to be accompanied by times of great blessing and glory are forced to interpret these visions along lines which insist on their fulfilment in the destruction of the city of Jerusalem and its temple in 70 AD (often called the 'preterist' view). The interpretation adopted here is one that views the *progress* of the gospel as taking place in parallel with an increasing hostility to God.

8

Sweet and Sour

*T*hen I saw another mighty angel coming down from heaven, wrapped in a cloud, with a rainbow over his head, and his face was like the sun, and his legs like pillars of fire. *² He had a little scroll open in his hand. And he set his right foot on the sea, and his left foot on the land, ³ and called out with a loud voice, like a lion roaring. When he called out, the seven thunders sounded. ⁴ And when the seven thunders had sounded, I was about to write, but I heard a voice from heaven saying, "Seal up what the seven thunders have said, and do not write it down."* *⁵ And the angel whom I saw standing on the sea and on the land raised his right hand to heaven ⁶ and swore by him who lives forever and ever, who created heaven and what is in it, the earth and what is in it, and the sea and what is in it, that there would be no more delay, ⁷ but that in the days of the trumpet call to be sounded by the seventh angel, the mystery of God would be fulfilled, just as he announced to his servants the prophets.*

⁸ Then the voice that I had heard from heaven spoke to me again, saying, "Go, take the scroll that is open in the hand of the angel who is standing on the sea and on the land." ⁹ So I went to the angel and told him to give me the little scroll. And he said to me, "Take and eat it; it will make your stomach bitter, but in your mouth it will be sweet as honey." ¹⁰ And I took the little scroll from the hand of the angel and ate it. It was sweet as honey in my mouth, but when I had eaten it my stomach was made bitter. ¹¹ And I was told, "You must again prophesy about many peoples and nations and languages and kings" (Rev. 10: 1–11).

There is a clear structure to the book of Revelation. Just as there was an interlude between the sixth and seventh seals (chapter 7), so there is a similar one between trumpets six and seven.

The sounding of the seventh trumpet will be described at 11:15, and the section which precedes it consists of two visions: the angel with the little scroll (10:1–11), and the two witnesses (11:1–14). As before, what is recorded for us in chapters 10 and 11 is not meant to be regarded as chronological, as though these visions describe something taking place after the blowing of the sixth trumpet. Rather, as in chapter 7, these visions cover the same period of time as those events described by the first six trumpets (and the first six seals). According to 10:6–7, whenever the seventh trumpet does sound, there will be no further delay in the plan and purposes of God. Consequently, in 11:15, whenever the seventh trumpet sounds, we are ushered into the arena of the Day of Judgment.

As many have recognized, the basic structure of Revelation can be described as a *recapitulatory* and *progressive parallelism*. That is, the book is constantly covering the same general ground, returning to survey it all over again, adding further insight on each new visit.

We have already noted, for example, that the first six seals and the first six trumpets describe the same events, but from different perspectives. The seals are concerned with history from the vantage point of earth, looking up into heaven. The trumpets, on the other hand, view the same history, but this time from the vantage point of heaven, looking down upon the earth. The two visions of chapters 10 and 11 provide us with an interlude before the cataclysmic description of the Day of Judgment which is signalled by the blowing of the seventh trumpet (11:15). This provides John with the motivation and challenge to continue as a faithful herald of God's truth. In particular, chapter 10 speaks of a re-commissioning of the apostle to the work of prophetic ministry. There are times when the greatest of God's servants need a word of encouragement to continue!

THE LION'S ROAR

As has become clear to us by now, the last book of the Bible makes full use of the Old Testament. It is tempting to think that its first readers were familiar with the Old Testament in a way we are not, but that is a huge assumption to make. Perhaps they found it as challenging as we do and were driven to search the Scriptures (or ask their teachers for information and help) as we are. Perhaps that is what God intends in the closing pages of the Bible: to give us an incentive to go back and read the Bible more carefully!

Chapter 10 opens in a way that reminds us of the opening of chapter 5 since both chapters describe a '*mighty angel*', who cries with '*a loud voice*' (10:1,3; 5:2) and both mention lion-like attributes (10:3; 5:5). Everything about the description of this angel would seem to indicate that Christ (rather than, say, Michael or Gabriel) is intended, though many commentators disagree. In that sense, it seems similar to the passages in the Old Testament where the 'angel of the Lord' is a theophany, or Christophany – a pre-incarnate appearance of Christ in human form in the Old Testament economy (for example, *Gen.* 16:7–13; 22:1–2, 11–18; 24:7, 40; *Exod.* 3:2–6; 13:21; 33:14).

The angel appears '*wrapped in a cloud*' (10:1). The imagery is reminiscent of Daniel 7 where the Son of Man comes on the clouds to receive authority from the Ancient of Days. Similarly, the description of the rainbow that overarched his head (10:1) is a powerful reminder of a similar description given in the opening chapter of Ezekiel (1:26–28), where God's glory is described in this multi-coloured way.

Both of these descriptions from Daniel and Ezekiel have already been alluded to in the opening chapter of Revelation (1:7, 13). John may now be repeating elements of the picture of the Son of Man from his first chapter as a conclusion to this first half of Revelation. Additionally, the descriptions of his face as '*like the sun*' and his legs like '*pillars of fire*' also remind us of the description of Christ in chapter 1 (1:15–16).

Daniel's vision of the Son of Man was intended to portray the presence and power of God with his people in the midst of severe persecution and trial. The concern facing John's readers, and the church ever since, has been similar. Jesus is 'coming down from heaven' to speak to John! God's servant needs a personal word of motivation and challenge.

The '*mighty angel*' stands with one foot on the land and the other on the sea (10:2, indicating, of course, his total sovereignty over the affairs of the earth) and carries in his hand a '*little scroll*', which may contain the contents of the remainder of the book. In chapter 5, a similar scroll contained the judgment and redemption that unfolded in chapters 6–8.

Some believe the two scrolls of chapters 5 and 10 are identical, but the fact that John uses a different word for scroll here from that in chapter 5 probably points to this scroll being a smaller, less general one. The scroll in chapter 5 had contained the purposes of God in redemption and judgment. This one seems more specifically orientated to the book of Revelation itself and to John's calling to be God's spokesman in delivering it.

The imagery is one of a mighty ruler whose dominion is over land and sea (10:2), and whose voice sounds like that of a lion roaring (10:3; see also *Amos* 3:8).

When a lion roars, it is already committed to the attack. The sound is meant to paralyse, in much the way that a car's headlights cause a deer caught in their beam to 'freeze'. It is a savage, terrifying word that signals the unleashing of devastating, blood–curdling images of death and destruction. John describes the sound of '*seven thunders*' that accompany the vision. Clearly, John's nerves are in need of being steeled for something altogether dreadful.

THE SEVEN THUNDERS

As John has been in the habit of recording what he hears, he intends to do the same again, but now he is forbidden to do so (10:4). Why? What did John hear that could not be recorded? The identification and meaning of the seven thunders is difficult.

• Does the prohibition to write down what he had heard mean that some things in the future are not to be revealed, in order that we might live more in dependence on God?

• Is this an example of the principle of Deuteronomy 29:29, that the secret things belong to God and we are to be content with that which he has disclosed to us in his revealed will?

• Was the message so extraordinary (ineffable) that, like the message Paul heard (referred to in 2 Corinthians 12), the church has no business knowing it?

[84]

- Is this an example of God delaying or even cancelling his proposed work of judgment in order to rescue more of mankind from the certain effects of sin by encouraging repentance?

- Are the seven thunders meant to be yet another parallel set of seven judgments along with the seven seals, trumpets and bowls (the contents of which, of course, are not revealed)?

- Is the passage recalling Psalm 29 where God is alluded to in terms of a seven-fold formula, 'The voice of the LORD . . . ', the first of which adds by way of explanation that, 'The voice of the LORD is over the waters; the God of glory thunders, the LORD, over many waters'?

Commentators have suggested all of these.

It is interesting that the seven thunders precede the seventh trumpet and therefore signify, along with the first six seals and the first six trumpets, judgments which take place throughout the course of the time that followed the first coming of Jesus Christ. When the multitude in John 12 heard the voice from heaven acknowledging the prayer of Jesus that the Father's name be glorified, they thought that it had thundered (*John* 12:28–29). Jesus' interpretation is significant: "'This voice has come for your sake, not mine. Now is the judgment of this world; now will the ruler of this world be cast out. And I, when I am lifted up from the earth, will draw all people to myself." He said this to show by what kind of death he was going to die.' (*John* 12:30–32). On this view, the death of Jesus was the first indication of judgment upon the impenitent.

No More Delay

As soon as the thunders have been revealed to John, the angel swears an oath, reminiscent of Daniel 12:7, regarding the imminence of the future Day of Judgment which the seventh trumpet will unleash: 'That there would be no more delay' (10:6). The King James Version renders this, 'that there should be time no longer'. This has led some to conclude that eternity will be timeless in nature. But it is doubtful, even if it is true, whether this verse is meant to convey that notion. Instead, John is being reminded that there is nothing left to happen after the six trumpets have sounded except the sounding of the seventh trumpet and the Day of Judgment that it ushers in.

In the sequence of events the New Testament portrays, following the outworking of God's judgments in history, there is nothing else that needs to happen *before* the Last Judgment. In that sense we can speak of the Second Coming of Jesus Christ as *imminent*. Not that it will necessarily occur within the next few minutes, or days, or even years; but, that once the six trumpets have sounded, nothing else remains to happen.[1] There will be no more delay. It is in this sense that the closing words of the book of Revelation, and of the Bible, are to be understood: 'I am coming soon' (22:20).

The book of Revelation is unfolding the course of history as the revelation of a 'mystery' (10:7). In the end (when the seventh trumpet sounds) the mystery of God will be fully disclosed. Things otherwise hidden from view will become apparent by God's initiation and explanation. We know nothing unless God discloses it to us.

But what *mystery* is this? It is the mystery of God's plan and purpose. The greatest mystery of all is the way of salvation presented in the gospel, something which Paul gives testimony to in Romans 16:25–26: 'Now to him who is able to strengthen you according to my gospel and the preaching of Jesus Christ, according to the revelation of the mystery that was kept secret for long ages but has now been disclosed and through the prophetic writings has been made known to all nations, according to the command of the eternal God, to bring about the obedience of faith.'

What John is testifying to here is that the end of time will reveal to us what God is doing in this world, namely fulfilling his plan of redemption. What Daniel and the other prophets (see verse 7) had not been able to show, given their place in the history of redemption, John is now disclosing to us: that the first coming of Jesus has

---

[1] The expectation of a personal Antichrist at the end of the age, and the conversion of the Jews, are problematic for this view. For this reason, some have a *premillennial* interpretation that maintains the nearness of the Second Coming whilst postponing these and other expectations until *after* the Second Coming. Others have adopted a *preterist* interpretation, seeing the references to things that happen 'without delay' or 'soon' as referring to the destruction of Jerusalem in 70 AD.

actually set in motion the process that leads to the final consummation. The picture of Jesus opening the sealed book in chapter 5 had
already established that perspective. In the end, whatever may be
the case now, Jesus will be seen to be victorious over all the forces
of evil. That which has been veiled will then be fully disclosed for
all to appreciate.

> *Jesus shall reign where'er the sun*
> *Does his successive journeys run;*
> *His Kingdom stretch from shore to shore,*
> *Till moons shall wax and wane no more.*
>
> Isaac Watts (*based on Psalm 72*)

SWEET AND SOUR

John is asked to take the scroll and eat it. That which tastes sweet
(see *Psa.* 119:103) can also turn bitter, something which reminds
us of Ezekiel 2:8–3:11. There the prophet was told to eat a scroll
which tasted sweet. 'It was in my mouth as sweet as honey', Ezekiel
said (*Ezek.* 3:3).

Everyone who meditates on Scripture is urged to experience
something similar: 'Taste and see that the LORD is good' (*Psa.*
34:8). But just as Ezekiel was to discover that his word would be
to a 'rebellious house' (*Ezek.* 2:8; 3:7), so John's discovery would
likewise be that what tastes sweet in the mouth can turn bitter in the
stomach (10:9; *Ezek.* 2:8–3:3). Jeremiah confessed that 'the word
of the LORD has brought me insult and derision all day long' (*Jer.*
20:8). John, like Ezekiel and Jeremiah, must proclaim a message
that contains the notes of doom. When this message is taken to the
nations of the world (see 10:11), the experience will be a bitter one.
This lesson is one that every preacher and witness to the gospel
knows all too well.

John's office and call had unique features about it, but we are
entitled to draw some principles that apply equally well to those
called to preach the gospel of Jesus Christ. John's commission is
to make known the contents of the '*little scroll*'. He is to be God's
prophetic minister in making his Word known. In that sense, he
is a paradigm of what God has intended from the start, that he

should advance his kingdom through the faithful exposition of his Word. Like Timothy, John is being urged to 'Preach the Word; be prepared in season and out of season; reprove, rebuke and exhort, with complete patience and teaching' (*2 Tim.* 4:2).

Luke records that one of the first things Jesus did after his resurrection was to 'open the Scriptures' (*Luke* 24:32, see also verse 27) to the two on the Emmaus Road, who promptly returned to Jerusalem and to the other disciples, where Jesus appeared to them, too, and 'opened their minds to understand the Scriptures' (verse 45), adding, 'Thus it is written' so that it might be 'proclaimed in his name to all nations' (verses 46–47). Over thirty years later, knowing that his own death was not far away, Paul would commission his friend to 'preach the Word' (*2 Tim.* 4:2). Peter put it this way: 'God made a choice . . . that by my mouth' the gospel would be made known (*Acts* 15:7).

Just as God's hand was behind the choice of Paul, Timothy and John, so too it lay upon Peter: his *mouth*, that is to say, his voice, his personality, his background. He had been shaped and formed for this special task of being the 'mouthpiece of God' through whom God would speak. These men's task, like that of the Old Testament prophets before them – and there seems to be a specific allusion to Ezekiel in particular in Revelation 10 – is to expound what God has first of all revealed to them. Ezekiel, like John, was asked to eat the scroll containing the divine word (*Ezek.* 2:8– 3:3). This was the best way to explain the task laid upon him.

John is being re-commissioned. He is told that he must '*again prophesy*' (10:11). The message which he is asked to proclaim is a hard one and he, like others before him, can expect opposition and ridicule (*Ezek.* 3:7; *2 Tim.* 4:3–4; *1 Tim.* 6:11–12). He is to be faithful to the *final word* God has spoken in Scripture. He must neither add to nor subtract from the Bible (22:18–19). His concern is not ultimately scholarship and erudition, but faithfulness and accuracy.

The purposes of God in history have a quality about them that we might consider harsh and difficult, and which we would sooner turn away from than give expression to. In the same way that Paul asks for prayer that he might make known the mystery of the gospel 'boldly' (*Eph.* 6:19–20 – twice), and confesses to being afraid and weak when he visited Corinth (*1 Cor.* 2:3–4), so John needs the

[88]

assurance of a divine call and enablement to fulfil his task of being an ambassador of Jesus Christ.

By being told to eat the scroll, John is being informed that the word which he must proclaim is also a word which nourishes and empowers him. He is dependent on the very Word of God that he must now proclaim. Jeremiah was told to look at an almond bud (Hebrew, *shaqad*) so that he might understand God's reassurance, 'I am watching (*shaqad*) over my word to perform it' (*Jer.* 1:11–12). Just as the power of God lies behind the bursting forth of spring's blossom, so the power of God's Spirit lies behind the ministry of John (and those commissioned in a similar way to John) in the accomplishment of God's purposes.

9

The Two Witnesses

*T*hen I was given a measuring rod like a staff, and I was told,
"Rise and measure the temple of God and the altar and
those who worship there, ² but do not measure the court outside
the temple; leave that out, for it is given over to the nations, and
they will trample the holy city for forty-two months. ³ And I
will grant authority to my two witnesses, and they will prophesy
for 1,260 days, clothed in sackcloth."

⁴ These are the two olive trees and the two lampstands that
stand before the Lord of the earth. ⁵ And if anyone would harm
them, fire pours from their mouth and consumes their foes. If
anyone would harm them, this is how he is doomed to be killed.
⁶ They have the power to shut the sky, that no rain may fall
during the days of their prophesying, and they have power over
the waters to turn them into blood and to strike the earth with
every kind of plague, as often as they desire. ⁷ And when they
have finished their testimony, the beast that rises from the bottomless pit will make war on them and conquer them and kill
them, ⁸ and their dead bodies will lie in the street of the great
city that symbolically is called Sodom and Egypt, where their
Lord was crucified. ⁹ For three and a half days some from the
peoples and tribes and languages and nations will gaze at their
dead bodies and refuse to let them be placed in a tomb, ¹⁰ and
those who dwell on the earth will rejoice over them and make
merry and exchange presents, because these two prophets had
been a torment to those who dwell on the earth. ¹¹ But after the
three and a half days a breath of life from God entered them,
and they stood up on their feet, and great fear fell on those who
saw them. ¹² Then they heard a loud voice from heaven saying to

*them, "Come up here!" And they went up to heaven in a cloud,
and their enemies watched them.* ¹³ *And at that hour there was
a great earthquake, and a tenth of the city fell. Seven thousand
people were killed in the earthquake, and the rest were terrified
and I gave glory to the God of heaven.*

¹⁴ *The second woe has passed; behold, the third woe is soon
to come.*

¹⁵ *Then the seventh angel blew his trumpet, and there were
loud voices in heaven, saying, "The kingdom of the world has
become the kingdom of our Lord and of his Christ, and he shall
reign forever and ever."* ¹⁶ *And the twenty-four elders who sit
on their thrones before God fell on their faces and worshipped
God,* ¹⁷ *saying,*

"We give thanks to you, Lord God Almighty,
who is and who was,
for you have taken your great power
and begun to reign.
¹⁸ *The nations raged,*
but your wrath came,
and the time for the dead to be judged,
and for rewarding your servants, the prophets and saints,
and those who fear your name,
both small and great,
and for destroying the destroyers of the earth."

¹⁹ *Then God's temple in heaven was opened, and the ark of
his covenant was seen within his temple. There were flashes of
lightning, rumblings, peals of thunder, an earthquake, and heavy
hail* (Rev. 11:1–19).

As we have seen in the previous chapter, the two visions of
chapters 10 and 11 provide us with an interlude before the
seventh trumpet is blown (11:15). These visions give John both
motivation and challenge to continue as a faithful herald of God's
truth. In chapter 10, we have seen how the apostle is re-commissioned to the work of prophetic ministry. John '*must again prophesy
about many peoples and nations and languages and kings*' (10:11).

Most significantly, these visions give a message of reassurance to the people of God who are surrounded by enemies. As they bear testimony to the gospel, and suffer the consequences of their faithfulness, God *will* protect them.

This was also the point of the interlude in chapter 7 between the opening of the *sixth* and *seventh* seal. In the midst of God's judgments and the activities of the evil one, such reassurance is necessary and welcome.

In keeping with the interpretation we have already adopted in this study of Revelation, the two witnesses referred to in chapter 11 comprise something which is apparent *throughout* the course of history that leads up to the second coming of Jesus Christ and the end of the age.[1]

THE NUMBERS GAME

The vision begins with a command to John to go and measure the temple with a '*measuring rod like a staff*' (11:1). He is to measure the temple and the altar, but not the outer court of the Gentiles (11:2). Why not the outer court? Because '*the nations*' will '*trample the holy city for forty-two months*' (11:2). The '*holy city*' is to experience a period of persecution for a period of time designated as '*forty-two months*'.

Intimidating as this is, it is less complicated than it appears. Numbers, as we have seen, play an important role in the symbolism of the

---

[1] The view we have been adopting in this study is an *idealist* one. In contrast with views which understand the contents of this chapter as taking place during a 'Tribulation Period' *following* the 'rapture' of the saints toward the end of the age, we interpret the contents of the six seals and six trumpets as events that have been taking place during the *entire period from the ascension of Christ to his final return*. What is being described in chapter 11 is, according to this view, something that is happening right now! This will become especially clear as we identify the 1,260 days of 11:3 with that period that followed the first coming of Jesus Christ as described in 12:5–6 (see 14:14–20).

Those who understand Revelation from a *futurist* point of view (the contents of the book largely describe a period just prior to the return of Christ) also view these two witnesses as appearing in the end times.

book of Revelation. The number 'seven' is especially important, as are multiples and divisions of seven. Hence the number '42' – *'forty-two months'* (which is 7 x 6; 11:2) which is *'1,260 days'* (assuming each month has 30 days; 11:3). Then there is the reference to 'time, and times, and half a time' (12:14, or three and a half, which is half of seven). John is playing with numbers!

The time periods are identical in length and have similarities to their usage in the book of Daniel. It might even be the case that John was reading and re-reading the second half of Daniel as he wrote this book!

The *'holy city'* (understood spiritually as 'the church', or 'the people of God', rather than the actual city of Jerusalem) is to experience persecution for a period of one half of the duration of seven years, or three and a half years. Why 'three and a half'? At the risk of oversimplification, it represents the period of time from the destruction of the temple in 70 AD until Christ's return.[2] In other words (!) the 'last days' (that is, the 42 months or three and a half years of Revelation 11: 2, from 70 AD until the second coming) will be marked by tribulation.

This looks enormously complicated (and it is!), and possibly did so to John's hearers as well, but in effect all it is saying (in apocalyptic

---

[2] Though interpreters differ widely here, the explanation for the view adopted above goes something like this: Daniel speaks of a period of crisis which will last for 'a time, times, and half a time' (that is, three and a half, *Dan.* 7:25). This 'crisis' plays out in the second century BC in the reign of the Hellenistic king, Antiochus Epiphanes. During his reign, a violent attack was made against the temple. John is 'mirroring' this concept, speaking of '42 months,' or '1,260 days' or 'three and a half years' during which there will be persecution and trial. Since John is writing at the close of the first century – the temple has already been destroyed in 70 AD – this period must refer to the time interval from its destruction until Christ's return. (The relevant texts to look up are: *Jer.* 25:12; 29:10; *Dan.* 7:25; 9:2, 24–27; 12:7, 11–12). Some have attempted to pin-point this in the period of time leading up to the destruction of the temple in 70 AD, rather than following it as we have done here, but according to Revelation 11:1, the inner part of the temple and the altar are preserved and there is nothing in the events of the first century to equate with that.

language) is this: 'In the last days there will come times of difficulty' (*2 Tim.* 3:1–13; *2 Thess.* 1:4–8), understanding 'last days' to include the entire period between the two advents of Christ.

THE SAFETY OF GOD'S PEOPLE

In the picture John paints for us, he is measuring the inner temple and the altar, and more significantly still, he is counting the worshippers.

We should not think of a literal temple, one that might be built in the future, for we are dealing here with symbolism. This is a representation of the people of God who are God's temple.

We have already noted how significant the number 144,000 was in chapter 7, representing as it did God's worshipping people. They are assembled around the throne in heaven in much the same way as the tribes assembled around the tabernacle in Numbers 2. They are symbolic of the church triumphant in heaven. Here in Revelation 11, the picture is not so much the departed (and martyred) saints in heaven as it is the saints who are still on earth during this persecution.

He is *not* to measure the outer court of the Gentiles (11:2). Why not? Because the assurance and security this passage affords relates *only* to the people of God, those who bear the seal of God (9:4).

Measuring often signifies in Scripture the care and protection God affords to all his children (see *Ezek.* 40–41). Whatever may be happening in the world, and however the church may be affected by it, there is no question as to God's care for his own. He superintends and governs his flock. His control is irresistible. His love is unremitting.

THE TWO WITNESSES

Another difficult metaphor follows. The point of ensuring God's care for his people in the opening two verses is to prepare us for what the church is to engage in during the inter-adventual age: the people of God are to witness in a hostile world to his word and his ways.

John introduces us to '*two witnesses*' (11:3) whose ministry takes place during this 42-month, 1,260-day period. Though their identity

is sometimes likened to others, including Enoch, Peter, Paul and
the two Jewish high priests killed in 68 AD (attractive to those who
place the 42 months as *prior* to the destruction of the temple in 70
AD), the description of their ministry resembles more that of Elijah
and Moses (11:6). Note that these figures are *like* Elijah and Moses;
they are not to be identified *as* Elijah and Moses.

A further clue is given to help us understand the symbolism:
'*These are the two olive trees and the two lampstands that stand before the
Lord of the earth*' (11:4). The allusion here is to the architecture of the
temple where the lampstands represented the presence of God, or the
Spirit of God (*Num.* 8:4; *Exod.* 25:30–31; *Zech.* 4:2–5). The church's
testimony or witness is to be by the power of the Holy Spirit. The oil
for the lampstands comes from the two olive trees (11:4), an allusion
to the prophecy of Zechariah 4 in which the prophet describes the
assurance of the completion of the Second Temple 'not my might,
nor by power, but by my Spirit' (*Zech.* 4:6).

During the last days, there is to be a powerful testimony to the
Word of God in the world reminiscent of the ministry of Elijah
and Moses. In the same way that John the Baptist came in the spirit of
Elijah (*Luke* 1:17), the people of God are likewise to exude the same
spirit. There are two of them in order to establish their authority
(the law required two witnesses for validation, *Num.* 35:30; *Deut.*
17:6; 19:15; *Matt.* 18:16; *1 Tim.* 5:19).

There is in this picture an allusion to the commission given to
the church in Acts 1:8: 'But you will receive power when the Holy
Spirit has come upon you, and you will be my witnesses in Jerusalem
and in all Judea and Samaria, and to the ends of the earth.' Rejected
as these witnesses will be by the world, their divine validity and
authenticity remains in no doubt.

There is an invincibility about their witness (11:5). They cannot
be ultimately harmed in any way. The fragile vessels which make
up God's church may be afflicted, perplexed, persecuted and struck
down, but not crushed or in despair or forsaken or destroyed (*2
Cor.* 4:7–9).

If the book of Revelation intends to encourage the people of God
as they face persecution, it could hardly do so with greater force than
by suggesting that the power of the gospel to which they witness is
like that of Elijah when he prevented the rain from falling (*1 Kings*

17:1), or Moses when he turned water into blood (*Exod.* 7:17–25). The church, as Jesus told Peter, has the power of the keys, a power that both liberates and condemns (*Matt.* 16:19; 18:18, 19).

The Word to which the church gives witness is the Word of God. It blesses those who heed it and curses those who do not.

THE BEAST THAT COMES FROM THE ABYSS: THE END GAME

Verse 7 introduces us to a figure alluded to in 9:11, and who will appear to a far greater extent in chapters 13 and 17. The '*angel of the bottomless pit*. His name in Hebrew is Abaddon, and in Greek he is called Apollyon' (9:11). Behind all anarchy and rebellion lies the activity of Satan, the prince of darkness. His malevolence knows no abatement during the 'last days'. God's people are to be mindful of his every stratagem and wile (*Eph.* 6:11,13; see also *1 Pet.* 5:8).

In the symbolism of this chapter, the intensity of the persecution by the '*beast that rises from the bottomless pit*' takes place over a shorter period of time, three and a half days, rather than forty-two months. This is usually interpreted as signalling an event that is to take place at the end of the forty-two-month period, that is, at the end of history itself. This would then corroborate a belief held by many that the final days of this age are to experience a singularly vicious period of persecution, led by a personal manifestation of Antichrist.

In that case, what we have here may reflect other New Testament statements regarding the appearance of an Antichrist figure, or what Paul refers to as the 'man of lawlessness' (*2 Thess.* 2:1–12; *1 John* 2:18), a figure who appears in some form or another throughout the last days, but seems to appear in a definite and personal way towards the close of this age. Other passages in Revelation will further suggest such a view, including the 'Battle of Armageddon' in chapter 16 and the releasing of Satan 'for a little while' in chapter 20.

However, some have suggested that this may not necessarily be the case, either here in this chapter or in the other references cited. In line with what has already been suggested, what is envisaged here may simply demonstrate a period of intense persecution without reference to the exact time of its occurrence. In fact, such occurrences may well repeat themselves as history unfolds. On reflection, this view seems unlikely to be what John is indicating here.

What follows is a parallel to Daniel 7:21, the prophecy of the final kingdom that will appear to persecute the people of God. It is the fourth beast of Daniel's vision, which has ten horns on its head and out of which emerges a 'little horn'. Its ferocity is depicted here, but further allusions to this figure will emerge in Revelation 12, 13 and 17. The Antichrist figure in John's reckoning is already at work in the Satanic eruptions that have occurred in the experience of the first century Christian church (*1 John* 2:18; 4:3).

These 'last days' are punctuated with periods of intense difficulty for the people of God. They sometimes occasion death. The picture given in verse 8, of the bodies of the witnesses lying in the streets of the '*great city*' for '*three and a half days*', is particularly gruesome (11:7–8).

Their bodies will lie in '*the great city*' (11:8). It is not to be identified with the '*holy city*' of verse 2, but with Babylon (also figuratively known as 'Sodom' and 'Egypt'). These names represent the Bible's trinity of evil.

The picture now changes and is reminiscent of Ezekiel 37, the valley of the dry bones coming to life. Three and a half days pass by during which onlookers seem to stare with scorn at the corpses of those who have died in the streets, when suddenly these bodies come to life (11:11). The cause? '*A breath of life from God entered them*' (11:11).

This is the end. A voice of command from heaven urges the bodies to rise into a cloud and disappear from the disbelieving gaze of their enemies (11:12). *There is no secret rapture!* While all this is going on, the city experiences an earthquake in which a tenth of the city collapses and seven thousand are killed (11:13–14).

All this is symbolism, of course. At the moment of Christ's return, death and destruction will occur in the godless city that is opposed to Christ's kingdom and his rule. The survivors will acknowledge his glory (11:13), though it is doubtful that this means that they will be converted. They will acknowledge God's glory, but it will be too late, for the seventh trumpet is about to sound (11:15).

Though the closing days of this age will be troublesome, the victory of God's people is assured: they will be taken to heaven.

There is coming a day when the people of God, those who have died and have been left rotting in the streets, will hear the voice that says, '*Come up here.*' Not even Satan can prevent this.

When the seventh and final trumpet sounds, the end has arrived (11:15). And there is rejoicing in heaven.

'The kingdom of the world has become
    the kingdom of our Lord and of his Christ,
  and he shall reign forever and ever'

                    (11:15).

And again:

'We give thanks to you, Lord God Almighty,
    who is and who was,
 for you have taken your great power
    and begun to reign.
The nations raged,
    but your wrath came,
And the time for the dead to be judged,
    and for rewarding your servants, the prophets
and saints, and those who fear your name,
    both small and great,
and for destroying the destroyers of the earth'

                  (11:17–18).

John sees in heaven 'the ark of the covenant' (11:19). God has kept his covenant! The explanation for the redemption of his people lies in his unfailing promise.

> *The work which His goodness began,*
> *The arm of His strength will complete;*
> *His promise is Yea and Amen,*
>   *And never was forfeited yet.*
> *Things future, nor things that are now,*
>   *Nor all things below or above,*
> *Can make Him His purpose forgo,*
>   *Or sever my soul from His love.*
>
>   Augustus Toplady (1740–78).

His purposes in redemption and judgment have been fulfilled.

10

The Great Red Dragon

*A*nd a great sign appeared in heaven: a woman clothed with the sun, with the moon under her feet, and on her head a crown of twelve stars. ² She was pregnant and was crying out in birth pains and the agony of giving birth. ³ And another sign appeared in heaven: behold, a great red dragon, with seven heads and ten horns, and on his heads seven diadems. ⁴ His tail swept down a third of the stars of heaven and cast them to the earth. And the dragon stood before the woman who was about to give birth, so that when she bore her child he might devour it. ⁵ She gave birth to a male child, one who is to rule all the nations with a rod of iron, but her child was caught up to God and to his throne, ⁶ and the woman fled into the wilderness, where she has a place prepared by God, in which she is to be nourished for 1,260 days.

⁷ Now war arose in heaven, Michael and his angels fighting against the dragon. And the dragon and his angels fought back, ⁸ but he was defeated and there was no longer any place for them in heaven. ⁹ And the great dragon was thrown down, that ancient serpent, who is called the devil and Satan, the deceiver of the whole world— he was thrown down to the earth, and his angels were thrown down with him. ¹⁰ And I heard a loud voice in heaven, saying, "Now the salvation and the power and the kingdom of our God and the authority of his Christ have come, for the accuser of our brothers has been thrown down, who accuses them day and night before our God. ¹¹ And they have conquered him by the blood of the Lamb and by the word of their testimony, for they loved not their lives even unto death. ¹² Therefore,

rejoice, O heavens and you who dwell in them! But woe to you, O earth and sea, for the devil has come down to you in great wrath, because he knows that his time is short!"

¹³ And when the dragon saw that he had been thrown down to the earth, he pursued the woman who had given birth to the male child. ¹⁴ But the woman was given the two wings of the great eagle so that she might fly from the serpent into the wilderness, to the place where she is to be nourished for a time, and times, and half a time. ¹⁵ The serpent poured water like a river out of his mouth after the woman, to sweep her away with a flood. ¹⁶ But the earth came to the help of the woman, and the earth opened its mouth and swallowed the river that the dragon had poured from his mouth. ¹⁷ Then the dragon became furious with the woman and went off to make war on the rest of her offspring, on those who keep the commandments of God and hold to the testimony of Jesus. And he stood on the sand of the sea (Rev. 12:1–17).

Revelation 12 begins the fourth in the series of seven visions (see p. xviii). Indeed, in some ways it can be thought of as the key to the entire book. Alluding as it does to the cosmic struggle between the forces of darkness and the kingdom of God, the chapter depicts a graphic account of just how malicious the opposition becomes.

The pattern of *sevens* continues:

i.   The conflict of the serpent with the woman and her seed (12:1–13:1a)
ii. Persecution by the beast from the sea (13:1b–10)
iii. Persecution by the beast from the land (13:11–18)
iv. The Lamb and the 144,000 standing on Mount Zion (14:1–5)
v.   The proclamation of the gospel and of judgment by three angels (14:6–13)
vi. The Son of Man's harvest of the earth (14:14–20)
vii. The saints' victory over the sea beast and their victory song (15:2–4)

Concerted opposition is a principle that underlies the whole of Scripture as it unfolds the purposes of God at every stage in its development. The seed of the serpent is endeavouring to destroy the seed of the woman (*Gen.* 3:15). Everything that happens is part of the cosmic battle between these two seeds: Christ and Satan. Jesus is building his church within the precincts of Hell and can therefore expect to know the brutal hostility of Satanic opposition (see *Matt.* 16:18). The assurance given, of course, is that Christ will be triumphant in all that he purposes to do. Of this there can be no uncertainty. Jesus reigns!

What has been implicit in chapters 1–11 is now made clear: Satan is the one who orchestrates the flurried and desperate attacks upon every attempt to bring the purposes of God to fruition.

There have been hints of this already: in 6:8 (the Rider who was called Death and Hades) and 9:11 (the King named Abaddon, or Apollyon), for example. The previous chapter, too, had mentioned a beast that ascends from the Abyss (11:7). But, now in chapter 12, his identity is revealed as *'that ancient serpent, who is called the devil and Satan, the deceiver of the whole world'* (12:9). The various manifestations of evil that follow: the beast, the false prophet and the whore of Babylon will ultimately be destroyed, because the doom of Satan himself is sure and certain.

Four truths are inter-woven here that repeat themselves elsewhere in the pages of Scripture:

i. Satan is implacably hostile to the purposes of Almighty God.

ii. Satan is a defeated foe whose doom is written (12:5, 7–12). This knowledge does not prevent him from venting his spleen in anger even though he knows that victory in the ultimate sense is an impossibility. He *'knows that his time is short'* (12:12).

iii. The people of God are inevitably caught up in this cosmic battle. Furthermore, there is no expectation in the Scriptures that we are to look forward to a time when the church will be removed from this battle. Not until the Second Coming itself will the battle be brought to its final dénouement when Satan and all who belong to him will be cast into 'the lake of burning sulphur' (20:10).

iv. Satan's power is contained within the overruling purposes of God. In the story of Job, Satan has authority to afflict Job only because God gives it to him (*Job* 1:12; 2:6). His influence is bound by the *decree* of God.

This twofold position, that Satan is *hostile* but *under restraint*, is what Revelation wants us to appreciate. There is a fight in which we are bound to take part. Some will suffer terribly and may even die as a consequence, but Satan will never achieve the ultimate victory he desires. 'The body he may kill' (as Luther says in his hymn, *A Mighty Fortress Is Our God*), but he can never destroy the kingdom that God builds. It is within that framework that the details of this opposition are now described.

The Woman Giving Birth

Greek mythology contains the story of the serpent-like monster Python and his attempt to prevent the birth of Apollo, son of Zeus the king of the gods. Python failed and was consequently killed himself by Apollo four days after his birth. Similarly, Revelation 12 depicts Satan's attempt to prevent the birth of Jesus Christ. In this event, the opposition of the seed of the serpent to the seed of the woman is at its fiercest.

The story that follows is described in terms of the twin *signs* of a pregnant woman about to give birth and '*a great red dragon, with seven heads and ten horns*' (12:1,3).

The woman is depicted as '*clothed with the sun, with the moon under her feet, and on her head a crown of twelve stars*' (12:1). The allusion reminds us of Jacob, his wife and the eleven stars that bow down to Joseph in his dream (*Gen.* 37). A similar picture, but with no stars, is found in Isaiah 60:19–20. It is a picture of the church as it emerges from the period we call BC into the period we call AD. The crown alludes to the fact that the church shares in Christ's kingship (see also 2:10; 3:11; 4:4, 10; 14:14).

Roman Catholics see in this woman a depiction of Mary, the mother of Jesus. But the allusion seems to be a more general one. Having been driven into the desert the woman gives birth to other children (12:17 – a point presenting considerable problems for those who believe in Mary's perpetual virginity!). It is best to see this remarkable figure as combining the allusions in Scripture to the church as a woman (*Jer.* 4:31; *Isa.* 52:2; 54:1–6; 61:10; 62:1–5, 11; 66:7–13; *Gal.* 4:26–27; *2 John* 1, 5; *3 John* 9). A contrast will be drawn in chapter 17 between the believing community of God's covenant people represented by this woman in birth pangs and the unbelieving community represented by a whore! John may have had in mind the passage in Isaiah 26 describing Israel's oppression by Assyria:

> Like a pregnant woman who writhes and cries out
>   in her pangs when she is near to giving birth,
> So were we because of you, O LORD;
> We were pregnant, we writhed,
>   but we have given birth to wind
>
> <div align="right">(<i>Isa.</i> 26:17–18).</div>

THE DRAGON

Obviously the description of the second sign as '*a great red dragon*' (12:3) is metaphorical. Even the most persistent of literalistic interpreters agree that a metaphor is being employed here!

A broad range of Old Testament pictures is being employed here: that of Egypt (and Pharaoh) as a 'sea dragon' (*Psa.* 74:13–14; 89:10; *Isa.* 30:7; 51:9; *Ezek.* 29:3; 32:2–3), and Rome as a beast with ten horns (*Dan.* 7:7, 24).

The colour red (as in 17:3–6 of the whore, and 6:4 of the red horse), is linked with blood, specifically, the blood of martyred saints (17:6; 6:9–10). Satan's work is deadly in nature. Furthermore, Satan is a pretender, living in denial of reality. Thinking himself king (the seven crowns, seven for completeness, arising from the creation and rest in seven days), he pretends to be *all*-powerful. With his tail, he sweeps away a third of the stars and throws them to the earth, and this *before* the birth of the Messiah is recorded.

The description so vividly describes King Herod's brutal attack on the Bethlehem children following the birth of Jesus and the flight of Jesus, Mary and Joseph into Egypt that followed, that it is difficult to see how this vision depicts anything else (*Matt.* 2:13–18). But as so often happens in these pictures, it is a little more complex than that.

What seems to be depicted here is the *entire* life of Jesus – from his birth to his death. The fact that he is '*caught up*' to heaven (12:5) would seem to describe Jesus' death and subsequent resurrection and ascension.

Revelation 12 attests to the reality of satanic opposition against Christ. Indeed, the work of Christ can be understood from the perspective of his conquest and final victory over satanic opposition. 'The reason the Son of God appeared was to destroy the works of the devil' (*1 John* 3:8).

What happens to the church as a consequence of Satan's inability to destroy the male child? Verse 6 tells us that the woman flees into the desert where she experiences the protection of God for 1,260 days – those days which culminate in his return at the end of history.

It is crucial to observe that the focus and motive of the book of Revelation is that during this period of warfare God protects his church.

In the desert, as God's people in the Old Testament knew well, they experience both trial and protection. 'God . . . led you through the great and terrible wilderness, with its fiery serpents . . . [God] fed you in the wilderness with manna . . . that he might humble you and test you, to do good in the end' (*Deut.* 8:14–16). God has ordained the life of the church in this world in such a way that trials form the way of pilgrimage, and divine protection is the means by which we are kept secure to the end of the journey.

The Heavenly Battle

The section 12:7–12 describes the same events as 12:1–6, but from the point of view of heaven. All of this may have been taking place on earth, but an even greater reality is taking place in heaven. Satan himself is defeated by the Son of Man with the aid of Michael and his angels. While battles take place in this world, a corresponding heavenly war takes place which gives another explanation for the trouble that besets the church here on earth.

Once again there is an allusion to the book of Daniel, in which the battle of Michael and the Son of Man against the wicked angels of Persia and Greece involves the opposition of forces outside of this world (*Dan*. 10:13, 21). We wrestle, not against flesh and blood, but against principalities and powers, against the spiritual forces of wickedness in high places (*Eph*. 6:12).

The battle between Michael and his angels and the dragon and his army ends up in the defeat of the latter and the expulsion of the dragon from heaven (12:7–8). The description is given in the very language of Daniel's prophecies (*Dan* 7:21; 10:20). It is only now that the metaphorical language is broken and the identity of the dragon revealed by the twin names, *'devil'* and *'Satan'*, names meaning 'slanderer' and 'deceiver' respectively (12:9).

The one who deceived Adam and Eve, slandering the character of God in the process, is now described as *'the deceiver of the whole world'* (12:9). As then, so now, he finds himself defeated: he is *'thrown down to the earth, and his angels [are] thrown down with him'* (12:9; see also *Gen*. 3:4–5). In anticipation of this, Jesus said, 'I saw Satan fall like lightning from heaven . . . ' (*Luke* 10:18).

The vision is not left to interpretative imagination. The hymn which follows gives a clear representation of what the previous verses have indicated. A *'loud voice'* is heard (12:10), the source of which appears to be the same as that in 6:10, namely, the martyred saints in their cry for vengeance.

What is in view is the fulfilment of the prophecy of the second Psalm (see also 11:15). The hymn in verse 10 is not anticipating the coming of kingdom rule on the part of Christ so much as celebrating the fact that his rule has already been established. *'Now the salvation and the power and the kingdom of our God and the authority of his Christ have come'* (12:10). 'He disarmed the rulers and authorities and put them to open shame, by triumphing over them in him' (*Col*. 2:15).

Revelation 12 provides us with a four-fold way in which the devil's work is manifested:

i.   He is the ancient serpent who has now grown into the
     Dragon (verses 3–4, 7–9) who sought to destroy the Christ,

but failed.

ii.   He is Satan, the prosecuting counsel against believers (verse 4).

iii.   He is the devil, who hurls his fiery darts of temptation against them (verse 4).

iv.   He is the accuser of the brethren who fills his diary with a record of their sins in order to blackmail them (verse 10).

Yet, the brethren overcame him (12:11). How? '*By the blood of the Lamb*', said the loud voice from heaven, '*and by the word of their testimony, for loved not their lives even unto death*' (12:10–12). Through his death, Christ disarms him who had the power of death, and releases his people from their lifelong satanic bondage to the fear of death (see *Heb*. 2:14–16). Satan's power over Christians (the fear of death) has been destroyed.

THE PROTECTION OF GOD'S PEOPLE

Verse 13 now fills out what had been hinted at in verse 6, namely that the church which flees into the desert is pursued by the now-angry dragon. He is angry because he has been hurled out of heaven. Having failed to destroy Christ he goes after those who belong to Christ. Satan can never accept the reality of his situation. He now attempts to destroy the security of the desert by '*pour*[ing] *water like a river*' (verse 15).

It is, of course, the same attempt that was made in the Exodus from Egypt, but Satan's plan backfired when the flood waters of the Red Sea came in deluge and judgment upon the Egyptians and not the Israelites. The intervention of God's power demonstrates his care for, and protection of, his people.

As we have just observed, Satan can never accept reality. Having failed against the church in the Old Testament, he continues his warfare against '*the rest of her offspring*' (verse 17), probably an allusion to the church in the last days, or inter-adventual period. It is a singular mark of the New Testament covenant community that they are described as '*those who keep the commandments of God and hold to the testimony of Jesus'* (12:17). The power that enables the church to stand 'in the evil day' (*Eph.* 6:13) comes from her relationship to Jesus, and is expressed in the quality of Christians' lives.

The closer we follow Jesus, the more likely we are to become Satan's target. But, equally, the more likely we are to know the protecting grace of our Father in heaven.

11

Beasts of Land and Sea

*A*nd I saw a beast rising out of the sea, with ten horns and
seven heads, with ten diadems on its horns and blasphemous names on its heads. *² And the beast that I saw was like a
leopard; its feet were like a bear's, and its mouth was like a
lion's mouth. And to it the dragon gave his power and his throne
and great authority. ³ One of its heads seemed to have a mortal
wound, but its mortal wound was healed, and the whole earth
marvelled as they followed the beast. ⁴ And they worshipped
the dragon, for he had given his authority to the beast, and they
worshipped the beast, saying, "Who is like the beast, and who
can fight against it?"*

*⁵ And the beast was given a mouth uttering haughty and
blasphemous words, and it was allowed to exercise authority for
forty-two months. ⁶ It opened its mouth to utter blasphemies
against God, blaspheming his name and his dwelling, that is,
those who dwell in heaven. ⁷ Also it was allowed to make war
on the saints and to conquer them. And authority was given it
over every tribe and people and language and nation, ⁸ and all
who dwell on earth will worship it, everyone whose name has
not been written before the foundation of the world in the book
of life of the Lamb that was slain. ⁹ If anyone has an ear, let
him hear:*

¹⁰ If anyone is to be taken captive,
         to captivity he goes;
     if anyone is to be slain with the sword,
         with the sword must he be slain.

   Here is a call for the endurance and faith of the saints.

[11] *Then I saw another beast rising out of the earth. It had two horns like a lamb and it spoke like a dragon.* *[12]* *It exercises all the authority of the first beast in its presence, and makes the earth and its inhabitants worship the first beast, whose mortal wound was healed.* *[13]* *It performs great signs, even making fire come down from heaven to earth in front of people,* *[14]* *and by the signs that it is allowed to work in the presence of the beast it deceives those who dwell on earth, telling them to make an image for the beast that was wounded by the sword and yet lived.* *[15]* *And it was allowed to give breath to the image of the beast, so that the image of the beast might even speak and might cause those who would not worship the image of the beast to be slain.* *[16]* *Also it causes all, both small and great, both rich and poor, both free and slave, to be marked on the right hand or the fore-head,* *[17]* *so that no one can buy or sell unless he has the mark, that is, the name of the beast or the number of its name.* *[18]* *This calls for wisdom: let the one who has understanding calculate the number of the beast, for it is the number of a man, and his number is 666* (Rev. 13:1–18).

Six hundred and sixty-six! Few things have fuelled more speculation than the biblical witness to the Antichrist, and especially the testimony given by John in Revelation 13, to a beast identified by the cryptogram 666. All kinds of bizarre interpretations are current.

At the close of chapter 12, the dragon was hurled out of heaven, intent on pursuing the church (12:13–17). He is standing on the shore of the sea.

But how does Satan accomplish his malice? What form does his persecuting and hounding of the people of God take? The answer given in this chapter involves the activity of two beasts: a '*beast . . . of the sea*' (13:1), and a '*beast . . . of the earth*' (13:11).

The mention of two beasts, of 'the sea' (Leviathan) and 'the land' (Behemoth), seems to have its origin in the closing pages of the book of Job (*Job* 40:15; 41:1). The identification of these two creatures in Job is a source of much debate. Jewish rabbis favoured the identification of them as the embodiment of the powers of evil, and the

Greek translation of Job with which John would have been familiar rendered 'Leviathan' as 'dragon'.

It may be that John is borrowing (once more) from Daniel 7 and its vision of *four* beasts. John sees two beasts, not four, but there are marked similarities, especially in the case of the first beast (the *sea*-creature): a ten-horned, seven-headed, seven-crowned creature (13:2; *Dan.* 7:4–6), '*uttering haughty and blasphemous words*' (13:5; see *Dan.* 7:6,8), appearing for '*forty-two months*' (13:5; *Dan.* 7:25).

THE BEAST OF THE SEA (13:1–10)

As the dragon stands on the shore, John sees a beast arising 'out of the sea' (13:1). It has ten horns and seven heads (see also 12:3). This beast is satanic in nature, but is not Satan himself. It is an *image* of Satan. Satan it is who gives this creature its authority (13:2).

On each of the beast's heads there is '*a blasphemous name*' (13:1). The background here may well be the fondness of the Roman emperors for being referred to by divine names. Domitian, for example, demanded to be called 'our Lord and our God'. The first readers of Revelation were familiar with ships coming to shore bearing the divine names of Roman emperors and establishing worship in the local port-cities. In Ephesus, for example, a gigantic statue was erected celebrating the cult of Domitian.

The beast of the sea, while based on the Roman persecutions of the first century, and therefore of immediate significance to the first recipients of Revelation, conveys a hostility of more general significance, one that prevails until the end of time. He exercises his power for a period of 42 months (13:5), the same period of time alluded to before (12:6; see also 11:2–3), the period between the Ascension and the Second Coming of Christ. He is given a mouth to utter '*blasphemies*' (13:5), and he does so against God, heaven, and all who are in it (13:6).

The beast represents political and secular forces that seek, however subtly, to destroy the testimony to Jesus Christ and oppose the building of the kingdom of Christ on earth. It has many shapes, many horns, now taking one form and now another.

One of the beast's seven heads bears a *mortal wound*, now healed (13:3), a wound caused by a sword (13:14). The death and resur-

rection of Jesus has caused a fatal blow. The beast is not dead, but
dying.

> In that day,
> The LORD with his hard and great and strong sword
>   will punish Leviathan the fleeting serpent,
> Leviathan the twisting serpent,
> And he will slay the dragon that is in the sea.
>   (*Isa.* 27:1; see also *Psa.* 74:13–14; *Hab.* 3:14–15).

The use of the language '*seemed to have*' in the ESV rendering of
verse 3, '*One of its heads seemed to have a mortal wound*', is not meant
to cast doubt on its reality or even its eventual fatality. It is a parallel
– perhaps a deliberate parody of John's vision of 'a Lamb standing
as though it had been slain' (5:6). Jesus' death had been all too real,
but he now stands in Resurrection triumph. The beast, too, bears a
mortal wound and appears to stand. But it will not be for long. His
eventual doom is certain. His reign is a pretence. He has '*authority*'
(13: 2, 4, 5, 7; see 12:12), he is '*allowed to make war*' (13:7; see also
verse 15), but the ultimate sovereignty belongs to Another.

Those not protected by God's seal (7:1–4; 9:4), who do not belong
to God's true temple (11:1–2; 13:1, 6, 14) succumb to the beast's
authority and worship him (13:4). They are those '*whose name has
not been written before the foundation of the world in the book of life of
the Lamb that was slain*' (13:8).

Using the instruments of deception and pretence, the beast man-
ages to fool and hoodwink the ignorant into giving him worship. It
is what he craves for, even offering to Jesus what he did not possess
in order to have him bow before him (see *Matt.* 4:9).

In the face of such deception, Christians will therefore need
'*the endurance and faith of the saints*' (13:10; see also *Heb.* 12:1–3).
Opportunities to exercise such qualities as these are to be prized as
character building, and ultimately God-glorifying.

THE BEAST OF THE EARTH (13:11–18)

Just as John had seen a beast arise out of the sea (13:1), so now he
sees another arise out of the earth (13:11). The parody in this image
is even more striking. The lamb-like figure, with two horns, speaks

like a dragon (13:11). Again, Daniel seems to provide the background idea: 'a ram . . . [that] had two horns' (*Dan.* 8:3).

The function of the beast of the earth is to encourage the worship of the beast of the sea (13:12). Those who refuse are condemned to death (13:15).

Whereas the beast of the sea appears to exercise *political* power, the beast of the earth, later referred to as 'the false prophet' (16:13; 19:20; 20:10), bears all the trappings of *religion*: he performs '*signs*' (13:13); he even has a 'sacrament' of his own – a bestial baptism of a cranial mark (13:16). And he has a '*number*': 666.

Just as the beast of the sea had imaged Satan, the beast of the earth parodies Christ himself! The parody is such that many have identified the 'beast of the earth' with the *anti*-Christ figure of other New Testament passages. Some, therefore, have identified the beast of the earth with the 'man of lawlessness' in 2 Thessalonians 2:3–7, indicating, therefore, a *particular figure* who will arise towards the end of this current age.

The sixteenth-century Reformers identified this figure as 'Antichrist', meaning (for them) the Roman Catholic church, and the papacy in particular. This identification found its way into the formulation of several confessions of faith, including the *Westminster Confession of Faith*.

Since the book of Revelation was intended to be of significance to persecuted Christians in every age, it would seem best to interpret Revelation 13 in a more general way, as indicative of *anti*-Christian forces urging worship of the demonic. In that sense, it is of a piece with what John has said elsewhere: that Antichrist is already present in the world (*1 John* 2:18; 2:22; 4:4; *2 John* 7) and will be up until Jesus' return. What seems to be in view here is not an Antichrist figure, one who can be pin-pointed in history, but a more general description of the *religious* character of Antichrist, just as the beast of the sea had alluded to the *political* character of Antichrist.

THE NUMBER 666

Attempts are often made to interpret the number '666' (13:18). Some have sought to do this by reference to the *Gematria* – the art of representing words and names by the addition of the numerical equivalent of each letter. Such 'equivalences' of numbers and names exist in the (North American) use of telephone numbers of the '1-800-CALL-JOE' variety. These represent a convenient way of remembering an otherwise unmemorable array of numbers.

According to the rules of the *Gematria*, the first nine letters of the alphabet are used to represent the numbers 1 to 9, and then the next nine letters to represent the numbers 10, 20, 30 etc., to 90, and the following nine letters to represent the numbers 100 to 900, and so on. Thus A=1, B=2, J=10, K=20, S=100, and T=200, and so on.

Those particularly keen on identifying the 'beast of the earth' as Nero (for example, those eager to give an early date for Revelation and to see most of its contents as referring to the period culminating in the destruction of the temple in 70 AD) have considerable difficulty getting the letters N-E-R-O to make 666 (in English, Latin or Greek!). However, if transliterated into Hebrew 'Caesar Nero' does add up to 666, though only by misspelling the name (and omitting one of the necessary Hebrew letters)! This has not deterred its loyal devotees.

Another attempt has involved the use of the first letter of the names of all the emperors from Julius to Vespasian, but the degree of arbitrariness in the choice of starting and finishing points renders it deeply suspicious.

The use of the *Gematria* is more than a little questionable when it comes to identifying the number 666. No such attempt, for example, is made in identifying other numbers, such as 7, 10, 42, 1,260, or 144,000. The process is too 'clever' for a book that is more concerned with discernment than specialist knowledge.

According to 13:18, the number 666 is a '*the number of a man*', and, tempting as it is to identify it with a *particular individual*, it is more in the spirit of this chapter as a whole that it should signify something broader. The reference could be to man considered universally, that is, man without God, *religious* man without God! What could '666' possibly represent?

Since the number 7 is used throughout Revelation as a number of completeness (the seven days of creation and rest), it is likely that John intends 666 to be a parody of 777. A number short of completeness repeated three times is a trinity of imperfection. The beast of the earth bears the spirit of utter imperfection. Despite his lofty claims he bears a deadly flaw.

OVERCOMING THE BEASTS

Revelation 12 and 13 provide some clear instruction for us on how we may overcome the influence of the beasts of the earth and sea.

i.   It is possible for a believer to overcome because Christ has overcome and now reigns. We are to live with this firmly in our minds and hearts. The victory of Christ is not in the future; he has already won the victory. It began in the past. Jesus Christ now reigns and that is why the beast is so furious. He knows his time is short. That is why he seeks to destroy the people of God.

ii.   We can overcome, so long as we develop spiritual insight (13:18). The wisdom that is called for is spiritual wisdom. We are to recognize that the source of all opposition is hellish. We are to remember that we wrestle against a power that is greater than flesh and blood (Eph 6:18-20).

iii.   We are to endure patiently (13:10). To appreciate this chapter, John does not intend the kind of wisdom needed for solving mathematical puzzles so much as the wisdom of knowing God and his ways – the wisdom that knows what godliness looks like. For such times as these (yes, these in which you and I live), three skills are required: patient endurance (13:10), faithfulness (13:10), and wisdom (13:18): they are the keys to living God's way.

12

One Hundred and Forty-Four Thousand

*T*hen I looked, and behold, on Mount Zion stood the Lamb,
*and with him 144,000 who had his name and his Father's
name written on their foreheads.* ² *And I heard a voice from
heaven like the roar of many waters and like the sound of loud
thunder. The voice I heard was like the sound of harpists playing on their harps,* ³ *and they were singing a new song before
the throne and before the four living creatures and before the
elders. No one could learn that song except the 144,000 who had
been redeemed from the earth.* ⁴ *It is these who have not defiled
themselves with women, for they are virgins. It is these who
follow the Lamb wherever he goes. These have been redeemed
from mankind as firstfruits for God and the Lamb,* ⁵ *and in their
mouth no lie was found, for they are blameless.*

⁶ *Then I saw another angel flying directly overhead, with an
eternal gospel to proclaim to those who dwell on earth, to every
nation and tribe and language and people.* ⁷ *And he said with
a loud voice, "Fear God and give him glory, because the hour
of his judgment has come, and worship him who made heaven
and earth, the sea and the springs of water."*

⁸ *Another angel, a second, followed, saying, "Fallen, fallen
is Babylon the great, she who made all nations drink the wine
of the passion of her sexual immorality."*

⁹ *And another angel, a third, followed them, saying with a
loud voice, "If anyone worships the beast and its image and
receives a mark on his forehead or on his hand,* ¹⁰ *he also will
drink the wine of God's wrath, poured full strength into the cup
of his anger, and he will be tormented with fire and sulphur in
the presence of the holy angels and in the presence of the Lamb.*
¹¹ *And the smoke of their torment goes up forever and ever, and*

they have no rest, day or night, these worshippers of the beast and its image, and whoever receives the mark of its name."
¹² Here is a call for the endurance of the saints, those who keep the commandments of God and their faith in Jesus.
¹³ And I heard a voice from heaven saying, "Write this: Blessed are the dead who die in the Lord from now on." "Blessed indeed," says the Spirit, "that they may rest from their labours, for their deeds follow them!"

¹⁴ Then I looked, and behold, a white cloud, and seated on the cloud one like a son of man, with a golden crown on his head, and a sharp sickle in his hand. ¹⁵ And another angel came out of the temple, calling with a loud voice to him who sat on the cloud, "Put in your sickle, and reap, for the hour to reap has come, for the harvest of the earth is fully ripe." ¹⁶ So he who sat on the cloud swung his sickle across the earth, and the earth was reaped.

¹⁷ Then another angel came out of the temple in heaven, and he too had a sharp sickle. ¹⁸ And another angel came out from the altar, the angel who has authority over the fire, and he called with a loud voice to the one who had the sharp sickle, "Put in your sickle and gather the clusters from the vine of the earth, for its grapes are ripe." ¹⁹ So the angel swung his sickle across the earth and gathered the grape harvest of the earth and threw it into the great winepress of the wrath of God. ²⁰ And the winepress was trodden outside the city, and blood flowed from the winepress, as high as a horse's bridle, for 1,600 stadia.

^{15:1} Then I saw another sign in heaven, great and amazing, seven angels with seven plagues, which are the last, for with them the wrath of God is finished.

² And I saw what appeared to be a sea of glass mingled with fire – and also those who had conquered the beast and its image and the number of its name, standing beside the sea of glass with harps of God in their hands. ³ And they sing the song of Moses, the servant of God, and the song of the Lamb, saying,

"Great and amazing are your deeds,
O Lord God the Almighty!
Just and true are your ways,
O King of the nations!

⁴ Who will not fear, O Lord,
*   and glorify your name?*
For you alone are holy.
*   All nations will come*
*   and worship you,*
for your righteous acts have been revealed"
                                    (Rev. 14:1–15:4).

I n the unfolding sequence of visions that John sees, a message is
building up. In the first few chapters, John has been shown the
condition of the churches in Asia Minor at the close of the first century. Then, in a series of 'wonderful' pictures, the triumph of Jesus
Christ is revealed to him in a most remarkable way. Then follows
another picture: a scroll with seven seals, taken out of the hand of
God. The only one (One!) who can open these seals is Jesus Christ.
As they are opened, seven trumpeters come on to the stage blowing
their trumpets of warning, thus moving the reader into the second
half of the book and prompting us to penetrate more deeply into
the mysteries that are being revealed.

Behind what John has so far seen and heard are even bigger
realities!

In a series of seven signs, John takes us behind the space-time
world with which we are familiar, to catch a glimpse of another reality, one in which a war is taking place between God and the powers
of darkness. Jesus is building his church within sight of the gates of
hell (*Matt.* 16:18). Beasts arise out of the earth and sea. Powers are
at work, seeking to destroy everything that Christ is endeavouring
to build.

The beasts represent the instruments that Satan (the 'great red
dragon') uses in order to impede the progress and ultimate triumph
of the kingdom of God. But the victory of God's kingdom is never
in doubt. The decisive battle has already been won at Calvary, a victory signalled by Christ's resurrection and ascension. It is because of
that certainty that Satan's rage is so fierce. Like a cornered animal,
he bares his teeth and growls.

In part, this explains what follows: God's people need assurance
of their ultimate safety.

The following pattern emerges:

i.   the conflict of the serpent with the woman and her seed (12:1–17)

ii.   persecution by the beast from the sea (13:1–10)

iii.   persecution by the beast from the land (13:11–18)

iv.   the Lamb and the 144,000 standing on Mount Zion (14:1–5)

v.   the proclamation of the gospel and of judgment by three angels (14:6–13)

vi.   the Son of Man's harvest of the earth (14:14–20)

vii.   the saints' victory over the sea beast and their victory song (15:2–4)

Four sub-sections, then, form the basic structure of 14:1–15:4 and take us to the Judgment Day once again. Each one begins with the words, '*Then I saw*' (14:1, 6, 14; 15:1; the ESV confusingly renders 14:1 and 14:14 as '*Then I looked*', though the Greek is identical in each case).

THE LAMB AND THE 144,000

The Lamb is seen standing on Mount Zion in the presence of 144,000 (14:1–5). This is, of course, in direct contrast to the mocking parody presented in 13:11 of the beast of the earth (the false prophet, as he will later be called, 16:13; 19:20) who had lamb-like features.

The Lamb is standing on Mount Zion. This has led some to expect a literal return of Jesus to Jerusalem (Mount Zion) at some point in the future. However, a quick glance at 21:2–3 indicates that Mount Zion is to 'descend' to the earth out of heaven. The Jerusalem that the saints of God long for is the ideal city, as depicted in other places in the New Testament (*Gal.* 4:25-27; *Heb.* 12:22-23). While Satan and his two henchmen are doing their worst on earth, Jesus is standing in heaven with his redeemed (represented by the number *144,000*).

Jesus marks those who belong to him just as Satan is said to mark his (13:17). The Lamb's followers have inscribed upon their foreheads the name of the Father and of the Son (14:1). As labels on garments identify origin and manufacturer, so the name of God on 'the foreheads' of every believer signifies their identity and their safe-keeping. Every believer bears the stamp: *Made in Heaven.*

The 144,000 praise God by 'playing harps' and singing a 'new song' (see also 5:8–9; 15:2–3). The praise is a response to the victory of God, 'new songs' always being in response to victories (*Psa.* 33:3; 40:3; 96:1; 98:1; 144:9; 149:1; *Isa.* 42:10). In this case, it is the victory over the two beasts of the previous chapter that is the cause of the celebration (though news of this must wait until 15:1–3). Their praise is so loud that it sounds '*like the roar of many waters and like the sound of loud thunder*' (14:2).

But who are these 144,000? A threefold description is given in verse 4:

i.   they are those who 'have not defiled themselves with women'.

ii. they are those who 'follow the Lamb wherever he goes'.

iii. they 'have been redeemed from mankind as firstfruits to God and the Lamb'.

Who exactly are the 144,000? 144,000 is 12 x 12 x 1000, or 10 x 10 x 10 x 12 x 12 [that is, 10^3 x 12^2] and represents *completeness.* But why are they called '*firstfruits*' (14:4)? Does this suggest they represent *a fraction of the whole* (as Paul uses the term in 1 Corinthians 15:20), perhaps referring to the martyred saints pictured in chapter 6?

We have already identified the 144,000 of chapter 7 as the whole of the redeemed. What, then, is the significance of the term '*firstfruits*' here? Possibly what is in view is a contrast between the believers as '*firstfruits*' and the rest of mankind, who will be judged (14:14–20). Sometimes, the term '*firstfruits*' connotes the idea of 'choicest' with no thought of more to come (as in Jeremiah 2:3).

The language of sexual purity may sound a little odd in this context, but Israelite soldiers were expected to maintain their ceremonial purity before battle (*Deut.* 23:9–10; *1 Sam.* 21:5; *2 Sam.* 11:8–11), and perhaps John is using the language as symbolic of the Christian warfare we are to engage in. The holy war requires consecration to the bridegroom and the expectation of a wedding to come is part of a New Testament theme (19:7; 21:2, 9; 22:17).

THE PROCLAMATION OF THE GOSPEL AND OF JUDGMENT BY
THREE ANGELS

After a description of the beast of the earth and the beast of the
sea, and a word of encouragement to the redeemed (the 144,000),
a warning to the unbelieving world follows.

An angel appears proclaiming the *'eternal gospel'* (14:6). This
is not a word of good news as such, but of judgment. Even so, it is
vital to bear in mind that the downfall of all that is contrary to the
purposes of God is, in the last analysis, good news for the believer,
however painful that thought might be. The gospel always contains
a dire warning of the consequences of rejecting the offer of grace
in Jesus Christ. The twin rôles of the covenant are that it contains
curses as well as blessings.

What follows is similar in nature to what is recorded earlier
in 8:13. Here, as there, the angel flies in mid-heaven, cries
with a loud voice, and addresses those dwelling on earth. The
unregenerate multitudes are in view, from 'every nation and tribe
and language and people'. The extent of God's sovereign rule over
evil is total.

The appeal of verse 7, 'Fear God and give him glory, because
the hour of his judgment has come', is meant to assert the Lord's
absolute sovereignty. 'At the name of Jesus every knee should bow,
in heaven and on earth and under the earth, and every tongue confess that Jesus Christ is Lord, to the glory of God the Father' (*Phil.*
2:10–11). It is also possible that it is to be viewed as an evangelistic
appeal to those who worship the beast instead of God. It would be
in keeping with such passages as 2 Peter 3:9–11.

A second angel appears declaring that Babylon (Rome and all
earthly systems raised in opposition to God) is fallen (14:8; see also
Isa. 21:9).

A third angel appears also announcing judgment. This time the
emphasis falls upon the eternal nature of the punishment that comes
upon those who worship the beast and his image. '*If anyone worships
the beast and its image and receives a mark on his forehead or on his hand,
he also will drink of the wine of God's wrath, poured full strength into
the cup of his anger, and he will be tormented with fire and sulphur in
the presence of the holy angels and in the presence of the Lamb. And the*

smoke of their torment goes up forever and ever, and they have no rest day or night, these worshippers of the beast and its image, and whoever receives the mark of its name' (14:9–11).

These words remind us of some words of Jesus about the fire which is not quenched and the wrath which abides (*Mark* 9:44–48). The punishment envisioned is eternal; it is *'forever and ever'* (literally, to ages and ages), just as Jesus in Revelation 4:9 is described as the one 'who lives forever and ever'.

Two verses follow to bring this section to a close, exhorting the faithful to patient endurance (as in the close of the previous chapter, 13:10 and 13:18). Warnings are always encouragements for the godly to persevere (14:12–13). Once again, the faithful are described as those *'who keep the commandments of God and their faith in Jesus'* (14:12; see also 12:17). As before, the hope held out for believers is not a rapture from the trouble that lies ahead, but a deliverance through it to the hope that is beyond it, in the new heavens and new earth to come.

Thus, the angel is heard to say, *"'Blessed are the dead who die in the Lord from now on." "Blessed indeed," says the Spirit, "that they may rest from their labours, for their deeds will follow them"'* (14:13). 'What comfort do you derive from the article of the *life everlasting*?' asks Question 58 of the *Heidelberg Catechism*; to which the answer is: 'That, since I now feel in my heart the beginning of eternal joy, after this I shall possess perfect bliss, such as eye has not seen nor ear heard, neither has entered into the heart of man – therein to praise God forever.'

Another truth emerges here with respect to the works that believers do in this life. Though they do not contribute towards their justification, these works are taken into account in the life to come. What we do in this life has eternal consequences in the life to come.

All of this would prove encouraging to the beleaguered Christians to whom John first wrote, but it is also a powerful incentive for us to persevere in the midst of our troubles.

THE SON OF MAN'S HARVEST OF THE EARTH

The sixth section (14:14–20), describes the judgment at the end of history in much the same way as the sixth seal and sixth bowl have done previously. What had been but a warning in verses 6–13 is now described as a present reality.

The vision introduces us to someone sitting on a cloud, '*one like a son of man, with a golden crown on his head, and a sharp sickle in his hand*' (14:14; see *Dan.* 7:13). This is Jesus (1:7, 13–20). He comes as King (hence the crown) and in judgment (hence the sharp sickle). Another angel issues a command from God to the Son of Man figure to take his sickle and reap, '*for the harvest of the earth is fully ripe*' (14:15). The judgment is described using a harvest metaphor. The image is repeated and expanded in the verses that follow. The fact that these sections, 14–16 and 17–20, have small differences has led some to advocate two *distinct* harvests. However, they are best viewed as mirror images of each other. Just as that day will bring salvation to the 144,000, it will involve the eternal punishment of the rest of mankind.

Behind the imagery lies Joel 3:13, 'Put in the sickle, for the harvest is ripe. Go in, tread, for the winepress is full. The vats overflow, for their evil is great.'

The statement in verse 20 that '*the winepress was trodden outside the city, and blood flowed from the winepress, as high as a horse's bridle, for 1,600 stadia*' needs some comment!

The spreading of blood for 1,600 stadia (4^2 x 10^2, approximately 184 miles or 300 kilometres) from the city is an approximate measurement of Palestine from the borders of Tyre to the borders of Egypt and could signal a comprehensive judgment of Palestine. But more likely, since both four and ten are numbers representing completeness (in this case, 4 becomes symbolic of the four corners of the earth: north, south, east, west), it is a way of describing world-wide judgment.

The imagery is that of unbelievers being judged outside of the true city of God. It is, once again, a compilation of two Old Testament passages: the Joel passage already cited, together with Isaiah 63:2–3, 'Why is your apparel red, and your garments like his who treads in the winepress? I have trodden the winepress alone, and from the peoples no one was with me; I trod them in my anger and trampled them in my wrath; their lifeblood spattered on my garments, and stained all my apparel.' This imagery will return again in chapter 19.

However gory this language may be, it is meant to convey the seriousness of the punishment that awaits unbelief. The war imagery is symbolic of the enmity that will exist between the seed of the serpent and that of the woman until the end of time.

But, the victory is not in doubt: *Jesus shall reign from shore to shore.*

THE VICTORY SONG OF THE REDEEMED

Just as the people of God who experienced deliverance from Egyptian bondage sang a song in celebration and victory by the Red Sea (*Exod.* 15), so John pictures the redeemed in heaven gathered by the crystal sea, singing a new song in celebration of the Lamb's triumph over evil.

> '*Great and amazing are your deeds,*
> > *O Lord God the Almighty!*
> *Just and true are your ways,*
> > *O King of the nations!*
> *Who will not fear, O Lord,*
> > *And glorify your name?*
> *For you alone are holy.*
> *All nations will come*
> > *and worship you*
> *for your righteous acts have been revealed.*'
>
> (15:3–4).

In the background are the echoes of another song, one which the church militant has been singing for centuries in anticipation of this new song of the church triumphant:

> 'I have set my King
> > on Zion, my holy hill.
> > . . . and I will make the nations your heritage,
> > and the ends of the earth your possession.
> You shall break them with a rod of iron
> > and dash them in pieces like a potter's vessel.'
>
> (*Psa.* 2:6, 8–9).

13

Armageddon

*A*fter this I looked, and the sanctuary of the tent of witness in heaven was opened, ⁶ and out of the sanctuary came the seven angels with the seven plagues, clothed in pure, bright linen, with golden sashes around their chests. ⁷ And one of the four living creatures gave to the seven angels seven golden bowls full of the wrath of God who lives forever and ever, ⁸ and the sanctuary was filled with smoke from the glory of God and from his power, and no one could enter the sanctuary until the seven plagues of the seven angels were finished.

¹⁶:¹ Then I heard a loud voice from the temple telling the seven angels, "Go and pour out on the earth the seven bowls of the wrath of God."

² So the first angel went and poured out his bowl on the earth, and harmful and painful sores came upon the people who bore the mark of the beast and worshipped its image.

³ The second angel poured out his bowl into the sea, and it became like the blood of a corpse, and every living thing died that was in the sea.

⁴ The third angel poured out his bowl into the rivers and the springs of water, and they became blood. ⁵ And I heard the angel in charge of the waters say,

"Just are you, O Holy One, who is and who was,
    for you brought these judgments.
⁶ For they have shed the blood of saints and prophets,
    and you have given them blood to drink.
It is what they deserve!"

⁷ *And I heard the altar saying,*

"Yes, Lord God the Almighty,
    true and just are your judgments!"

⁸ *The fourth angel poured out his bowl on the sun, and it was allowed to scorch people with fire.* ⁹ *They were scorched by the fierce heat, and they cursed the name of God who had power over these plagues. They did not repent and give him glory.*

¹⁰ *The fifth angel poured out his bowl on the throne of the beast, and its kingdom was plunged into darkness. People gnawed their tongues in anguish* ¹¹ *and cursed the God of heaven for their pain and sores. They did not repent of their deeds.*

¹² *The sixth angel poured out his bowl on the great river Euphrates, and its water was dried up, to prepare the way for the kings from the east.* ¹³ *And I saw, coming out of the mouth of the dragon and out of the mouth of the beast and out of the mouth of the false prophet, three unclean spirits like frogs.* ¹⁴ *For they are demonic spirits, performing signs, who go abroad to the kings of the whole world, to assemble them for battle on the great day of God the Almighty.* ¹⁵ *("Behold, I am coming like a thief! Blessed is the one who stays awake, keeping his garments on, that he may not go about naked and be seen exposed!")* ¹⁶ *And they assembled them at the place that in Hebrew is called Armageddon.*

¹⁷ *The seventh angel poured out his bowl into the air, and a loud voice came out of the temple, from the throne, saying, "It is done!"* ¹⁸ *And there were flashes of lightning, rumblings, peals of thunder, and a great earthquake such as there had never been since man was on the earth, so great was that earthquake.* ¹⁹ *The great city was split into three parts, and the cities of the nations fell, and God remembered Babylon the great, to make her drain the cup of the wine of the fury of his wrath.* ²⁰ *And every island fled away, and no mountains were to be found.* ²¹ *And great hailstones, about one hundred pounds each, fell from heaven on people; and they cursed God for the plague of the hail, because the plague was so severe* (Rev. 15:5–16:21).

We now come to the fifth of the seven visionary cycles of Revelation (see p. xviii). The Battle of Armageddon!

The 'problem' with the book of Revelation is the reader! Or, perhaps we should say, certain readers in particular. Bizarre interpretations abound when it comes to Revelation.

Some have seen it as one huge cryptic puzzle to be solved by the initiated. Thus, 'the ten horns of the beast' in chapter 13 have been taken to symbolize the European Community, the 'mark of the beast' and '666' in the same chapter have been taken to indicate anything from credit cards to the Internet or personal subcutaneous identity markers, and the Antichrist figure of 6:2 has been interpreted as any one of a long line of candidates from Adolf Hitler or Benito Mussolini to Henry Kissinger or Bill Clinton.

This 'crystal ball' view of the book of Revelation currently interprets the gathering of '*the kings from the east*' to Armageddon (16:12–16) as a reference to communist China.

The problem with such an approach is the way in which each generation interprets the book from events current within its own time. There is, therefore, no end to the possibilities that can arise.

As we have already seen in the opening chapter of Revelation, John has given us three clues as to what the book of Revelation is about: it is, firstly, a 'revelation of Jesus Christ' (1:1), secondly, it testifies to 'all that he saw' (1:2), and thirdly, it is a word of 'prophecy' (1:3). John has faithfully recorded the details of what he saw, in the order in which he saw them, unfolding, as these details do, the redemptive and judgmental purposes of God throughout history.

Revelation tells us what Jesus intends to do for his people and against his enemies as he brings to fruition the promise given to Peter at Caesarea Philippi: 'On this rock I will build my church and the gates of hell will not prevail against it' (*Matt.* 16:18). History will unfold in one terrible scene of judgment after another, but Christians are to be assured that it does so in accordance with his purpose! Nothing happens without God willing it to happen, and willing it to happen *in the way that it happens*, and willing it to happen *before* it happens. Since the description of the judgments which unfold following the seven bowls are particularly graphic and disturbing, it is all the more important to recall that Jesus Christ is in complete control of everything.

We have already had the seven seals (6:1–8:5) and the seven trumpets (8:6–11:19) of wrath. Now the pattern is repeated once more with '*seven golden bowls full of the wrath of God*' (15:7). In language reminiscent of the description of the Egyptian plagues in the opening chapters of Exodus, John outlines a picture of judgment more graphic and terrifying than anything that has gone before.

Since these are the last of the 'sevens' in the book of Revelation, some interpreters (usually classified as 'Futurists') see in these plagues descriptions of the final stages of history. Along similar lines, some understand these seven bowls as the *content* of the *seventh trumpet* (the trumpets being seen as an expansion of the seventh seal). In that way the bowls represent a narrowing of the camera lens to pinpoint events at the closing stages of history. It is more likely, however, that the seals, trumpets and bowls all depict the same events, but from different points of view. Each group of seven recapitulates what has been seen before. The order implied in each group of seven is the order *in which John saw them* rather than a sequential, historical order in which they are to be fulfilled.

One clue that this is indeed the case is the obvious reference at the end of each sequence of seven to the Day of Judgment (for the seals, see 6:12–17, and 8:1; for the trumpets, see 11:15–19; for the visions of chapters 12-14, see 14:8-11; and for this sequence of seven bowls, see 16:17–21).

These are the '*last*' plagues (15:1), in the sense, perhaps, that they belong to the 'last days.' Based as they are upon the Egyptian plagues, these belong to the age of the Spirit (see *2 Cor.* 3:8) rather than to the day of Moses, to the new covenant rather than to the old.

THE SEVEN BOWLS OF JUDGMENT

The vision begins with the temple, or '*sanctuary of the tent of witness*' (15:5). This is the heavenly reality of which the tabernacle in the wilderness was an earthly replica. It represented the presence of God amongst his people (*Acts* 7:44). When the tabernacle contained the ark of the covenant, God's judgment and mercy were both symbolized. The focus now, however, is the impending judgment.

The seven angels emerge from the temple dressed in priestly garments and are given the seven bowls, symbolic of the wrath of

God that is to be poured out. The judgments do not come from the angels; they are only the messengers. Bowls of wrath are *given to them*. The temple is filled with smoke (symbolic of God's power and glory, 15:8). God alone is able to remain in the presence of his unmitigated wrath.

The judgments follow the same order as those depicted by the trumpets in chapter 8: the earth, the sea, rivers, the sun, the realm of the wicked, the Euphrates, and the final judgment (following the same imagery of lightning, sounds, thunders, earthquake and great hail). The similarity here is based upon the underlying similarity we have noted to the plagues of the Exodus.

Like the trumpets, the bowl-plagues are answers to the prayers of the martyrs in 6:9–11 for the vengeance of Almighty God upon their enemies. The fear that such vengeance may involve injustice has already been answered by the declaration that all of God's ways are '*just*' and '*true*' (15:3; 16:5, 7).

In response to the initial judgments, the angels express the *justice* of God's judgments. Everything about this scene is expressive of God's holiness. No one can say of God's judgments that they are unfair. These are acts of the '*Holy One*' (16:5).

THE RECIPIENTS OF THE JUDGMENTS

Three categories may be singled out as recipients of the bowls of wrath.

1. *Those who bear the mark of the beast and worship his image*. The cause of the first bowl of wrath is idolatry. It is poured on those who have the mark of the beast (666, the mark of imperfection) and worship his image (16:2; see also 13:16–18).

The effects of this first bowl are similar to that of the sixth Egyptian plague: boils and sores (*Exod*. 9:9–11).

Like the second and third trumpets (8:8–9, 10–11), the imagery of the second and third bowls is that of death in a watery grave ('*sea*', '*rivers and springs*'). The allusion is to the turning of the Nile into blood and the consequent death of the fish (*Exod*. 7:17–21). But, whereas the effects of the trumpets' judgment was partial, the effect of the bowls' is total: '*Every living thing died that was in the sea*' (16:3).

Any accusation of injustice is immediately answered. An angel declares that God is *'just'* in *'these judgments'* (16:5). It is an echo of the *'righteous acts'* of 15:4. A similar cry comes from another angel in verse 7, '*Yes, Lord God the Almighty, true and just are your judgments!*' A variation takes place in the formula used to describe God: instead of the usual, 'who is and who was and who is to come' (1:4, 8; 4:8; see also 11:17) we now have, '*O Holy One, who is and who was*'.

The fourth bowl is poured on the sun causing it to '*scorch people with fire*' (16:8). Again it is the Lord who does this: it is he who has '*power over these plagues*' (16:9). This is the opposite of the beautiful imagery of Revelation 7:16, which promises that the sun will not smite, nor the heat destroy those who have been sealed by God (see also *Isa.* 49:10). This judgment does not bring about repentance, but a continuation of the blasphemy that had initiated it in the first place.

2. *The dragon, the beast and the false prophet.* The fifth bowl is poured upon the *'throne of the beast'* (16:10). The very seat of his government is challenged, plunging his kingdom into darkness. It is reminiscent of the plague of darkness over Egypt. In the Exodus story, the plague was a direct attack upon Pharaoh who was believed to be an incarnation of the sun god, Ra. The fifth bowl identifies God's total sovereignty over Satan and his forces. Again, despite the intense imagery of pain and suffering, there is no repentance (16:11).

The sixth bowl brings us to the battle of Armageddon (16:16). The imagery is introduced using language that reminds us of the drying up of the Red Sea at the time of the Exodus, only this time it is the river Euphrates. Old Testament prophets had spoken of the drying of the river (*Isa.* 11:15; 44:27; *Jer.* 50:38; 51:36) and there is a fulfilment of it in the history of King Cyrus who diverted the river allowing his army to cross, enter Babylon unexpectedly, and defeat it. The victory of Cyrus over Babylon was to be the means of Israel's deliverance from exile. The fact that Isaiah refers to Cyrus as 'one from the east' (*Isa.* 41:2) prepares the way here in Revelation 16 for a similar picture, this time of *'kings from the east'* who cross the dry bed of the river Euphrates.

That a figurative interpretation is in order can be seen by glancing at 17:1, where the Babylonian harlot '*is seated on many waters*', which is another way of describing '*the great river Euphrates, and its water*' (16:12). The '*many waters*' of 17:1 are further explained as '*peoples and multitudes and nations and languages*' (17:15).

Things now get a little complicated! Three antagonists arise: the dragon, the beast and the false prophet. These are usually thought to be parallel to the 'great red dragon', 'the beast of the sea' and 'the beast of the earth' of chapters 12 and 13 (that is, Satan, Satanic politics and Satanic religion).

This trinity of evil spits out three frog-like '*unclean spirits*' (16:13) who deceive the people into idolatry. They are able to perform miracles (as the second beast, or false prophet of chapter 13 is said to perform 'great signs' (13:13)). That these frogs affect only the kings of the earth is a reminder that in the Exodus story, it was the king (*Exod.* 8:3–4) who was first affected.

By means of this great disguise, the kings of the earth are gathered for '*the battle on the great day of God Almighty*' (16:14; see also 19:19; 20:8). This is the same war that has been referred to earlier in 11:7, but it is now taking on a greater significance. It is the battle of Armageddon, in which the forces of the dragon and beast are destroyed. More will be said about it in 19:14–21 and 20:7–10.

Since Babylon and the river Euphrates are not to be taken in a literalistic way, neither should the reference to Armageddon. What, then, does this all mean?

Several things are worth noting that should help us come to some understanding of this sequence:

i.   The story of redemption is one of war and hostility, whether it be of Moses against the Amalekites, or Joshua against the Philistines or, as here, of Jesus against the Dragon and the beast and the false prophet. 'I am persuaded', wrote the Lutheran bishop, Gustaf Aulén, in the closing pages of his book, *Christus Victor*, 'that no form of Christian teaching has any future before it except such as can keep steadily in view the reality of evil that is in the world, and go to meet the evil with a battle song of triumph.'[1]

---

[1] G. Aulén, *Christus Victor* [1931], translated by A. G. Hebert, London: SPCK, 1965, p. 159.

ii.   The site of Megiddo as the last battlefield of redemptive history is consonant with biblical imagery thus far. Megiddo was a large fortress city, strategically placed at the foot of Mount Carmel, which acts as a sentinel over the plain of the Esdraelon Valley of Jezreel. It was *the* battlefield of Israel. Overlooking it was Mount Tabor where Deborah and Barak mustered the tribes for their triumphant assault on the Canaanites. Down the plain to the east was Gilboa where Saul met his doom. Josiah lost his life here in a battle with Pharaoh Neco. Jehu's chariot chase took place in this valley. And on the mount that rises behind Megiddo, Elijah entered into battle with Jezebel. It is, then, altogether appropriate that Megiddo should symbolize the location of the battle of the Lord against the forces of darkness and that the final, cataclysmic battle should be pictured as taking place here, even though no such literal battle need be expected.

iii.   An expectation of a future golden age before the return of Christ does not do justice to the continuing tension in the history of the world between the kingdom of God and the forces of evil as depicted in these scenes of Revelation. It is true that some interpreters apply these scenes, including the battle of Armageddon, to the final overthrow of the city of Jerusalem in 70 AD, but the connection of the battle with the sixth bowl, coming as close as it does to the seventh (an obvious representation of the Day of Judgment), would seem to cast doubt on this position. The parable of the Tares (or Weeds) in Matthew 13:36–43 teaches that we can expect hostility and trouble right up to the return of Jesus Christ. The enmity of the seed of Satan continues until the very end of history. This is what the Battle of Armageddon (16:13–16) and, later, the Battle of Gog and Magog (20:7–9) both indicate. Satan's kingdom will continue to exist and grow as long as God's kingdom grows, until Christ comes again. To suppose that before Christ's return evil 'will be reduced to negligible proportions' would seem to be a simplistic analysis of history not warranted by the biblical data.

iv.   There is a pastoral desire on John's part to intersperse messages of hope and encouragement in the middle of a message of alarming proportions. Thus, in verse 15, there is the pronouncement of blessing (the third of seven such blessings, see also 1:3;

14:13; 19:9; 20:6; 22:7, 14) upon those who '*stay awake*' and are therefore ready for the return of Jesus Christ. We are not to be found '*naked*' whenever Jesus returns. It is the biblical injunction to be prepared, expecting that Jesus may come '*like a thief*,' suddenly and unannounced.

Yet the reality symbolized by the Battle of Armageddon comes to pass *before* Jesus returns. The Bible's stress is not so much on the precise 'when', as much as the certainty of Christ's return: we are to be ready no matter when it transpires.

3. *Babylon*. Much of the imagery of the final judgment scene, the seventh bowl (16:17–21), reflects the Exodus narrative once again. '*Flashes of lightning, rumblings, peals of thunder, and a great earthquake*' (16:18) are all reminiscent of the description of Sinai in Exodus 19:16–18. It is imagery that we have seen before in Revelation 4:5 and 11:19.

As another reference to Daniel 12:1 shows, there is something altogether unique about this Day: nothing quite like it has ever been seen before. Babylon, representing the consummation of evil, is destroyed. Interestingly, as we noted earlier, there is more in view here than the mere destruction of the ancient city of Rome. Not only Babylon the Great, but also '*the cities of the nations*' collapse (16:19). '*Every island fled away, and no mountains were to be found*' (16:20). The hail storm descends from heaven on the entire world in hostility against God (16:21), suggesting that there is something cosmic and climactic about this judgment.

To understand the significance of Babylon we need to return to Genesis 11:1–9 and the story of the tower of Babel. The great city of Babylon owes its origin to the confusion brought about by God following man's attempt to reach God by the grandest scheme of all: building a tower, or *ziggurat* that would penetrate heaven itself. It was pride in its fullest expression. The intent of the men concerned was to '*make a name*' for themselves (*Gen.* 11:4). It was to signal to all who happened to pass by in the plain of Shinar (the Fertile Crescent) that here were folk worthy of note. It was 'skyscraper theology' come to fullest expression!

But God judged it! And ever since, the principle of Babylon versus Jerusalem has symbolized the hostility between man's religion and

God's. That hostility has here reached its zenith. Babylon is given a cup filled with '*the wine of the fury of his wrath*' (16:19).

All that now awaits her is the shout: '*Fallen! Fallen is Babylon the great*' (18:2).

LIKE A THIEF

When the judgment spoken of comes, there will be no repentance: '*they did not repent*' but '*cursed God*' (16:9, 11, 21). They have despised the judgment of God in their hearts and when it comes it finds them incapable of repentance. They die as they live: cursing the name of God. The judgments of God catch them unprepared. He comes '*like a thief*' (16:15). And the day of grace and evangelism is over!

In the midst of this scene there are words of comfort. John hears Jesus express a beatitude: '*Blessed is the one who stays awake, keeping his garments on, that he may not go about naked and be seen exposed*' (16:15). Like the wise virgins, they have their lamps burning whenever the bridegroom comes (*Matt.* 25:1–13).

This is the watchfulness to which the Scriptures, the New Testament in particular, calls us (*Matt.* 24:42; 26:41; *Luke* 12:37). Being ready for the coming of Christ is the right way, the wise way, to live.

And it is the wise way to die! It is that which lies at the heart of the child's bed-time prayer taken from the *New England Primer* of 1737:

> *Now I lay me down to sleep,*
> *I pray the Lord my soul to keep;*
> *If I should die before I wake,*
> *I pray the Lord my soul to take.*

14

A Tale of Two Cities

*T*hen one of the seven angels who had the seven bowls came
and said to me, "Come, I will show you the judgment of
the great prostitute who is seated on many waters, ² with whom
the kings of the earth have committed sexual immorality, and
with the wine of whose sexual immorality the dwellers on earth
have become drunk." ³ And he carried me away in the Spirit
into a wilderness, and I saw a woman sitting on a scarlet beast
that was full of blasphemous names, and it had seven heads and
ten horns. ⁴ The woman was arrayed in purple and scarlet, and
adorned with gold and jewels and pearls, holding in her hand a
golden cup full of abominations and the impurities of her sexual
immorality. ⁵ And on her forehead was written a name of mystery: "Babylon the great, mother of prostitutes and of earth's
abominations." ⁶ And I saw the woman, drunk with the blood
of the saints, the blood of the martyrs of Jesus.
When I saw her, I marvelled greatly. ⁷ But the angel said to me,
"Why do you marvel? I will tell you the mystery of the woman,
and of the beast with seven heads and ten horns that carries her.
⁸ The beast that you saw was, and is not, and is about to rise
from the bottomless pit and go to destruction. And the dwellers
on earth whose names have not been written in the book of life
from the foundation of the world will marvel to see the beast,
because it was and is not and is to come. ⁹ This calls for a mind
with wisdom: the seven heads are seven mountains on which the
woman is seated; ¹⁰ they are also seven kings, five of whom have
fallen, one is, the other has not yet come, and when he does come
he must remain only a little while. ¹¹As for the beast that was

and is not, it is an eighth but it belongs to the seven, and it goes to destruction. ¹² And the ten horns that you saw are ten kings who have not yet received royal power, but they are to receive authority as kings for one hour, together with the beast. ¹³ These are of one mind and hand over their power and authority to the beast. ¹⁴ They will make war on the Lamb, and the Lamb will conquer them, for he is Lord of lords and King of kings, and those with him are called and chosen and faithful."

¹⁵ And the angel said to me, "The waters that you saw, where the prostitute is seated, are peoples and multitudes and nations and languages. ¹⁶ And the ten horns that you saw, they and the beast will hate the prostitute. They will make her desolate and naked, and devour her flesh and burn her up with fire, ¹⁷ for God has put it into their hearts to carry out his purpose by being of one mind and l handing over their royal power to the beast, until the words of God are fulfilled. ¹⁸ And the woman that you saw is the great city that has dominion over the kings of the earth" (Rev. 17:1–18).

The next three chapters (17-19) in the book of Revelation describe the systematic destruction of every enemy of God. They include the 'enormous red dragon' (Satan), the beast of the sea (the powers of this world), the beast of the earth (the false prophet, representing false spirituality), the city of Babylon and those who bear the mark of the beast. Chapter 17 is concerned with the nature of the city of Babylon whose destruction is described in chapter 19. This is the sixth of the seven visions of Revelation.

'*Babylon the great*' (17:5). As we saw in the previous chapter, Babylon (Babel) emerges as the stereotypical act of rebellion on man's part in the pages of Genesis: 'Come, let us build ourselves a city and a tower with its top in the heavens, and let us make a name for ourselves, lest we be dispersed over the face of the whole earth' (*Gen.* 11:4).

'Let us make a name for ourselves . . . ' That just about sums it all up. The Babylonians themselves conveniently explained the name as *babili*, meaning 'gate of God'; but *babel* is an echo of the Hebrew for 'confused', recalling that God turned mankind's common language into a confusion of tongues. It is a small picture of what man has tried to do ever since: build his way to God and thereby boast of his achievements and significance before others.

Just as modern cities have their grandiose symbols (Paris has its Eiffel Tower, Washington, D.C. its Washington Monument, Toronto its Canadian National Tower), so the Fertile Crescent had its *ziggurat* which boasted of oversized ambition. It is pride gone to seed. It is passion for power, prestige, and pomposity all in one. It signals man apart from God and in opposition to God. It is the godless city.

Three years after the city of Rome fell to the Visigoth king, Alaric, in 410, Augustine began his best known work, *The City of God*. He worked on it for thirteen years and it instantly became a classic. It still is. In it he attempts to convey a comprehensive philosophy of history. The first half of the book is an attempt to answer a charge that Rome had fallen because it had embraced Christianity (the emperor Constantine had converted to Christianity following his victory at the Milvian Bridge in 312 AD).

In the second half of the book Augustine begins to argue that the whole of history can be seen as one of a battle between two rival societies, one allied to the god of this world, another allied to the King of kings. There are two loves, he argued, one that is proud and arrogant and godless; another that is 'heavenly' and even contemptuous of self. The whole of history can be symbolized by these two cities, Babylon and Jerusalem.

Augustine is not alone in the use of the 'city' to describe history. There have been many authors who have described an idealistic utopia in the form of a city, Plato's *Republic* and Henry David Thoreau's *Walden* among them. Others have warned of the consequences of unchecked evil by representing cities in chaos, among them Aldous Huxley in his *Brave New World* and George Orwell in his *Nineteen Eighty-Four*.

John's visions are so complex that he once again cries, '*This calls for a mind with wisdom*' (17:9; see 13:18)!

John does not necessarily mean what we might think he means! At least a part of what he means is that without the revelation of Scripture, particularly the Old Testament, together with the illumination of the Holy Spirit on particular passages in Exodus, Daniel and Jeremiah, we are sure to be led astray in our interpretations!

A cursory analysis of these three chapters will reveal some interesting features. In the Exodus story in the Old Testament, deliverance sets the people of God free to worship. Thus, Exodus 14 describes the deliverance from Egypt and chapter 15 contains the song of Moses and Miriam recounting this fact. In similar style, the description of the destruction of the *'great prostitute'* in chapter 17 is followed in chapters 18 and 19 by a song recounting the fact.

Babylon is described as a *'great prostitute'* (17:1; 'whore' in other versions). She allures and controls from a sitting position (17:1,3,9,15). *'I sit as queen'* (18:7). The kings of the earth have fornicated with this harlot (17:2), they have *'drunk the wine of the passion of her sexual immorality'* (18:3). The three-fold combination of the drunken stupor, the spiritual compromise and the idolatrous alliances ensures the maximum effect in the description of Babylon's degeneracy.

The issue here is not so much illicit sex as false worship (though the two often have a connection). Giving ourselves to the dragon is an act of spiritual prostitution. It is a failure to maintain loyal relationships with God. To flirt with Babylon is to betray disloyalty to the ways of God. It is to believe the satanic lie that love can be purchased, that a relationship can be maintained at the purely commercial level. It is the myth of relationships without commitment, of transaction without personal involvement. It is how so many desire religion to be: a fail-safe mechanism that operates without taxing demands or demanding lifestyle changes. The harlotry of false religion exacts, however, a price so great that death and disaster inevitably follow in its wake.

Isaiah 21 seems to be in the background here, especially the portrayal by the prophet of Babylon as fallen (*Isa.* 21:1–2, 9). John is carried to a *'wilderness'* (17:3). Elsewhere he has been 'carried' to earth (1:9–10), sea and earth (10:8–9), heaven (4:1), seashore (13:1) and later, mountaintop (21:9–10). Of greater importance is the fact that in the desert John sees a woman sitting on a scarlet beast that has seven heads and ten horns (evidently, the beast of the sea as described in chapter 13).

The woman '*is seated on many waters*' (17:1) and is in the '*wilderness*' (17:3) which, difficult as it is to imagine, seems to involve allusions to Isaiah 21 and Jeremiah 51:13, rather than describing distinct physical localities. The association of words with certain images is more important here than the geographical pinpointing of places on a map. Thus, the many waters of Babylon, including the great Euphrates River, symbolize the immense irrigation and fertility provided. The desert, by contrast, suggests that despite these advantages, Babylon remained infertile ground. Later in this chapter, the waters will be identified as 'peoples and multitudes and nations and languages' (17:15).

The woman is dressed in the very same materials (clothes and jewellery) mentioned among the trade products of 18:12–14. What is being described is a wealthy trading system, which in the first century was Rome ('code name', Babylon). The entire world depended on the ability of Rome to ply her trade. Dressed in fine apparel, she remains, nevertheless, a whore. She is a persecutor, and carries this out to great effect in league with the beast and the dragon. Her description is in vivid contrast to the Lamb's bride, again portrayed as a city '*adorned for her husband*' (21:2) and clothed in '*fine linen, bright and pure*' (19:8).

Babylon promises economic prosperity, life that has 'never been so good'. But it is a cup full of '*abominations and impurities*' (17:4) – imagery which echoes Jeremiah 51.

We have seen the phenomenon of names written on foreheads before: the relationship of believers to God (7:3; 14:1; 22:4), the relationship of others to Satan (13:16; 14:9; 20:4). The woman, too, has a name written on her forehead:

MYSTERY

BABYLON THE GREAT

MOTHER OF PROSTITUTES

AND OF EARTH'S ABOMINATIONS

It is believed that prostitutes in Roman times wore name bands on their heads and this may account for the allusion here. The word 'mystery' may not be part of the title given to the woman, and the

verse may be read: 'And on her head was written a name of mystery
. . .' What is apparent is that we are to take into consideration here,
not just the identity of the whore, but that of her progeny also. She
is the '*mother*' of prostitutes (17:5). Just as the woman in chapter 12
gives birth to the church (the bride of chapter 19), so the woman of
chapter 17 gives birth to those who would destroy the church. This
woman makes herself drunk with the blood of the saints, which is
her most heinous crime of all (17:6).

John himself is astonished at this vision (17:6).

An explanation follows.

The beast is described as one who was, is not and yet will be (17:8,
10), and in verse 10, the '*kings*' are described similarly in terms of
past, present and future, thereby indicating a connection between
the beast and the kings. Clearly, this is a parody of the formula,
'*who is and who was and who is to come*', as applied to God (1:8; 4:8;
11:16; 16:5). It is a formula which mocks the beast's attempts at
coronation.

The formula itself conveys the beast's present demise in compari-
son with what has been and what will be before the end comes. To
borrow the language of chapter 20, where Satan is being spoken of,
the beast is on a chain and, to some extent, 'is not'. And even though
he may have his day before the end, he will not end in triumph. His
end will be the lake of fire.

Behind this mockery is a serious point. The beast (and evil gen-
erally) is forever attempting to mimic Christ. But he overplays his
hand. His promises go beyond his ability to perform. And his failure
to accomplish his objectives sends him into a rage of warfare against
Christ, in a final attempt to stamp out all traces of his ancient foe
(17:14).

The beast is said to have seven heads and ten horns (17:7, 9).
They are further described as '*seven kings*' (17:10).

IDENTIFYING THE SEVEN HEADS

Many interpreters of Revelation have attempted to identify the
seven kings (17:10), five of whom '*have fallen, one is, the other has not
yet come*' (17:10), with specific emperors. But it would be strange,
given the interpretation thus far, for the vision suddenly to identify

the Roman Empire of the mid-first century. The point seems to be that five of seven heads of the beast have already been slain. He is not totally defeated, though it is true that he once *'was'*, and now *'is not'* (17:8). In that sense, the beast is a defeated foe bearing fatal wounds. But a sixth head and a seventh head remain.

Some fairly complicated formulas have been employed to try and identify the sixth and seventh heads, not always heeding the warning of verse 9, '*This calls for a mind with wisdom*'!

Two assumptions often made are: that each 'head' refers to a Roman emperor, and that the statement, '*Five have fallen, one is, the other has not yet come*' (17:10), implies that the sixth was still alive at the time Revelation was written.

Since we have no agreement on when Revelation was written (though this book has assumed a date) this further complicates accurate identification. As to the identity of the fifth (and still living) emperor, those that have found support include Nero (54-68 AD), Galba (68-69 AD), Vespasian (69-79 AD), and Domitian (81-96 AD).

Some have taken an entirely different course and suggested that each 'head' represents an *empire* rather than *emperor*. These would be Egypt, Assyria, Babylon, Persia, Greece and Rome (the sixth and still living 'head'). The seventh empire is then taken to be symbolic of all world empires between Rome and the Second Coming of Christ.

The reference to the beast itself being an *'eighth'* king (17:11) is most likely an attempt to capture the idea that it personifies the totality of evil represented by its predecessors. The one to be reckoned with, at the end of the day, is the eighth king – Satan himself.

The Ten Horns

The clue to the interpretation of the '*ten horns*' (17:3) as '*ten kings*' (17:12), or '*the kings of the earth*' (17:18), is to be found in an earlier description of the Lamb's '*seven horns*' as indicative of his perfect power (5:6). Once more, Daniel's prophecy seems to set the background (*Dan.* 7:4–8, 20, 24). The '*ten kings*' are representative of the agents of the beast and Satan; they represent the power that the beast and Satan have. They represent such things as art, education, commerce, industry and government in so far as they operate according to an ungodly agenda. They help the beast in the accomplishment of his grand design to bring down the kingdom of God.

The horns are said to be 'kings' who receive authority along with the beast for '*one hour*', a short period of time (17:12). Since the ten horns are (at the time of writing) still future – they have 'not yet received a kingdom' (17:12) – this seems to imply that they are to be found *only* on the seventh beast.[1] This vision again testifies to a period of intense battle against the forces of the Lamb prior to Christ's return.

Once again, though the battle is intense and fierce, the Lamb, who is Lord of lords, will be victorious (17:14). The wording is almost exactly that of Daniel 7:21, but with a glorious twist. Whereas Daniel is describing the partial and momentary victory of the beast over the saints (as do Revelation 11:7 and 13:7), the language here is of the Lamb's victory over the kings. The great question of 13:4 – 'Who is like the beast, and who can fight against it?' – is now answered. The Lamb can!

The Waters

One more feature of the vision needs explanation: the waters upon which the great harlot sits (17:1). Jeremiah 51:13 may be the background to this picture. The reference is to the economic wealth brought into the city of Babylon along the Euphrates and its tributaries. The beast and the ten horns combine to bring down the harlot before they attempt to attack the Lamb. Evil is implicitly self-destructive. This is the lesson of the closing verses of Revelation 17. The horn-kings in league with the beast now begin to loathe the harlot and eventually '*devour her flesh and burn her with fire*' (17:16). Three powerful images – nakedness, being devoured, and fire combine to spell her doom. Images from Ezekiel and Jeremiah seem to be in the background (see *Jer.* 2:20–4:30; *Ezek.* 16:37–41; 23: 25–29).

Ezekiel 23 is the story of two sisters: Oholah and Oholibah who engage in prostitution in Egypt. It is a powerful indictment of the

---

[1] In chapters 12 and 13, the ten horns would seem to be distributed among the seven heads (12:3; 13:1).

unfaithfulness of Israel in her liaison with foreign (pagan) deities. Revelation 17 now picks up this metaphor, describing the apostate church as a harlot.

The Woman

The final verse of Revelation 17 identifies the woman as '*the great city that has dominion over the kings of the earth*' (17:18). She has been interpreted as the entire evil economic-religious system that operates in the world throughout the last days. She is the exact opposite of the pure bride that is the church.

Several lessons can be drawn:

1.   The Bible gives us a graphic description of sexual commerce (harlotry) as descriptive of unfaithfulness in worship. False worship is as tawdry and cheap as prostitution. It deserves the same ignominy and rejection. It is also self-destructive: bringing tawdry and fleeting pleasures, but carrying a deadly sting too.

2.   The powers of evil are inherently self-destructive. There is a restlessness about the beast and his cohorts; Satan is always 'going to and fro on the earth' (*Job* 1:7; 2:2). Evil has no peace. There is no resolution of the insecurity that is at the heart of rebellion. Finding no way to defeat the Lamb, the forces of evil turn upon each other. Alliances of evil last for only a brief time. It is only in Jesus that fullness and light are to be found (see *John* 8:12).

3.   God's sovereignty operates even in these ungodly and vicious realms. Self-destructive powers of darkness operate according to a plan that is divine in nature. They accomplish his purpose (17:17). Nothing is outside of the over-ruling plan of God. His providence extends to the overthrow of wickedness and sin. This, too, will be a fulfilment of prophecy.

15

'Fallen, Fallen Is Babylon
the Great!'

A fter this I saw another angel coming down from heaven,
having great authority, and the earth was made bright with
his glory. ² And he called out with a mighty voice,

"Fallen, fallen is Babylon the great!
She has become a dwelling place for demons,
a haunt for every unclean spirit,
a haunt for every unclean bird,
a haunt for every unclean and detestable beast.
³ *For all nations have drunk the wine of the passion of her*
sexual immorality,
and the kings of the earth have committed immorality with her,
and the merchants of the earth have grown rich from the power
of her luxurious living."

⁴ *Then I heard another voice from heaven saying,*

"Come out of her, my people, lest you take part in her sins,
lest you share in her plagues;
⁵ *for her sins are heaped high as heaven,*
and God has remembered her iniquities.
⁶ *Pay her back as she herself has paid back others,*
and repay her double for her deeds;
mix a double portion for her in the cup she mixed.
⁷ *As she glorified herself and lived in luxury,*
so give her a like measure of torment and mourning,
since in her heart she says,
'I sit as a queen, I am no widow, and mourning I shall never
see.'

[8] *For this reason her plagues will come in a single day,*
death and mourning and famine,
and she will be burned up with fire;
    for mighty is the Lord God who has judged her."

[9] *And the kings of the earth, who committed sexual immorality*
and lived in luxury with her, will weep and wail over her when
they see the smoke of her burning. [10] *They will stand far off, in*
fear of her torment, and say,

"Alas! Alas! You great city,
    you mighty city, Babylon!
For in a single hour your judgment has come."

[11] *And the merchants of the earth weep and mourn for her, since*
no one buys their cargo anymore, [12] *cargo of gold, silver, jewels,*
pearls, fine linen, purple cloth, silk, scarlet cloth, all kinds of
scented wood, all kinds of articles of ivory, all kinds of articles
of costly wood, bronze, iron and marble, [13] *cinnamon, spice, in-*
cense, myrrh, frankincense, wine, oil, fine flour, wheat, cattle and
sheep, horses and chariots, and slaves, that is, human souls.

[14] *"The fruit for which your soul longed has gone from you,*
    and all your delicacies and your splendors
    are lost to you, never to be found again!"

[15] *The merchants of these wares, who gained wealth from her,*
will stand far off, in fear of her torment, weeping and mourn-
ing aloud,

[16] *"Alas, alas, for the great city that was clothed in fine linen,*
    in purple and scarlet, adorned with gold,
    with jewels, and with pearls!
[17] *For in a single hour all this wealth has been laid waste."*

And all shipmasters and seafaring men, sailors and all whose
trade is on the sea, stood far off [18] *and cried out as they saw the*
smoke of her burning,

"What city was like the great city?"

[19] *And they threw dust on their heads as they wept and mourned,*
crying out,
"Alas, alas, for the great city

where all who had ships at sea
grew rich by her wealth!
For in a single hour she has been laid waste.
[20] *Rejoice over her, O heaven,*
and you saints and apostles and prophets,
for God has given judgment for you against her!"

[21] *Then a mighty angel took up a stone like a great millstone*
and threw it into the sea, saying,
"So will Babylon the great city be thrown down with vio-
lence,
and will be found no more;
[22] *and the sound of harpists and musicians, of flute players*
and trumpeters,
will be heard in you no more,
and a craftsman of any craft
will be found in you no more,
and the sound of the mill
will be heard in you no more,
[23] *and the light of a lamp*
will shine in you no more,
and the voice of bridegroom and bride
will be heard in you no more,
for your merchants were the great ones of the earth,
and all nations were deceived by your sorcery.
[24] *And in her was found the blood of prophets and of saints,*
and of all who have been slain on earth"
(Rev. 18:1–24).

The fall of Babylon, first announced in 14:8, 'Fallen, fallen is Babylon the great!', and then again in 16:19, 'God remembered Babylon the great, to make her drain the cup of the wine of the fury of his wrath', now reaches its climax in chapters 18 and 19. Babylon has so far been represented as a harlot (prostitute) who sits astride a seven-headed, ten-horned beast, and who is drunk with the blood of martyred saints (17:1–6). She is a temptress, alluring and seductive. Her goal is to turn people away from God. Her influence is cosmic; she rules over the kings of the earth (17:18).

Babylon appears therefore to be a symbol for the pleasure-mad, arrogant world, with all its seductive luxuries and pleasures, with its antichristian philosophy and culture.

Some interpreters have been equally insistent that Babylon represents a worldly element within the church itself, and that therefore Babylon is representative of Jerusalem! There is some justification for this line of reasoning. After all, when Babylon is finally destroyed (18:21), the apostles and prophets whom she has destroyed are called upon to rejoice. The pages of Scripture certainly do reveal that it was often the church – the worldly church – that abused the servants of God more than the world in general. And there are clear echoes of Jeremiah 25:10 in verses 22 and 23 of this chapter, a passage in which Jeremiah is clearly talking about Jerusalem.

One thing is certain: ungodliness, wherever it manifests itself, whether it is in the church or in the world, is doomed.

THE CURSE OF BABYLON

The chapter opens with something else that John '*saw*' (18:1). An angel descends from heaven, and as a consequence, '*the earth was made bright with his glory*' (18:1). The word '*glory*' is used to describe God or Christ in Revelation (4:9, 11; 5:13 for God; 1:6; 5:12-13 for Christ).

In the background lies yet another Old Testament passage. The closing chapters of Ezekiel depict in some detail the new temple. Chapter 43 describes the descent of the LORD to the temple in terms strikingly similar to Revelation 18:1. In particular, the earth is said to shine as a consequence of the '*glory*' of the LORD as he enters the temple structure.

However alluring Babylon may be, the splendour of this '*angel*' belongs to another sphere of reality. Some have insisted that this is Christ. The light and the voice are both meant to suggest a power far greater, and far more threatening, than Babylon: God is pronouncing a curse on Babylon and her doom is written: '*Fallen, Fallen is Babylon the great!*' (18:2; see also 14:8; *Isa*. 21:9). Where once her beauties allured and dazzled, her streets will be empty and her fine buildings ruined. She will be fit only for the demonic (18:2). 'Babylon shall become a heap of ruins, the haunt of jackals, a horror and a hissing, without inhabitant' (*Jer.* 51:37). There are several allusions in this chapter to Jeremiah 50–51 (prophesying the fall of Babylon) and Ezekiel 27 (prophesying the fall of Tyre).

'COME OUT OF HER' – THE CALL FOR SEPARATION AND HOLINESS

The true church of Christ is exhorted to separate from the alluring tentacles of Babylon. *'Come out of her, my people . . .'* pleads another voice (18:4; there are similar exhortations in *Isa.* 48:20; 52:11; *Jer.* 50:8; 51:6, and especially *Jer.* 51:45). The reason for this separation is solemn enough: lest the church be caught in the impending judgment (18:5).

The church is in the world, but the world must *never* be in the church. Some form of involvement in the world is a responsibility and duty. The church is to be salt and light in the world. Equally, however, the church has no business being of the world. She is to be different. Holiness demands separation from the idolatry that characterizes Babylon.

Babylon is to receive in judgment *'double'* of that which she herself inflicted (verse 6). The word translated 'double' can also mean 'duplicate' and this would fit in with what follows in verse 7, stating as it does the principle that the punishment should meet the crime. There is equity in God's justice.

Such judgment will bring despair to those who remain under Babylon's alluring spell. The lover weeps when his beloved is destroyed. Those who have engaged in adultery with Babylon now find themselves bereft of the harlot. Hence the cry:

Alas! Alas! You great city,
    You mighty city, Babylon!
For in a single hour your judgement has come!
                                                    (18:10).

And again:

Alas, alas, for the great city,
That was clothed in fine linen, in purple and scarlet,
Adorned with gold, with jewels and with pearls!
For in a single hour all this wealth has been laid waste
                                                    (18:16–17).

LAMENTATIONS AND WOES

The sight of the city on fire (18:9) is terrifying to her supporters (18:10). Despair arises, due either to the suddenness of the demise, '*In a single hour . . .*' (18:10, 17, 19), or to its effect upon themselves: '*No one buys their cargo anymore*' (18:11). The point is that the demise comes swiftly and decisively. And the mourners here catch a glimpse of the reality that faces all worshippers of the beast, and participants in the economic schemes of Babylon: they, too, will be judged. If God is to cause Babylon to burn, the final condemnation of Babylon's traders will not be far behind in his purposes.

In language of graphic simplicity, John pictures the traders who have profited from Babylon. They no longer have a place to do their trading. No one buys their goods any more: gold, silver, precious stones, pearls etc (18:11–13). The picture extends out into the sea, to ship captains beholding the pall of smoke hanging over the city, and they, too, lament uttering a cry similar to earlier ones in this chapter (18:19, see also 10, 16–17).

CERTAIN AND IRREVOCABLE DESTRUCTION

In a further graphic description, which repeats much of the imagery of earlier verses, the final section of the chapter (18:21–24) depicts an angel throwing a huge boulder into the sea. It depicts the '*violence*' with which Babylon will be overthrown. Despite all her great claims, she will be brought to utter desolation. The sound of music, and trade, and the allurement of bright lights will be gone. Like the eerie spectacle of the *Titanic* on the ocean floor as a camera slowly passes over her carbuncled remains, so the glory of Babylon will be gone. 'Will never . . . will never . . . will never . . . be heard in you again' tolls like some faint echo of a distant bell signalling her eternal doom.

Prostitution is tawdry. It cheapens and commercializes something sacred. The exchange of money adds insult and offence to something beautiful and covenantal. It brings something heavenly to the level of the gutter. But now, in this chapter, the whore has been destroyed and her lovers are distraught. From the traffic of her bed they had made a rich life for themselves. The merchants had cashed in on a ready market. But the promise of everlasting gain is shattered. Salvation by cheque-book is impossible.

The lessons are not all negative, however. Behind the destruction of this archetypal city of wickedness, lies the truth that God is all-powerful and sovereign. Nothing can thwart his determination to build his church. The gates of Hades will not prevail; nor will the gates of Babylon. Only God's kingdom endures forever. All temporal things, despite sometimes great and substantial appearances are, at best temporal.

> *These things shall vanish all;*
> *The city of God remaineth.*
> Martin Luther

16

Hallelujah!

*A*fter this I heard what seemed to be the loud voice of a great multitude in heaven, crying out,

"Hallelujah!
 Salvation and glory and power belong to our God,
  2 for his judgments are true and just;
 for he has judged the great prostitute
  who corrupted the earth with her immorality,
  and has avenged on her the blood of his servants."

3 Once more they cried out,

"Hallelujah!
The smoke from her goes up forever and ever."

4 And the twenty-four elders and the four living creatures fell down and worshipped God who was seated on the throne, saying, "Amen. Hallelujah!" 5 And from the throne came a voice saying,

"Praise our God,
 all you his servants,
you who fear him,
 small and great."

6 Then I heard what seemed to be the voice of a great multitude, like the roar of many waters and like the sound of mighty peals of thunder, crying out,

"Hallelujah!
 For the Lord our God the Almighty reigns.
 7 Let us rejoice and exult and give him the glory,
  for the marriage of the Lamb has come,
  and his Bride has made herself ready;

Hallelujah!

⁸ it was granted her to clothe herself with fine linen, bright and pure" – for the fine linen is the righteous deeds of the saints.

⁹ And the angel said to me, "Write this: Blessed are those who are invited to the marriage supper of the Lamb." And he said to me, "These are the true words of God." ¹⁰ Then I fell down at his feet to worship him, but he said to me, "You must not do that! I am a fellow servant with you and your brothers who hold to the testimony of Jesus. Worship God." For the testimony of Jesus is the spirit of prophecy.

¹¹ Then I saw heaven opened, and behold, a white horse! The one sitting on it is called Faithful and True, and in righteousness he judges and makes war. ¹² His eyes are like a flame of fire, and on his head are many diadems, and he has a name written that no one knows but himself. ¹³ He is clothed in a robe dipped in blood, and the name by which he is called is The Word of God. ¹⁴ And the armies of heaven, arrayed in fine linen, white and pure, were following him on white horses. ¹⁵ From his mouth comes a sharp sword with which to strike down the nations, and he will rule them with a rod of iron. He will tread the winepress of the fury of the wrath of God the Almighty. ¹⁶ On his robe and on his thigh he has a name written, King of kings and Lord of lords.

¹⁷ Then I saw an angel standing in the sun, and with a loud voice he called to all the birds that fly directly overhead, "Come, gather for the great supper of God, ¹⁸ to eat the flesh of kings, the flesh of captains, the flesh of mighty men, the flesh of horses and their riders, and the flesh of all men, both free and slave, both small and great." ¹⁹ And I saw the beast and the kings of the earth with their armies gathered to make war against him who was sitting on the horse and against his army. ²⁰ And the beast was captured, and with it the false prophet who in its presence had done the signs by which he deceived those who had received the mark of the beast and those who worshipped its image. These two were thrown alive into the lake of fire that burns with sulphur. ²¹ And the rest were slain by the sword that came from the mouth of him who was sitting on the horse, and all the birds were gorged with their flesh (Rev. 19:1–21).

Revelation 19 is the response to the exhortation of the previous chapter, to 'Rejoice' at the destruction of Babylon, the godless city (18:20). The sights and sounds of God's wrath upon Babylon bring forth joyful strains of worship from the hosts of heaven. It is an indication of how far removed we often are from the biblical testimony to the character of God that we can so often recoil in horror at the graphic portrayals of God's wrath. But heavenly saints see things differently.

The judgment of Babylon signals the triumph of Jesus. The destruction of the beast and the false prophet is proof that God is the ultimate ruler. The cries of the citizens of Babylon highlight the victory of the purposes of God.

What we have in Revelation is the original Hallelujah chorus! There is something almost indescribable about the worship of heaven. John has to resort to such comparisons as '*what seemed to be* ' and '*like*' (19:1, 6, 12). There is no language that adequately describes heavenly worship!

Hallelujah! This is what they sing in heaven (19:1, 3, 4, 6). Surprising as it may seem, the word 'Hallelujah' occurs for the very first time in the Bible at this point! But this way of stating it somewhat obscures the fact that the Hebrew equivalent, often translated 'Praise the LORD' occurs frequently in the Old Testament (mainly in the Psalms, and over half of these occurrences are in the six Psalms 135, 146–150).

The word has become so much a part of our Christian vocabulary, we might easily miss the appropriateness of its occurrence (four times) in this chapter. Coming as it does from the Hebrew, 'Praise JAH [or JEHOVAH]' it indicates the desire of the heavenly multitude (19:1) to praise the Lord for the downfall of evil's tyranny. It is the Lord who has done this great thing.

REJOICING IN THE JUDGMENTS OF GOD!

The fourfold hallelujah is worth noting, for each repetition has something significant to teach us.

i. The *first* hallelujah celebrates *the righteousness of the act of judgment:*

Hallelujah!
Salvation and glory and power belong to our God,
      for his judgments are true and just;
For he has judged the great prostitute
      who corrupted the earth with her immorality,
And he has avenged on her the blood of his servants.

(19:1–3)

God's ways in judgment are *'true and just'*. Everything about this action is pure. No evil motive can be imputed to any of God's actions. The vengeance of God is an act of purity. At last, the cry of the martyred saints in 6:10, 'O Sovereign Lord, holy and true, how long before you will judge and avenge our blood on those who dwell on the earth?', has been answered. He 'has avenged on her the blood of his servants' (19:2). Justice has been seen to be done.

ii. The *second* hallelujah signals *the finality of God's judgment:*

Hallelujah!
The smoke from her goes up forever and ever.

(19:3)

The rising smoke that ascends over the burnt ruins of the city of Babylon is evidence of a battle fought and lost: Babylon is fallen never to rise again (19:21–23). Her doom has come (19:10). She has been brought to ruin (19:17). There is no phoenix rising from the ashes here; Babylon's influence has been obliterated. God's people will never again have to fear her.

iii. The *third* hallelujah reminds us that *worship is always God-centred.* It is sung by the twenty-four elders and the four living creatures (cherubim) alone. The twenty-four elders we have met before (4:4, 10; 5:8; 11:16). They are more than likely angels, twelve identifying the twelve tribes and twelve representing the twelve apostles, thus collectively representing the entire community of the Lord's people in both Old and New Testaments. The four living creatures, described earlier as cherubim, remind us of the picture given in Ezekiel 1 (see also 4:6, 8, 9; 5:6, 8, 11, 14).

Together, these angelic figures lead in the worship of God, underlining, confirming ('Amen' 19:4; see also 1:4) what has been said already. They focus their worship exclusively upon the Lord and his character. They form a community of praise encircling the throne of God. They are our constant encouragers as we worship God. Their appeal is followed by an antiphonal call from the throne itself (19:5). If we compare these verses with Revelation 6:6, 16:1 and 16:17, it seems that the voice that speaks in response is that of Jesus:

> [*Choir:*]   Amen, Hallelujah!
> [*Jesus:*]   Praise our God, all you his servants,
>   you who fear him, small and great.
>
> (19:4–5)

iv. The *fourth* hallelujah is the response of the heavenly choir to the call to worship. It is a *celebration of the union of Christ to the church*.

> Hallelujah! For the Lord God
>   the Almighty reigns.
> Let us rejoice and exult
>   and give him the glory!
> For the marriage of the Lamb has come,
>   and his bride has made herself ready;
>   it was granted her to clothe herself
>   with fine linen, bright and pure.
>
> (19:6–8)

This final hallelujah introduces us to a wedding banquet. The trials of persecution have been a preparation for a wedding. Christ and his people are to be married for eternity and the banquet is upon us!

The bride is to make herself ready (19:7), but in reality, the righteous acts she displays are '*granted her*' (19:8). The tension here is only apparent; the saints are justified by faith alone, but the faith which justifies is never alone; it is always followed by works.

God is about to bring to pass a new creation, a church unsullied by her contact with Babylon. A pure bride is to emerge, one fit for God's perfect Son wearing garments of white linen (19:8; see also 7:13–15).

The first song had proclaimed '*salvation*' (19:1). The other songs follow in its wake. God has rescued his people from certain destruction, 'plucked [them] from the fire' (see *Zech.* 3:2). The imagery of the smoking earth (see also *2 Pet.* 3:10) now gives way to the festal sounds of a wedding celebration.

In the Gospel of John, the first thing Jesus did when he began his public ministry was to attend a wedding in Cana (*John* 2:1–11). This is more significant than it looks. The entire ministry of Jesus is a preparation for a wedding. The Old Testament background has prepared us for this:

> I will greatly rejoice in the LORD;
>> my soul shall exult in my God,
> for he has clothed me with garments of salvation;
>> he has covered me with a robe of righteousness,
> as a bridegroom decks himself like a priest
>> with a beautiful headdress,
> and as a bride adorns herself with her jewels.
>
> (Isa. 61:10)

What a joy it is to be invited to this marriage supper (19:9)! The Lord's Supper is an anticipatory meal of this coming union. We eat and drink 'until he comes' (*1 Cor.* 11:26). We anticipate what is before us as much as we look back in remembrance of what he has already done. As in the Lord's Supper, so everywhere else in the Christian life, there is a tension between the 'now' and the 'not yet', between that which has already happened and that which remains to appear.

WORSHIP GOD!

John's response to this vision of heaven, and the worship he observes there, is to *join in with them!* He falls down at the foot of the angel only to find himself instantly rebuked! '*You must not do that! I am a fellow servant with you and your brothers who hold to the testimony of Jesus. Worship God!*' (19:10; see also 22:9).

What is happening here? In part, John is responding to a sight so full of wonder that he thinks it must be divine. But this is not a sight of God, but of an angel, and God *alone* is to be worshipped. It is never right to worship angels, no matter how wonderful they are.

Angels, of course, know a thing or two about worship. The angel's swift response is worth noting. '*I am a fellow servant with you and with your brothers . . .*' (19:10) indicates that we, just as the angels, are meant to bow before the Lord. When John bowed to the angel, he was robbing God of the glory that was his. False worship, however unintentional, always does that. Just as Paul reacted so intensely to the false worship of Athens, so the angel reacts here. (see *Acts* 17:16). When Henry Martyn, the Cambridge translator of the Scriptures into Persian, discovered a drawing of Jesus bowing in the presence of Mohammed, he turned aside and wept. When some thought he was overcome by the heat, he responded: 'I could not endure existence if Jesus was not glorified; – it would be hell to me, if he were to be always thus dishonoured.'[1]

Jesus is to be worshipped, '*For the testimony of Jesus is the spirit of prophecy*' (verse 10). The meaning of this verse is not as difficult as it may appear! It is saying one of two things: either that the Holy Spirit (taking 'spirit' as 'Spirit') reveals Jesus as Lord, or that prophecy (lower-case 'spirit') does so. In either case Jesus is to be worshipped. God-glorifying worship places Jesus at the centre.

THE DIVINE WARRIOR

'*Come, gather for the great supper of God, to eat the flesh of kings, the flesh of captains, the flesh of mighty men, the flesh of horses and their riders, and the flesh of all men, both free and slave, both small and great*' (19:18). Passages employing such vivid and horrific imagery as this cause us to reflect upon our doctrine of God. Is the God we worship like this?

Christ is the Divine Warrior (see *Hab.* 3:11–15; *Zech.* 9:14–17; 14:1–5). His '*robe*' is '*dipped in blood*' (19:13). As he wages war against his enemies, he treads '*the winepress of the fury of the wrath of God the Almighty*' (19:15). The '*blood*' here is not his own, but that of his enemies. It has been spattered upon his garments in the battle. Jesus is destroying his enemies!

Why is your apparel red,
and your garments like his who treads the winepress?

[1] John Sargent, *The Life and Letters of Henry Martyn*, 1862 (reprinted Edinburgh: Banner of Truth, 1985), p. 343.

Hallelujah!

I have trodden the winepress alone,
  and from the peoples no one was with me;
I trod them in my anger
  and trampled them in my wrath;
their lifeblood spattered on my garments,
  and stained all my apparel.

(*Isa.* 63:2–3)

Even though in this battle '*the armies of heaven, arrayed in fine linen, white and pure, were following him on white horses*' (19:14) – probably angels, but they may also include the glorified saints – the focus is upon Christ. He is '*Faithful and True*', and battles '*in righteousness*' (19:11). Against the forces of darkness, led as they are by the Beast and the False Prophet (19:20), he is Victor.

Righteousness distinguishes this battle. He sees the true condition of the human heart because his eyes are like '*flaming fire*' (19:12; see also 1:14; 2:18). His authority to judge is shown by the '*many diadems*' he wears (19:12). As 'Word of God' he is Creator and Sustainer (*Gen.* 1:3; *Psa.* 33:6; *John* 1:1; *Heb.* 1:3) and is able to bring to a conclusion that which he has brought into being and maintained. The outcome is not in any doubt, for he is

KING OF KINGS AND LORD OF LORDS
(19:16; see also 17:14; *1 Tim.* 6:15)

His intention is to fulfil the terms of Psalm 2 and rule over the nations with '*a rod of iron*' (19:15; see *Psa.* 2:9). This had been the theme announced right at the very opening of the book of Revelation (2:9), and repeated in the vision of chapter 12 as the seed of the woman triumphs over the hostile intent of the Great Red Dragon (12:5). Clearly, Psalm 2 is decisive in our understanding of the book of Revelation.

It is interesting to note the weapon employed in this massacre of the enemies of Jesus Christ. It is '*a sharp sword*' (19:15, 21) which, once again, is the way in which Christ is portrayed in the opening verses of the book (1:16; 2:12, 16). Elsewhere in the Bible, the sword is a metaphor for the Word of God (*Isa.* 11:4; *Eph.* 6:17; *Heb.* 4:12). Christ who creates by an effectual word also destroys by an equally effective word.

THE FINAL BATTLE

An angelic messenger stands 'in the sun' and summons birds to a *'great supper'* (19:17). *'Come, gather for the great supper of God, to eat the flesh of kings, the flesh of captains, the flesh of mighty men, the flesh of horses and their riders, and the flesh of all men, both free and slave, both small and great'* (19:18). This language, strange to us, reflects the picture already painted in Ezekiel 39:

'As for you, son of man, thus says the LORD God: Speak to the birds of every sort and to all beasts of the field: "Assemble and come, gather from all around to the sacrificial feast that I am preparing for you, a great sacrificial feast on the mountains of Israel, and you shall eat flesh and drink blood. You shall eat the flesh of the mighty, and drink the blood of the princes of the earth – of rams, of lambs, and of he-goats, of bulls, all of them fat beasts of Bashan. And you shall eat fat till you are filled, and drink blood till you are drunk, at the sacrificial feast that I am preparing for you. And you shall be filled at my table with horses and charioteers, with mighty men and all kinds of warriors," declares the LORD God.'

(*Ezek.* 39: 17–20)

There is deep significance to this. Deuteronomy 28:26 (in a sustained listing of covenant curses) warns: 'Your dead body shall be food for all birds of the air and for the beasts of the earth, and there shall be no one to frighten them away.' The final battle is portrayed as a covenantal curse (see also *1 Sam.* 17:44; *1 Kings* 14:11).

The beast and false prophet are defeated and thrown *'alive into the lake of fire that burns with sulphur'* (19:20). One by one, the enemies of God are being destroyed. After chapter 19 there is only one left: Satan. And he, too, will join the beast and the false prophet in this burning lake in the next chapter (20:10).

One by one, Jesus is defeating every opponent. He is ensuring the triumph he has promised to his people.

17

The Millennium

*T*hen I saw an angel coming down from heaven, holding in his hand the key to the bottomless pit and a great chain. *2 And he seized the dragon, that ancient serpent, who is the devil and Satan, and bound him for a thousand years, 3 and threw him into the pit, and shut it and sealed it over him, so that he might not deceive the nations any longer, until the thousand years were ended. After that he must be released for a little while.*

4 Then I saw thrones, and seated on them were those to whom the authority to judge was committed. Also I saw the souls of those who had been beheaded for the testimony of Jesus and for the word of God, and who had not worshipped the beast or its image and had not received its mark on their foreheads or their hands. They came to life and reigned with Christ for a thousand years. 5 The rest of the dead did not come to life until the thousand years were ended. This is the first resurrection. 6 Blessed and holy is the one who shares in the first resurrection! Over such the second death has no power, but they will be priests of God and of Christ, and they will reign with him for a thousand years.

7 And when the thousand years are ended, Satan will be released from his prison 8 and will come out to deceive the nations that are at the four corners of the earth, Gog and Magog, to gather them for battle; their number is like the sand of the sea. 9 And they marched up over the broad plain of the earth and surrounded the camp of the saints and the beloved city, but fire came down from heaven and consumed them, 10 and the devil who had deceived them was thrown into the lake of fire and sulphur where the beast and the false prophet were, and they will be tormented day and night forever and ever.

[11] *Then I saw a great white throne and him who was seated on it. From his presence earth and sky fled away, and no place was found for them. [12] And I saw the dead, great and small, standing before the throne, and books were opened. Then another book was opened, which is the book of life. And the dead were judged by what was written in the books, according to what they had done. [13] And the sea gave up the dead who were in it, Death and Hades gave up the dead who were in them, and they were judged, each one of them, according to what they had done. [14] Then Death and Hades were thrown into the lake of fire. This is the second death, the lake of fire. [15] And if anyone's name was not found written in the book of life, he was thrown into the lake of fire* (Rev. 20:1–15).

Dr Alexander Whyte, the famous 19th century Scottish preacher and author, had an unusual understanding with his book supplier. Whenever the bookseller received a new commentary on Romans, Whyte would be allowed to read the comments on chapter seven. If the commentator did not interpret Romans 7:14–25 as a description of a Christian, Whyte would return the book!

Similar stories, no doubt, could be told in relation to the twentieth chapter of Revelation and the identification of the '*thousand years*' (20:2). No passage has highlighted in greater relief the differences between the various schools of millennial interpretation. The passage is, then, something of a *cause célèbre*. It forms part of the seventh and final vision of Revelation (see p. xviii).

Part of the problem with this, and other passages in Revelation, has to do with the phrase which introduces the next vision sequence: '*Then I saw . . .*' (20:1). As we have already noted, wherever this expression, or a similar one occurs (for example, 4:1; 8:2; 9:1; 13:1; 15:2; 19:17), it indicates the order in which *John saw these visions*. It does not imply that there is an historical sequence of events from the end of chapter 19 to the beginning of chapter 20.

So far, in the section which began at 17:1, we have been told of the destruction of Babylon (17:1-19:3), and the beast and the false prophet (19:11-21). The focus now turns to Satan, *the root of all the trouble.*

So long as Satan is at large, there is no assurance of victory. A threat still exists to Christ's ultimate triumph so long as the devil exercises any influence on the outcome of the kingdom of God.

John glimpses the battle from four particular angles, each of which demands a more detailed examination.

THE BINDING OF SATAN

The vision begins with Satan being bound for a thousand years (verses 1–3). As we will see, this binding was accomplished by Christ in his first coming. However, the fact that it is mentioned *following* the destruction of Babylon, the beast and the false prophet has led many to interpret this scene in conjunction with a view that expects a future millennial reign of Christ on earth. The binding of Satan, in this interpretation, takes place during the millennial reign, following Christ's return.

This view, though popular, fails to appreciate the inner structure of these visions. What is being revealed to John is the destruction of the Kingdom of Darkness, beginning with its external manifestation (Babylon), its driving forces (the beast and the false prophet), and ultimately its source and origin, Satan himself. The order is not chronological but theological.

This curtailment for a period of '*a thousand years*' has given rise to what has been called *millenarianism* (or *chiliasm*: the Greek for thousand is *chilioi*, 20:2, 3, 4, 5, 6, 7) in its many forms. This raises a question: Is the period of '*a thousand years*' to be taken in a literal sense? And if so, *when* does this take place?

Given the use made of number patterns in the book of Revelation (for example, 3, 4, 7, 10, 12, 666, 144,000) it would be fitting that a symbolic use of *thousand* is intended here also. In that case, 1000 (= 10 x 10 x 10, or 10^3) is a combination of the 'ideal' numbers, 3 and 10. Rather than seeing the '*thousand years*' as referring to a time at the end of the age (either *before* Christ's return – as in *post*millennialism, or *after* Christ's [initial] return – as in *pre*millennialism), it should be understood as a figurative expression denoting the period of time from the first to the second advents of Christ. We are therefore living in this millennial (one-thousand-year) period.

Another problem arises. Since evil abounds everywhere, how is it possible to interpret this 'binding' of Satan as something that has happened (and has been true since the birth of Christ)?

Despite warnings in the New Testament about Satan's continued malevolence, there are some pointed indications that his present influence is drastically restrained. What are these indications? According to this passage, Satan no longer deceives the nations (20:3). From the point of view of the history of redemption, Satan's power over the nations of the world is no longer what it was during the period of the Old Testament. Then, apart from some notable proselyte conversions, the kingdom of God was limited to one particular location and ethnic group, *Israel*. The Gentiles were, on the whole, excluded from the kingdom and 'sat in darkness and in the shadow of death' (*Psa.* 107:10). Gentile conversions (such as Ruth's) were the exceptions, not the rule. But prophets like Isaiah foresaw a day when the Gentiles would flow into the kingdom (*Isa.* 9:1; 42:6; 49:2, 22). That began *after* the first coming of Christ into the world. Christ's command to 'go and make disciples of all nations' implies that Satan's grip upon the Gentile nations has now been curtailed (*Matt.* 28:19).

Indications of this curtailment are present in various statements that Jesus made. Defending his ministry against accusations of collusion with Satan, Jesus asked: 'How can someone enter a strong man's house and plunder his goods, unless he first binds the strong man?' (*Matt.* 12:29). The expression 'binds' is the same word rendered '*bound*' in Revelation 20:2.

When the seventy disciples returned from a preaching tour, they were ecstatic: 'Lord, even the demons are subject to us in your name.' Jesus replied: 'I saw Satan fall like lightning from heaven.' (*Luke* 10:17–18). Satan's fall is surely the same event spoken of as a 'binding' in this chapter. When certain Greeks came asking to see Jesus, he indicated that this could only mean that Satan's kingdom among the deceived nations was being pillaged: 'Now is the time for judgment on this world; now will the ruler of this world be cast out. And I, when I am lifted up from the earth, will draw all people to myself' (*John* 12.31–32). The verb 'cast out' is from the same root as the verb in Revelation 20:3: the angel '*threw him into the pit*'. Here, too, those who are drawn to Christ are to come from every nation.

All this belongs to the same order of thought as the words of Paul to the Athenians in Acts 17: 'The times of ignorance God overlooked, but now he commands all people everywhere to repent' (*Acts* 17:30). When Jesus told his disciples that they must 'go . . . to the lost sheep of the house of Israel' (*Matt.* 10:6), he underlined the fact that the widespread inclusion of the Gentiles would only come *after* Pentecost. Until then Satan held 'the nations' in blindness and unbelief. At that time, there was no 'church' in Africa, or Asia or Europe, or the Americas! But now there is! Satan's power, therefore, is currently restrained. All around us, we are seeing the fulfilment of the cry of Psalm 2:8: 'Ask of me, and I will make the nations your heritage, and the ends of the earth your possession.' Satan's binding ensures and enables the evangelism of the world.

It is not that Satan has *no* power at all; rather, his freedom is limited. He is on a chain. He is cast into the '*pit*' (20:1, 3; later '*prison*' 20:7). The 'lake of fire' mentioned later in the chapter (20:10, 14, 15) is the final place of punishment assigned to Satan, whilst the '*pit*' of verses 1 and 3 refers to some intermediate condition. Perhaps, given the symbolic nature of Revelation, we should avoid thinking of some *physical* expression of the Abyss. It is a figurative description of Satan's curtailment.

THE REIGN OF THE SAINTS

The second thing that John sees ('*I saw* . . . ' 20:4) is described as '*thrones, and seated on them [were] those to whom the authority to judge was committed*' (20:4). Some interpret this as corroboration of a promise of an earthly reign of resurrected saints '*with* Christ', described later in the same verse ('*And I saw . . . They came to life and reigned with Christ for a thousand years*', 20:4). This resurrection is usually thought to occur in Jerusalem. Various features of an end-time sequence of events must, of course, be inserted to complete this picture – a return of Christ *before* this event in Jerusalem being one of them. But this is unnecessary, for the following reason.

The assumption that this vision *follows chronologically* the vision already given of the binding of Satan in verses 1–3 is a faulty one. It is altogether feasible that John intends to say something like this: *at the same time* as Satan is bound, the saints *are* reigning. That means that the saints are reigning now, in the period of time between the two advents.

How can this be? Where are they reigning? Where are these thrones?

The answer, of course, is an obvious one: they reign *in heaven*! With one exception – the cathedral seat of Satan mentioned in 2:13 – all references to 'thrones' in Revelation are to seats of power that exist *in heaven*. Corroboration for this view is given in verse 4, where John tells us that he '*saw the souls of those who had been beheaded* . . .' This gives yet another reply to a question posed by the first readers of Revelation, and that lies just beneath the surface of this book: what has happened to those Christians who have been killed for their testimony to Jesus Christ? This pressing pastoral concern has been answered again and again, and now receives this glorious answer: they are reigning with Christ in heaven and entering into judgment upon their persecutors! They have '*come to life*' and have experienced '*the first resurrection*' (20:5). Though it is possible that John includes all believers who have died in Christ, it certainly *includes* the martyrs – friends and family of Revelation's first readers! They have died, as they lived, *in Christ*. They are sharing in the fruits of his resurrection from the dead. It is difficult to imagine an answer better calculated to produce encouragement for those who remain than this one.

What does John mean by saying that '*the rest of the dead did not come to life until the thousand years were ended*' (20:5)? If a *spiritual resurrection* is meant in verse 4 (those presently reigning with Christ), a *physical* resurrection of unbelievers is meant in verse 5. Some have protested, insisting that if a *physical* resurrection is implied in verse 5, then a *physical* resurrection must be in view in verse 4 (this would involve a literal, physical resurrection of believers on earth prior to the consummation). But this is unnecessary. The switch from *spiritual* to *physical* resurrection in the New Testament is not uncommon. Consider the following:

' . . . just as Christ was *raised* from the dead . . .' we too might walk in newness of *life*. For if we have been united with him in a death like his, we shall certainly be united with him in a *resurrection* like his . . . Now if we have died with Christ, we believe that we will also *live* with him . . . but the life he *lives* he *lives* to God. So you also must consider yourselves dead to sin and *alive* to God in Christ Jesus . . . present yourselves to God as those who have been brought from death to *life*' (*Rom.* 6:4–13, emphasis added).

Throughout this passage, Paul is switching from a physical to a spiritual idea of resurrection!

Saints are reigning (spiritually) with Christ in heaven now, and unbelievers will be raised (physically) to Christ's judgment at the end of the age.

A blessing is pronounced upon those who have died, for they take part in the '*first resurrection*', and over them the '*second death*' has no power (20:6). This 'second death' is a reference to eternal punishment (see also 20:14). The martyred saints – loved ones of many of the first readers of this vision – are safe now and for ever!

THE JUDGMENT OF SATAN

The closing verses of this chapter describe the defeat of Satan and the '*second death*' to which he is subjected (20:7–15). Following the thousand year reign (which we have seen is a reference to the period of time which began at the resurrection of Jesus), Satan is released from prison (earlier called the '*pit*', verse 1). His inability to deceive the nations (20:8; see also verse 3) is now altered. Once more he will wield his power. The language of Ezekiel 38 and 39 returns again, with a reference to Gog and Magog gathering in war against Israel. God's people and Jerusalem are the focus of their hatred.

The expectation that at the end of history a battle of immense proportions will take place between the kingdom of God and the kingdom of evil (Armageddon in 16:13–16, and Gog and Magog here in 20:7–10) is one of those factors which makes a postmillennial interpretation of history difficult to sustain. A period of time in which all (or a good proportion) of the opposition levelled against the kingdom of God is to cease is a paradigm that is difficult to substantiate.

There is to be a '*little while*' in which Satan will wage war (20:3). When will this take place? The 'obvious' answer would be that it takes place just prior to the second coming of Christ. In that case, the releasing of Satan 'for a while' is synonymous with the

LET'S STUDY REVELATION

expectation of the appearance of Antichrist at the end of the age. We have already had cause to refer to this in the reference to the death of the 'Two Witnesses' in chapter 11, as well as the 'Battle of Armageddon' in chapter 16.

The number of nations assembled is '*like the sand of the sea*' (20:8). The language is borrowed from Ezekiel's description, emphasizing the impossible odds arrayed against the people of God. But the battles of the kingdom of God have always been unevenly matched. It is not the power of man that prevails, but the power of God. In this battle, as in every other, it is the power of the Warrior Jesus that overcomes.

The defeat is sudden and dramatic. Fire descends and devours the hostile army of forces. Satan is cast into the '*lake of fire and sulphur*' where the beast and false prophet have already been cast. The general judgment scene that follows includes a depiction of the dead (not just unbelievers) raised and standing before the throne (20:12). As in 4:2, the throne is described in terms calculated to emphasize the greatness of God. The throne of God is the ultimate answer to the problem of evil.

THE FINAL JUDGMENT

Another section begins, '*Then I saw . . .*' (20:11). In this John sees '*a great white throne and him who was seated on it*'. This is the final judgment of mankind. We have seen it many times in Revelation already, but this is its final manifestation. The ultimate basis for rescue from the '*lake of fire*' (20:14) is the inclusion of our names in what John calls '*the book of life*' (20:12, 15). It contains the names of the elect (see 13:8).

Salvation is not achieved by our good works, but by the free grace of God. The words of the final verse are solemn: '*If anyone's name was not found written in the book of life, he was thrown into the lake of fire*' (20:15; see also 3:5; 21:27).

The question may arise: how can I be sure that my name is written in this book? The consistent answer of the Scriptures is that this certainty can only be achieved by *believing in Jesus Christ*. Those who exercise faith are assured of their election. As Calvin put it, *Christ is the mirror of our election*. We cannot read the book of life, but we can look to Christ who freely offers pardon and justification to all who will believe in him.

The alternative to faith is a certain, and endless, judgment: '*They will be tormented day and night forever and ever*' (20:10). Their deeds, including their unbelief, will condemn them (20:12–13).

Grace *alone* can ensure deliverance from the fiery lake of God's eternal wrath.

18

A Place Called Home

*T*hen I saw a new heaven and a new earth, for the first heaven and the first earth had passed away, and the sea was no more. ² And I saw the holy city, new Jerusalem, coming down out of heaven from God, prepared as a bride adorned for her husband. ³ And I heard a loud voice from the throne saying, "Behold, the dwelling place of God is with man. He will dwell with them, and they will be his people, and God himself will be with them as their God. ⁴ He will wipe away every tear from their eyes, and death shall be no more, neither shall there be mourning nor crying nor pain anymore, for the former things have passed away."

⁵ And he who was seated on the throne said, "Behold, I am making all things new." Also he said, "Write this down, for these words are trustworthy and true." ⁶ And he said to me, "It is done! I am the Alpha and the Omega, the beginning and the end. To the thirsty I will give from the spring of the water of life without payment. ⁷ The one who conquers will have this heritage, and I will be his God and he will be my son. ⁸ But as for the cowardly, the faithless, the detestable, as for murderers, the sexually immoral, sorcerers, idolaters, and all liars, their portion will be in the lake that burns with fire and sulfur, which is the second death."

⁹ Then came one of the seven angels who had the seven bowls full of the seven last plagues and spoke to me, saying, "Come, I will show you the Bride, the wife of the Lamb." ¹⁰ And he carried me away in the Spirit to a great, high mountain, and showed me the holy city Jerusalem coming down out of heaven from God, ¹¹ having the glory of God, its radiance like a most

rare jewel, like a jasper, clear as crystal. ¹² *It had a great, high
wall, with twelve gates, and at the gates twelve angels, and on
the gates the names of the twelve tribes of the sons of Israel were
inscribed –* ¹³ *on the east three gates, on the north three gates,
on the south three gates, and on the west three gates.* ¹⁴ *And the
wall of the city had twelve foundations, and on them were the
twelve names of the twelve apostles of the Lamb.*

¹⁵ *And the one who spoke with me had a measuring rod of
gold to measure the city and its gates and walls.* ¹⁶ *The city lies
foursquare; its length the same as its width. And he measured
the city with his rod, 12,000 stadia. Its length and width and
height are equal.* ¹⁷ *He also measured its wall, 144 cubits by
human measurement, which is also an angel's measurement.*
¹⁸ *The wall was built of jasper, while the city was pure gold,
clear as glass.* ¹⁹ *The foundations of the wall of the city were
adorned with every kind of jewel. The first was jasper, the second
sapphire, the third agate, the fourth emerald,* ²⁰ *the fifth onyx,
the sixth carnelian, the seventh chrysolite, the eighth beryl, the
ninth topaz, the tenth chrysoprase, the eleventh jacinth, the
twelfth amethyst.* ²¹ *And the twelve gates were twelve pearls,
each of the gates made of a single pearl, and the street of the city
was pure gold, transparent as glass.*

²² *And I saw no temple in the city, for its temple is the Lord
God the Almighty and the Lamb.* ²³ *And the city has no need
of sun or moon to shine on it, for the glory of God gives it light,
and its lamp is the Lamb.* ²⁴ *By its light will the nations walk,
and the kings of the earth will bring their glory into it,* ²⁵ *and
its gates will never be shut by day—and there will be no night
there.* ²⁶ *They will bring into it the glory and the honour of the
nations.* ²⁷ *But nothing unclean will ever enter it, nor anyone
who does what is detestable or false, but only those who are
written in the Lamb's book of life.*

^{22:1} *Then the angel showed me the river of the water of life,
bright as crystal, flowing from the throne of God and of the
Lamb*

² *through the middle of the street of the city; also, on either side
of the river, the tree of life with its twelve kinds of fruit, yielding
its fruit each month. The leaves of the tree were for the healing*

of the nations. *³ No longer will there be anything accursed, but the throne of God and of the Lamb will be in it, and his servants will worship him.* *⁴ They will see his face, and his name will be on their foreheads.* *⁵ And night will be no more. They will need no light of lamp or sun, for the Lord God will be their light, and they will reign forever and ever* (Rev. 21:1–22:5).

Jesus reigns over every evil force. As we come to chapter 21, each one of Christ's enemies has been vanquished. Every opposition to the purposes of God has been rendered obsolete. Jesus is Lord!

He *'who was seated on the throne'* speaks (21:5), identifying himself as the *'Alpha and Omega, the beginning and the end'* (21:6; 22:13). The fact that John had heard this at the very beginning of the book seems to indicate that we have come full circle (1:8, 17).

A description of the *'new Jerusalem'* follows. The beast, the false prophet and Satan have been cast into the lake of fire, along with death and the grave (19:20; 20:10, 14). All that was (and is!) destructive of the present existence is removed from the picture. All that is left is the creation itself. What is to become of it?

Just as the cosmos shared in the results of Adam's fall – 'the creation was subjected to futility' (*Rom.* 8:20) – so, too, the cosmos shares in Christ's redemptive accomplishment. Jesus reverses the effects of the fall! Creation already stands 'on tiptoe' (as J. B. Phillips put it), stretching out its neck to catch a glimpse of its new mode of existence (*Rom.* 8:19). This eager expectation is for liberation from its present bondage (*Rom.* 8:19). Peter even tells us *how* this will come about: 'The heavens will pass away with a roar, and the heavenly bodies will be burned up and dissolved, and the earth and the works that are done on it will be exposed' (*2 Pet.* 3:10–11). The cosmos itself will experience a 'regeneration' (*Matt.* 19:28, KJV), or 'restoration' (*Acts* 3:21).

'I am making all things new!' (*Rev.* 21:5). Behind this vision lie some words of Isaiah:

'For behold, I will create
    new heavens and a new earth,
And the former things shall not be remembered
    or come to mind.

But be glad and rejoice forever
    in that which I create . . .
No more shall there be in it
    an infant who lives but a few days,
    or an old man who does not fill out his days . . .

The wolf and the lamb shall graze together;
    the lion shall eat straw like the ox,
    but dust will be the serpent's food.
They shall not hurt nor destroy
    in all my holy mountain,' says the Lord.
                      (*Isa.* 65:17–25).

The new heaven and new earth will be a place 'in which righteousness dwells' (*2 Pet.* 3:13). All that was ruined in the old is repaired and beautified in the new. It is Paradise restored – and more (21:4–5). There will be access to the Tree of Life (22:2). There will be no curse or death (21:4; 22:3). Fellowship with God will be transparent (21:3). The '*river of the water of life*' will irrigate and sustain (22:1). Best of all, the new heaven and earth will provide the Lord's people with a vision of the Lamb unparalleled in its beauty (22:3), and unhindered by tears (7:17; 21:4).

Some interpreters of this passage have suggested that the present world order will be utterly destroyed (annihilated) in order to make way for the new heavens and new earth, appealing to the words, 'The heavens will be set on fire and dissolved, and the heavenly bodies will melt as they burn', in 2 Peter 3:12. However, this may not be correct. The word for '*new*' in '*new heavens and a new earth*', both here in Revelation 21:1 and in 2 Peter 3:13 is one that suggests newness in kind and quality rather than in origin or time. From one point of view, Satan will not have the satisfaction of seeing God destroy his creation. God will instead transform it so that it may reflect its intended glory and magnificence.

This will be heaven on earth! Here, 'the earth shall be full of the knowledge of the Lord as the waters cover the sea' (*Isa.* 11:9). The vision of heaven depicted in the Bible is an *earthly* one! The 'meek . . . shall inherit the *earth*' (*Matt.* 5:5; see also *Psa.* 37:11). It is not completely the same, of course. The eradication of sin will have consequences that make it difficult for us to fully imagine what perfection will be like.

Among the more intriguing aspects of the new earth which hint at *difference* is the phrase in verse 1 that the new earth will have '*no sea*'. From any point of view, this seems a very odd thing to say. It would be hard to imagine a world without the sea. And what does this say to all the creatures whose existence depends on the ocean?

Sea-merchants apart, the sea is not our *natural* habitat. We cannot survive in it without artificial means of support. For a land-dwelling people as the Jews were, the sea had always posed a threat. Death is often portrayed in the Old Testament as drowning (*Psa.* 42:7; 69:1; *Jon.* 2:3). The sea is synonymous with threat and hostility, from which the sea-beast had emerged to threaten the land (13:1).

It is into this tranquil existence that the new Jerusalem descends from heaven. She comes as a bride prepared for a wedding (21:2).

> You shall be a crown of beauty in the hand of the LORD,
>   a royal diadem in the hand of your God.
> You shall no more be termed Forsaken,
>   and your land shall no more be termed Desolate,
>   but you shall be called, My delight is in her,
>   and your land, Married;
>   for the LORD delights in you,
>   and your land will be married.
> For as a young man marries a young woman,
>   so shall your sons marry you,
>   and as the bridegroom rejoices over the bride,
>   so shall your God rejoice over you.
>
> (*Isa.* 62:3–5)

The church's final resting place is in fellowship with Jesus Christ on *earth* – a *new* earth. The union is described in terms of the closest possible intimacy, one which the Bible has been repeating in every period of redemptive history, and now again in the closing chapters of the final book of the Bible: '*They will be his people, and God himself will be with them as their God*' (21:3). The effect of this covenantal bond of intimacy is to reassure the people of God that no harm can ever come to them, no ill disturb their serenity. It is the fulfilment of the redemptive purposes of God from the very beginning.

'And I will establish my covenant between me and you and your offspring after you throughout their generations for an everlasting covenant, to be God to you and to your offspring after you' (*Gen.* 17:7).

'This is the covenant that I will make with the house of Israel after those days,' declares the LORD: 'I will put my law within them, and I will write it on their hearts. And I will be their God, and they shall be my people' (*Jer.* 31:33).

'But you are a chosen people, a royal priesthood, a holy nation, a people for his own possession, that you may proclaim the excellencies of him who called you out of darkness into his marvellous light. Once you were not a people, but now you are God's people; once you had not received mercy, but now you have received mercy' (*1 Pet.* 2:9–10).

There are no tears in this new world (21:4; see also 7:17). God wipes them away, reassuring his people that every source of evil is vanquished, and all the pain is gone! Death is now banished.

THE INHABITANTS OF THE CITY

John is particularly fond of using water as a symbol of life and sustenance. It is he who records Jesus as saying: 'Whoever believes in me shall never thirst' (*John* 6:35). Now he pictures the city in similar terms: '*To the thirsty I will give from the spring of the water of life without payment*' (21:6). A similar picture follows in the next chapter:

'*Let the one who is thirsty come; let the one who desires take the water without price*' (22:17).

Prophecies of Isaiah lie in the background:

They shall not hunger or thirst,
    neither scorching wind nor sun shall strike them,
For he who has pity on them will lead them,
    and by springs of water will guide them.
                                        (*Isa.* 49:10).

'Ho! Everyone who thirsts,
    Come to the waters;
And you who have no money
    Come, buy and eat.
Yes, come, buy wine and milk
    Without money and without price.'

(*Isa.* 55:1, NKJV)

The Isaiah passage just cited goes on to speak of the making of a new covenant after the pattern of the 'steadfast, sure love for David' (*Isa.* 55:1–3; see also *2 Sam.* 7:14). This is what God now promises: '*The one who conquers will have this heritage, and I will be his God and he will be my son*' (21:7). A line of continuity from the Old to the New is established in these closing pages of the Bible.

Who exactly will dwell in the new heaven and new earth? It is the one who '*conquers*' (21:7). It is language we have heard before:

'*To the one who conquers, I will grant to eat of the tree of life, which is in the paradise of God*' (2:7); '*[he] will not be hurt by the second death*' (2:11); '. . . *I will give some of the hidden manna and I will give him a white stone, with a new name written on the stone that no one knows except the one who receives it*' (2:17); '. . . *I will give authority over the nations*' (2:26); '. . . *[he] will be clothed thus in white garments, and I will never blot his name out of the book of life. I will confess his name before my Father and before his angels*' (3:5); '. . . *I will make a pillar in the temple of my God*' (3:12); '. . . *I will grant him to sit with me on my throne, as I also conquered and sat down with my Father on his throne*' (3:21).

Those whom grace catches hold of, grace transforms into Christ's image. Thus, '*As for the cowardly, the faithless, the detestable, as for murderers, the sexually immoral, sorcerers, idolaters, and all liars, their portion will be in the lake that burns with fire and sulphur*' (21:8). '*Nothing unclean will ever enter it, nor anyone who does what is detestable or false . . .* ' (21:27).

'*Outside are the dogs and sorcerers and the sexually immoral and murderers and idolaters and everyone who loves and practises falsehood*' (22:15). Paul says something similar: 'Do not be deceived: neither the sexually immoral, nor idolaters, nor adulterers nor men who practise homosexuality, nor thieves, nor the greedy, nor drunkards nor revilerers, nor swindlers will inherit the kingdom of God' (*1 Cor.* 6:9–10).

The guarantee of heaven for the redeemed does not lessen one whit the need for a diligent pursuit of holiness. Heaven is gained through perseverance and not apart from it.

ADORNED IN BEAUTY

Heaven is a beautiful place. The bride is described in terms of precious stones and foundation stones. A temple-like picture follows, in which the glory of God is expressed in terms of a dazzling array of jewels which are reminiscent of those on the breastplate which the high priest wore (21:18–19; see also *Exod.* 28:15–21), and the gold of Solomon's temple (21:18; *1 Kings* 6:20–22).

High walls (21:12) ensure protection and security; twelve gates inscribed with the names of the twelve tribes of Israel (21:12), and twelve foundations to the twelve walls of the city inscribed with the names of the twelve apostles (21:14), ensure the continuity and completeness of the Old and New Covenants. God has one people, one church, one purpose, one covenant of grace.

The city is represented as a cube, as was the Most Holy Place of the temple (*1 Kings* 6:20). In the new Jerusalem, however, the entire city is a holy place.

The proportions of the city are staggering. The city measures 12,000 *stadia* (a *stadion* is approximately 200 yards or 185 metres) in every direction (21:16). The walls measure, in length, about 1,400 miles each! The thickness of the walls is measured using a different unit, 144 cubits [a cubit is approximately 21.5 inches, or 0.55 metres] (21:17). This would make the walls approximately 216 feet thick.

Clearly, this is symbolic language. Multiples of twelve and ten are being used to describe a city of huge proportions, big enough to contain the vast company of the redeemed.

Clearly, as verse 17 suggests, there is accommodation taking place to 'man's way of looking at things'. The reality is beyond our ability to grasp. What we are meant to feel is the sheer wonder of it all.

The Absence of a Temple, the Sun, and the Moon

There is no temple in the new Jerusalem (21:22). There is no need for one! Jesus' death has rendered a place for sacrifice obsolete. '*Its temple is the Lord God the Almighty and the Lamb*' (21:22). Jesus had said in the temple of his day: 'Destroy this temple, and in three days I will raise it up' (*John* 2:19).

Further features of the new Jerusalem are curious: there is no sun or moon (21:23; see also *Isa.* 60:19). Are we to think that the new earth will have no luminaries in the sky? Probably not! The picture is intended to suggest that Jesus dominates the horizon in every direction. The glory of the Lord is everywhere, providing light for the temple and the new city (see *Ezek.* 43:2,5).

The picture continues, describing open gates and a tranquil existence. There is no night where evil lurks unseen. The nations are flocking to the presence of God, bringing their glory and honour into the city (21:26). What was first glimpsed at Pentecost, when the 'nations' gathered in Jerusalem and were baptized with the Spirit (*Acts* 2:9–11), is now seen on a grander scale. The promise to Abraham, that he would be a father 'of many nations' is fulfilled (*Gen.* 17:4, 5, 6; 18:18). The leaves of the tree of life are for the healing of the nations (22:2).

> All the nations you have made
>   shall come and worship before you, O Lord,
>   and shall glorify your name.
>
> (*Psa.* 86:9)

This is not a picture of a future millennial age; rather, it is an idealist picture of what the life following this one will be like. Its physical, earthly aspect expresses a corporeal existence. Its symbolical development tells us that we know only a little of its true nature. One thing is sure: Jesus will be at the centre of everything.

Summary

Three features require further elaboration:
First, the new city is cube-shaped, with city walls over 200 feet thick. The city is impregnable. Its vast dimensions speak of security. As

to its beauty, its gates are made of pearls (imagine a pearl the size of a city gate!). As to its destiny: this city is destined to become a bride!

Second, the new temple is descriptive of the fellowship the redeemed will enjoy. The language (in 21:3) is covenantal. God intends to create a people who will respond to him in worship and adoration. This has been God's intention from the beginning. In the new heaven and new earth the worship of God will be pure. There will be no source of evil left. It will also be international. The 'nations' will walk there (21:24, 26). There is no temple, because *everything* will be temple!

Third, the world which God will create for his glory is 'new'. Nothing threatens, there is no curse (21:23). The Lamb has borne all of the curses. There are no tears in this world because the Son has borne them on behalf of his people.

The Bible has come full circle. The Tree of Life appears once more (22:2; see *Gen.* 2:9; 3:22). The wilderness is transformed into a garden. But it is much more than Eden ever was. The garden is also a city. The light has expelled the night. Healing and restoration are everywhere evident. The purposes of God have been fulfilled. Everything in the garden is *wonder*-ful (22:1–5).

In a sense, this has been the intention of the book of Revelation from the very beginning: to increase our anticipation of heaven. As we read these closing lines and its description of the New Jerusalem, our hearts ache for it. When we see the beauty of heaven every deep longing will be satisfied in this condition of bliss and glory. The curse has been removed – borne by the Lamb who occupies heaven's throne.

At the very centre of the new existence are God and the Lamb. From the throne flows life-giving water – a picture that has now grown to full maturity (see *Gen.* 2:10–14; *Psa.* 46:4; *Ezek.* 47:1–12; *Joel* 3:18). And among the redeemed are the nations of the world. God's grace in all its richness is now apparent. The new creation is richer in its population than the literal seed of Abraham.

But it is not the garden that is the focus of attention. It is the glory of God shining in the face of Jesus Christ (22:5). We shall see his face (22:4). This surely takes our breath away. The words are read with such consummate ease, and yet reflect the very essence of grace. It is this enjoyment of fellowship in the presence of Christ that makes heaven what it is – and explains why we long for it!

The Bride eyes not her garment,
But her dear bridegroom's face
I will not gaze at glory,
But on my King of Grace –
Not at the crown He gifteth,
But on his piercèd hand:
The Lamb is all the glory
Of Emmanuel's land.

Anne Ross Cousin
(*based on words*
of Samuel Rutherford).

19

The End Game

*A*nd he said to me, "These words are trustworthy and true. And the Lord, the God of the spirits of the prophets, has sent his angel to show his servants what must soon take place."

⁷ *"And behold, I am coming soon. Blessed is the one who keeps the words of the prophecy of this book."*

⁸ *I, John, am the one who heard and saw these things. And when I heard and saw them, I fell down to worship at the feet of the angel who showed them to me,* ⁹ *but he said to me, "You must not do that! I am a fellow servant with you and your brothers the prophets, and with those who keep the words of this book. Worship God."*

¹⁰ *And he said to me, "Do not seal up the words of the prophecy of this book, for the time is near.* ¹¹ *Let the evildoer still do evil, and the filthy still be filthy, and the righteous still do right, and the holy still be holy."*

¹² *"Behold, I am coming soon, bringing my recompense with me, to repay everyone for what he has done.* ¹³ *I am the Alpha and the Omega, the first and the last, the beginning and the end."*

¹⁴ *Blessed are those who wash their robes, so that they may have the right to the tree of life and that they may enter the city by the gates.* ¹⁵ *Outside are the dogs and sorcerers and the sexually immoral and murderers and idolaters, and everyone who loves and practices falsehood.*

¹⁶ *"I, Jesus, have sent my angel to testify to you about these things for the churches. I am the root and the descendant of David, the bright morning star."*

¹⁷ The Spirit and the Bride say, "Come." And let the one who hears say, "Come." And let the one who is thirsty come; let the one who desires take the water of life without price.
¹⁸ I warn everyone who hears the words of the prophecy of this book: if anyone adds to them, God will add to him the plagues described in this book, ¹⁹ and if anyone takes away from the words of the book of this prophecy, God will take away his share in the tree of life and in the holy city, which are described in this book.
²⁰ He who testifies to these things says, "Surely I am coming soon." Amen. Come, Lord Jesus!
²¹ The grace of the Lord Jesus be with all. Amen.

(Rev. 22:6–21).

These are the last words of the last book of the Bible! And what memorable words they are! '*Behold, I am coming soon . . . Behold, I am coming soon . . . Surely I am coming soon.*' Amen. Come, Lord *Jesus* (22:7, 12, 20).

The final chapter of the Bible begins with a continuation of the theme begun in the previous chapter. Chapter 21 introduced us to a vision of the new Jerusalem in all its beauty and splendour. What is heaven like? Chapter 21 and the opening verses of chapter 22 unfolded a description in which several images coalesced: a city, a temple, a bride, a garden, a new heaven and a new earth.

Now that the book has run its course, John wants us to know that however strange the visions may have been, he has been faithfully recording what he had been shown; the words are '*trustworthy and true*' (22:6), just as he had said right at the very start of the book (1:2). The book of Revelation can be judged by its covers!

It is fascinating that in this final chapter of the Bible the parting words of Jesus are recorded for us in triplicate: '*I am coming soon*' (22:7, 12, 20). This is an echo of the opening sentence of the book: it speaks of things 'that must soon take place' (1:1, and repeated in 22:6). At both ends of the book, like a tolling bell, we are warned, '*The time is near*' (1:3; 22:10).

But, what do the words, 'near' and 'soon' mean? Two thousand years later, the return of Christ still has to occur. Does that not raise considerable doubt about the commonly accepted meaning of these words?

Some have suggested that the New Testament writers were of two minds, expecting Jesus to return quickly, but having to adjust their writings as the years went by and no return occurred. Some have even suggested that Jesus himself changed his mind as to his own second coming! What we have in the New Testament, then, according to this view, is a mixture of 'primitive' and supposedly 'mature' understandings of the way history will develop.

In response to this errant conclusion, some evangelical and Reformed Bible scholars have suggested a thorough reappraisal of passages in the New Testament which *seem* to speak about the second coming. Some have adopted a view which suggests that passages which seem to imply a 'soon' or 'near' coming of Jesus refer to the judgment that came upon Jerusalem in the years 67–70 AD. While this does have the advantage of dispelling some tensions, it has not been the view adopted in the course of this study of Revelation. There are too many indications to suggest that the book of Revelation was written *after* 70 AD, when Jerusalem had already been destroyed!

What then, are we to make of these pronouncements as to the nearness of Christ's coming, and of the shortness of the time? The answer seems to lie along the following lines. The New Testament teaches that the death, resurrection and ascension of Jesus ushered in 'the last days' (see *Heb.* 1:1–2). The 'end of the ages' has already dawned (*Heb.* 9:26). The last days began at Pentecost (*Acts* 2:17). We are on the last lap of human history. However long that lasts from our perspective, on Christ's calendar his return is soon. Since the outpouring of the Holy Spirit at Pentecost, only one significant (redemptive) event remains: the second coming of Jesus Christ!

The nearness of the return of Jesus is to be measured, not by human chronology, but by events in the timetable of God's plan of redemption in history. From this perspective, the return of Christ is always *near*.

Something interesting happens in verse 10, adding weight to the interpretation given above. John is told: '*Do not seal up the words of the prophecy of this book*' (22:10). This is the very opposite of what Daniel was told (*Dan.* 12:4)! His prophecies lay in the distant future. Jesus' prophecies concern here and now – after all, much of what we have seen in Revelation concerns the time in which we live!

Three sections are discernible, each of which contain an allusion to the 'nearness' of Christ's return.

OBEDIENCE

'*Blessed is the one who keeps the words of the prophecy in this book*' (22:7). This statement is full of echoes of the Old Testament. It is reminiscent of something Moses says repeatedly in the book of Deuteronomy as the Israelites prepare to move into Canaan: 'Remember the whole way that the LORD your God has led you these forty years in the wilderness, that he might humble you, testing you to know what was in your heart, whether you would keep his commandments or not' (*Deut.* 8:2, and some twenty other references!). In fact, the books of Deuteronomy and Revelation are specifically *covenantal*: they promise blessing to the obedience of *faith* and curses to the disobedience of *unbelief*.

This is God's covenantal pattern. To those who respond to the words of Jesus' near-coming there is held out the promise of rich blessing. And what blessing it is! John has seen it in these last twenty-one chapters. John has glimpsed *heaven*. He has been allowed to take a look over the wall of this world and glimpse the realities of the age to come. He has been shown how God will lead his faithful ones to the very fountain of the water of life that flows from the throne of God and of the Lamb (22:1).

Once again John is tempted to fall down and worship the giver of this revelation, and once again he is told not to do it (22:8; see 19:10).

There is also another side, a shadow-side: '*Let the evildoer still do evil, and the filthy still be filthy, and the righteous still do right, and the holy still be holy*' (22:11). There is no 'second-chance' on the other side of this world. The consequences of faith or unbelief follow us into eternity. '*Behold, I am coming soon, bringing my recompense with me, to repay everyone for what he has done*' (22:12; see also *Matt.* 16:27; *Rom.* 2:6; *2 Cor.* 5:10). The '*right to the tree of life*' and the right to '*enter the city by the gates*' (22:14) belongs only to those who exercise faith in Jesus Christ in this life and who demonstrate its reality with diligent holiness and Christ-like behaviour.

But there is a dark side: '*Outside are the dogs and sorcerers and the sexually immoral and murderers and idolaters, and everyone who loves and practises falsehood*' (22:15). The ugliness of the '*outside*' is in stark contrast to the beauty of the '*inside*'. The outside is undesirable and ugly, offensive and destructive. There is no grace of any kind. Everything about the outside is contrary to God. There is no possibility of change. There is no help offered. This is hell.

These are serious words, but they come from One who is '*the Alpha and the Omega, the first and the last, the beginning and the end*' (22:13; see also 1:8, 17; 2:8; 21:6), '*the root and the descendant of David, the bright morning star*' (22:16).

God's promise to Abraham, that those who bless him would be blessed and those who curse him would be cursed (*Gen.* 12:1–3), now seems to have reached its fulfilment.

It is fitting that the Bible should close with words of invitation: '*Let the one who is thirsty come; let the one who desires take the water of life without price*' (22:17). This side of death and the Day of Judgment, there is still room for repentance. God longs for sinners to come to Christ. Jesus, as John Owen said, is the 'safest place in the universe'.

A COMPLETED CANON

Covenant documents are not to be tampered with – they contain matters that cannot be undone. Hence, words of warning are added to the book of Revelation – the last words of the Bible: '*I warn everyone who hears the words of the prophecy of this book: If anyone adds to them, God will add to him the plagues described in this book*' (22:18).

There is a history to this warning. Moses, the first major writer of the Bible, uses the expression on several occasions (*Deut.* 4:2; 5:22; 12:32; 18:18; *Num.* 11:25). Here, in Revelation, the covenant Lord is issuing a final blessing and curse.

These are solemn words that have often gone unheeded. God will not tolerate any tampering with that which he has revealed. The canon which he has given us is sacred. We are not at liberty to alter it to suit our own purposes.

All that is left is a prayer: '*Come, Lord Jesus*' (22:20; this may be compared with the cry in Aramaic, *Maranatha*, *1 Cor.* 16:22). John may well be rendering the Greek equivalent here, of a prayer that had long since been used in the early church as an expression of deepest piety and longing. The *Didache*, the earliest known manual of liturgy, indicates that this prayer formed a part of the liturgy of the Lord's Supper in the early church.

When John Wesley was asked what he might do if he knew Jesus was to return on a certain date, he apparently looked at his diary for that day, read out his engagements, and said, 'That is what I would do.'

Living in preparation for the Lord's coming is the way of wisdom.

Can you say '*Amen* . . . ' (22:21)?

Group Study Guide

SCHEME FOR GROUP BIBLE STUDY
(Covering 13 Weeks)

	Study Passage	Chapters
1.	Revelation 1:1–20	1
2.	Revelation 2:1–3:22	2–3
3.	Revelation 4:1–5:14	4
4.	Revelation 6:1–8:5	5–6
5.	Revelation 8:6–9:21	7
6.	Revelation 10:1–11:19	8–9
7.	Revelation 12:1–13:18	10–11
8.	Revelation 14:1–15:4	12
9.	Revelation 15:5–16:21	13
10.	Revelation 17:1–18:24	14–15
11.	Revelation 19:1–20:15	16–17
12.	Revelation 21:1–22:5	18
13.	Revelation 22:6–21	19

This Study Guide has been prepared for group Bible study, but it can also be used individually. Those who use it on their own may find it helpful to keep a note of their responses in a notebook.

The way in which group Bible studies are led can greatly enhance their value. A well-conducted study will appear as though it has been easy to lead, but that is usually because the leader has worked hard and planned well. Clear aims are essential.

AIMS

In all Bible study, individual or corporate, we have several aims:

1. To gain an understanding of the original meaning of the particular passage of Scripture;

2. To apply this to ourselves and our own situation;

3. To develop some specific ways of putting the biblical teaching into practice.

2 Timothy 3:16–17 provides a helpful structure. Paul says that Scripture is useful for:

(i)   teaching us;

(ii) rebuking us;

(iii) correcting, or changing us;

(iv) training us in righteousness.

Consequently, in studying any passage of Scripture, we should always have in mind these questions:

What does this passage teach us (about God, ourselves, etc.)?

Does it rebuke us in some way?

How can its teaching transform us?

What equipment does it give us for serving Christ?

In fact, these four questions alone would provide a safe guide in any Bible study.

PRINCIPLES

In group Bible study we meet in order to learn about God's Word and ways 'together with all the saints' *(Eph.* 3:18). But our own experience, as well as Scripture, tells us that the saints are not always what they *are* called to be in every situation – including group Bible study! Leaders ordinarily have to work hard and prepare well if the work of the group is to be spiritually profitable. The following guidelines for leaders may help to make this a reality.

Group Study Guide

Preparation:

1. Study and understand the passage yourself. The better prepared and more sure of the direction of the study you are, the more likely it is that the group will have a beneficial and enjoyable study.
Ask: What are the main things this passage is saying? How can this be made clear? This is not the same question as the more common 'What does this passage "say to you"?', which expects a reaction rather than an exposition of the passage. Be clear about that dis-tinction yourself, and work at making it clear in the group study.

2. On the basis of your own study form a clear idea *before* the group meets of (i) the main theme(s) of the passage which should be opened out for discussion, and (ii) some general conclusions the group ought to reach as a result of the study. Here the questions which arise from 2 Timothy 3:16–17 should act as our guide.

3. The guidelines and questions which follow may help to provide a general framework for each discussion; leaders should use them as starting places which can be further developed. It is usually help-ful to have a specific goal or theme in mind for group discussion, and one is suggested for each study. But even more important than tracing a single theme is understanding the teaching and the implications of the passage.

Leading the Group:

1. Announce the passage and theme for the study, and begin with prayer. In group studies it may be helpful to invite a different person to lead in prayer each time you meet.

2. Introduce the passage and theme, briefly reminding people of its outline and highlighting the content of each subsidiary section.

3. Lead the group through the discussion questions. Use your own if you are comfortable in doing so; those provided may be used, developing them with your own points. As discussion pro-ceeds, continue to encourage the group first of all to discuss the significance of the passage (teaching) and only then its application (meaning for us). It may be helpful to write important points and applications on a board by way of summary as well as visual aid.

4. At the end of each meeting, remind members of the group of their assignments for the next meeting, and encourage them to come prepared. Be sufficiently prepared as the leader to give specific assignments to individuals, or even couples or groups, to come with specific contributions ('John, would you try to find out something about the church at Ephesus for the next meeting?' 'Fiona, would you see what you can find out about how Daniel 7 is referred to in Revelation 10?').

5. Remember that you are the leader of the group! Encourage clear contributions, and do not be embarrassed to ask someone to explain what they have said more fully or to help them to do so ('Do you mean . . . ?').

Most groups include the 'over-talkative', the 'over-silent' and the 'red-herring raisers'! Leaders must control the first, encourage the second and redirect the third! Each leader will develop his or her own most natural way of doing that; but it will be helpful to think out what that is before the occasion arises!

The first two groups can be helped by some judicious direction of questions to specific individuals or even groups (*e.g.*, 'How do those who are not preachers or pastors apply this?' 'Jane, you know something about this from personal experience . . .'); the third by redirecting the discussion to the passage itself ('That is an interesting point, but isn't it true that this passage really concentrates on . . . ?').

It may be helpful to break the group up into smaller groups sometimes, giving each subgroup specific points to discuss and to report back on. A wise arranging of these smaller groups may also help each member to participate.

More important than any techniques we may develop is the help of the Spirit enabling us to understand and to apply the Scriptures. Have, and encourage, a humble, prayerful spirit.

6. Keep faith with the schedule; it is better that some of the group wished the study could have been longer than that others are inconvenienced by it stretching beyond the time limits set.

7. Close in prayer. As time permits, spend the closing minutes in corporate prayer, encouraging the group to apply what they have learned in praise and thanks, intercession and petition.

STUDY 1: Revelation 1:1–20

AIM: To consider the absolute supremacy of Jesus Christ.

1. What is the significance of the opening words of Revelation, 'The revelation of Jesus Christ . . . '? What does this tell us about the book as a whole?

2. In what way is Revelation different from, say, Romans or the Gospel of Mark? What function do the word pictures of Revelation have in the overall understanding of the book?

3. How is the phrase, 'the time is near' (1:3), to be understood? What does this say about the time in which we live today? How might this phrase relate to the statement in 1 Corinthians 10:11, that we are those upon whom the 'fulfillment of the ages has come'?

4. What does John's use of the title 'son of man' (1:13) tell us about his understanding of who Jesus is?

5. The second verse to the hymn *Amazing Grace* begins with the words, ''Twas grace that taught my heart to fear . . . ' How does grace cause us to fear? Why does John's glimpse of the risen Lord cause him to fall prostrate (verse 17)? What does this have to say concerning our worship?

6. The author contends that two aspects of this chapter are the supremacy of Christ (verses 1, 5, 12–18) and the suffering of the first-century church (verse 9). Is there any connection between these two? How is the supremacy of Christ a comfort to troubled Christians? How is John's exile a 'blessing'?

FOR STUDY 2: Read Revelation 2–3 and chapters 2 and 3 of this book.

STUDY 2: Revelation 2:1–3:22

AIM: To see that Jesus knows and loves his bride, the church, and how this both comforts and confronts us.

1. What does the fact that chapters 2 and 3 are written to 'churches' rather than to individuals tell us? What is significant about the fact that Revelation begins with a series of letters? How is it related to what follows in the book?

2. Jesus is described as walking among the lampstands (2:1), which we interpreted as the seven representative churches, and as he does so it is obvious that he *knows* the condition of each church. What does this say about the local church to which we are attached? How is that a comfort? Also, what is the general format that John uses to address each church?

3. Jesus says of the church at Ephesus, 'I know your works' (2:2). What might the works of the church to which you belong be, if he were to outline them? How can we maintain a biblical attitude towards heterodoxy without being guilty of a loveless expression of Christianity? What are some of the non-negotiables of the Christian faith (consider the diagnosis of the other churches as well)?

4. It could be said that suffering is a 'mark' of true Christianity. Outline from the letter to the church at Smyrna (2:8–11) how this might be so. What does this say about modern expressions of Christianity? How does Jesus reassure the Christians in the church at Philadelphia (3:7–13) in the face of their weakness (3:8)? Outline the ways in which encouragement may be obtained even when the forces of opposition are considerable.

5. Revelation 3:20 is a well known text in New Testament. Can this verse be used as an evangelistic appeal to the unconverted to come to Christ? If not, how would you understand it?

6. Taking the assessment of the seven churches collectively, what does it say about the state of the church in the first century? Outline some of the positive and negative features of the church today as you think Jesus might assess them.

7. What did Jesus mean by the verb 'conquer' (2:7, 11, 26; 3:5, 12, 21)? How (and *what*!) are we to *conquer*?

FOR STUDY 3: Read Revelation 4–5 and chapter 4 in the book.

STUDY 3: Revelation 4:1–5:14

AIM: To see what heavenly worship is like.

1. Cotton Mather, the New England pastor/preacher of 300 years ago said, 'The great design and intention of the office of a Christian preacher [is] to restore the throne and dominion of God in the souls of men.' What is the significance of the fact that chapters 4 and 5 of Revelation give us a glimpse of heaven's throne? What might this say of the importance of the doctrine of the sovereignty of God in the Scriptures?

2. If our worship, both personal and corporate, both private and formal, is to be patterned after the worship of God in heaven, what might chapters 4 and 5 teach us about *how* we worship God? Read Hebrews 12:22–24 and consider our participation in this heavenly worship now. Can it be said that when we worship God we are joining in this scene in heaven?

3. What was the interpretation given of the 'scroll written within and on the back, sealed with seven seals' (5:1)? Who is able to open it? What is the correlation between the singular ability of Jesus to open the scroll and the worship he receives?

4. What is it about *singing* that is particularly appropriate in the worship of God? What do the following verses teach us about how such singing ought to be done (4:8, 11; 5:9–10, 12, 13)?

5. A central theme of the Bible is *knowing God*. What do we learn about who God is *and* what God is like in these two chapters of Revelation?

6. What can we learn from the use of the 'Amen' in these chapters (5:14)?

FOR STUDY 4: Read Revelation 6:1–8:5 and chapters five and six in the book.

STUDY 4: Revelation 6:1–8:5

AIM: To see how assurance can be maintained amid scenes of judgment.

1. Is there any significance to the fact that immediately after the scene of worship in heaven in chapters 4 and 5 we are introduced to a scene that depicts trouble of various kinds in chapter 6? What might this say about what we can expect in the period between Christ's first and second comings? How might this have encouraged the original readers? How does it encourage us?

2. How does Mark 13:7–8 help us understand what might be taking place in the description of the four horsemen of Revelation 6? How might these verses be applied appropriately today? What would be an inappropriate application?

3. What pastoral effect might be produced by telling us that martyred souls are before the throne of God (6:9–11)? Why is Revelation 6:11 described in this book as important for the understanding of the entire book of Revelation? How does Revelation 6 help us reconcile the desire for the salvation of others and *at the same time* a desire for justice?

4. How does chapter 7 function as an answer to the question posed at the close of chapter 6, 'For the great day of his wrath has come and who can stand?' (verse 17)?

5. How is chapter 7 to be understood chronologically in relation to chapter 6? How does the 'seal' of Revelation 7:2 *differ* from the seals referred to in chapter 6?

6. Who are the 144,000 mentioned in 7:4–8? How does this relate to verse 9? Does your answer help you understand something about the style of writing employed by John in composing this book of Revelation? Does it help you interpret other features of Revelation?

7. Daniel 12:1, Matthew 24:21 and Revelation 7:14 all refer to a 'great tribulation'? What interpretation of this 'event' was employed in this book?

FOR STUDY 5: Read Revelation 8:6–9:21 and chapter 7 in the book.

STUDY 5: Revelation 8:6–9:21

AIM: To consider the warnings given to the unsealed.

1. What is the relationship between the seven seals and the seven trumpets? How do they view the same reality from different perspectives?

2. How does the Old Testament depict the use of trumpets? How is this of help to us in interpreting chapters 8 and 9?

3. How does Romans 8:18–21 help us understand the first four trumpets of Revelation 8:6–12)? How do the trumpets relate to the plagues in Egypt? What are some of the similarities and differences?

4. What is the judgment of the *unsealed* as described in the blowing of the fifth trumpet? Who are the unsealed (compare Revelation 6–7 and the corresponding discussion of the 'sealed').

5. How does Ephesians 6:12 help us understand Revelation 9:7–10? How does this help us understand something of what we might expect the Christian life to look like? What does spiritual warfare look like in daily living?

6. There is an evident reference in the opening of the sixth trumpet to Jeremiah 46. The passage seems to describe a purpose of God

in judgment of the unrepentant. What does this tell us about the darkness of man's unrepentant heart? What does it tell us about God's character?

FOR STUDY 6: Read Revelation 10-11 and chapters 8 and 9 in the book.

STUDY 6: Revelation 10:1–11:19

AIM: To understand something of the nature of the time between the two comings of Christ.

1. Chapters 10 and 11 form an interlude. Explain what this might mean, and have we seen a similar pattern in previous sections of Revelation?

2. How does the particular interpretation of Revelation 10:6, 'there would be no more delay', help us understand the way in which the New Testament as a whole depicts the age between the first coming of Christ and his second coming? Why is the unfolding of the purposes of God in history described as a 'mystery' in 10:7?

3. Why did the scroll which John ate taste both sweet and sour? John's office as an apostle was unique, but, like him, we are all commissioned to obedience. That being the case, what are some of the sweet and sour things about being a faithful Christian living in this world?

4. Chapter 11 is much debated – what are the various views concerning the time of the events? What perspective does Thomas take? More importantly and various interpretations aside, what is the 'message' of chapter 11? How does it help us be assured of the final victory of God in this world?

5. Explain the significance of the number *42* in 11:2. How is this related to Daniel 9:24 and the prophecy of the 'seventy weeks'? How does 2 Timothy 3:1 help us to make sense of all this?

6. What is it about the two witnesses that resembles the ministry of Elijah and Moses? Why would these two Old Testament characters be significant?

7. Who is Abaddon or Apollyon and the 'beast that rises from the bottomless pit' (11:7, 9:11)? What is the significance of this vision to that of Revelation 19:19–21? Why does the vision mention Sodom, Babylon and Egypt? What does this tell us about the nature of the times in which we live?

FOR STUDY 7: Read Revelation 12 and 13 and chapters 10 and 11 in the book.

STUDY 7: Revelation 12:1–13:18

AIM: To see how these chapters, and particularly Revelation 12, are an interpretative key to unlock the book of Revelation.

1. In what way does this vision of the woman and her battle with the great red dragon help us understand what the book of Revelation is about?

2. What are some of the characteristics of the dragon depicted in chapter 12 and how might that help us live the Christian life today? Who or what is the 'beast . . . out of the sea' as described in Revelation 13:1–10? Who or what is the 'beast . . . out of the earth' as described in Revelation 13:11–18? How are the beasts overcome (this question encompasses chapters 10 and 11 in the book)? How can this encourage Christians today?

3. How are the two sections, 12:1–6 and 12:7–12 related?

4. If verse 13 of chapter 12 depicts the persecution of the church, how does this section bring us a consolation or assurance of victory?

5. How do 1 John 2:18, 1 John 4:1–4 and 2 Thessalonians 2:3–9 help us understand Revelation 13?

6. One of the seven heads of the beast of the sea bears a mortal wound now healed (13:3). How (and why) is this a parody of what is said of Christ in 5:6?

7. Why is it unlikely that the number *666* in Revelation 13:18 is meant to depict a particular individual?

FOR STUDY 8: Read Revelation14:1–15:4 and chapter 12 in the book.

STUDY 8: Revelation 14:1–15:4

AIM: To see how judgment can lead to praise.

1. How does the number *144,000* that appears in chapter 14 (verses 1, 3) relate to the same number in chapter 7 (verse 4) and the number *666* that appeared in chapter 13 (verse 17)? Does the interpretation that *144,000* represents *completeness* sound convincing to you?

2. Three features of the 144,000 are singled out in 14:4, including the idea that they are 'not defiled . . . with women, for they are virgins'. How, on the one hand, do we avoid Augustine's view that there is something inherently sinful about sex and sexuality, and on the other, maintain the view that purity in all relationships is a hallmark of the Christian life?

3. The message of the angel preaching the 'eternal gospel' (14:6–7) was interpreted as being a message of judgment rather than of salvation. How is this good news for the believer? Is there a sufficient emphasis upon judgment in contemporary Christianity?

4. What does the fact that the faithful are described as those 'who keep the commandments of God' (14:12) say about a Christian's attitude to the law?

5. The author says, 'The hope held out for believers is not a rapture from the troubles that lie ahead, but a deliverance through it to the hope that is beyond it in the new heavens and new earth of

the existence to come.' How is this statement contrary to many of the prevailing notions concerning the end times? Which perspective is more biblically realistic and faithful to the witness of Scripture?

6. The reaping scene (14:14–20) describes a harvest which contains the twin ideas of an ingathering (the image of the sickle) and judgment (the image of trampling grapes). How does such a picture relate to the way the Bible speaks of God's love and compassion?

7. How does Psalm 2 help us understand Revelation 14:1–15:4? [see also Revelation 12–13]? What is the effect of this teaching?

FOR STUDY 9: Read Revelation 15:5-16-:21 and chapter 13 in the book.

STUDY 9: Revelation 15:5–16:21

AIM: To grasp the fact that we live in a time of battle.

1. Why is it misguided to view the book of Revelation as a cryptic puzzle to be solved only by the initiated? What is the testimony of the book of Revelation to itself?

2. How are the seven seals and seven trumpets related to the seven bowls of wrath that are poured out in this section of Revelation? Is there a specific difference of perspective between the seven trumpets and the seven bowls? Another commentator has said that trumpets warn of judgment and bowls pour out wrath; does this accord with the author's view?

3. How does the imagery of the Exodus from Egypt help explain the way in which this section of Revelation is written? Who are the three recipients of God's wrath?

4. The fifth bowl is poured upon the 'throne of the beast'. What does this tell us about the relationship of evil (and more especially, Satan) to God? What does it say about how we should view the future?

5. The author says, 'The accomplishment of redemption involves a war against sin and evil.' Another writer has said that the peace (*shalom*) of God means 'God wins, and his enemies are defeated.' Are such statements disturbing? Who suffered such 'defeat' to pay for the sins of Christians (see Galatians 3:13)?

6. The case was made that the Battle of Armageddon (16:16) should be understand figuratively. What did that mean? Can you suggest ways in which this battle is being fought today?

7. The interpretation of the Battle of Armageddon suggested a difficulty for those who saw the future as a 'golden age'. Why is this so?

FOR STUDY 10: Read Revelation 17 and 18 and chapters 14 and 15 in the book.

STUDY 10: Revelation 17:1–18:24

AIM: To understand what the destruction of the wicked will be like.

1. Describe the way in which the Old Testament has established for us an interpretation of the city of Babylon. How is this related to the story of the erection of the tower of Babel in Genesis 11? Why is Babylon described as a 'prostitute' (17:1, 3, 9, 15)? Recalling Calvin's words, that man's mind is a perpetual factory of idols, how does the Bible relate idolatry and prostitution?

2. How does the fact that the beast is described as the one who 'was, is not and is about to rise . . . ' parody something that is said of Jesus Christ (17:8, 10)?

3. The interpretation given of the 'seven kings' of chapter 17 is only valid if Revelation was written after the destruction of Jerusalem in 70 AD. Why is this so? Is it of any importance (consider the Introduction)?

4. Contrast the woman who is identified in the final verse as 'the great city that has dominion over the kings of the earth' (17:18) with the bride of the church as described, say, in Revelation 21:9–14. How do the pictures of these two women help to capture the difference between sin and righteousness?

5. How does Revelation 17:14 help us appreciate once again the major theme of this book?

6. How has the expression, 'After this I saw . . . ' (18:1) been consistently interpreted throughout this book? What does this have to teach us about the structure of Revelation?

7. On the basis of the call given in 18:4 to 'come out' of Babylon, to what extent should Christians separate from the world and worldliness? You may want to consider what Augustine has to say about this in his *City of God* where he tells the story of redemption using the figures of Babylon and Jerusalem.

FOR STUDY 11: Read Revelation 19–20 and chapters 16 and 17 in the book.

STUDY 11: Revelation 19:1–21

AIM: To see the victory of Christ.

1. To what extent does the word 'Hallelujah' convey what is central to all of worship? What does it mean? The judgments of God in chapters 17 and 18 are followed by rejoicing in heaven. How is it possible to rejoice at the judgments of God? Will the redeemed in heaven rejoice over the fate of unrepentant friends and relatives? How could this be so?
2. Outline the significance of the heavenly gathering of the redeemed being described as a 'marriage supper'.

3. The description of the judgment in 19:18 has been described as 'blood-curdling'. How does the idea that Jesus is a Divine Warrior change your understanding of your relationship with him?

4. Revelation chapter 20 is something of a *cause célèbre*. Why is this so? To what extent do 'difficult' chapters, involving several alternative interpretations, affect the way we approach a passage of Scripture?

5. Why is it argued that the binding of Satan described in these verses is something that has already taken place? What are the biblical indicators that this is so? What is the practical effect of this interpretation?

6. Revelation 20 describes the present reign of saints in heaven. How is this so, and to what extent might this message appeal to the first readers of Revelation? How does this provide succour and prompt us to worship? How are Revelation 20:11 and Revelation 1:1 related?

7. At the end of Revelation 20, all of Christ's enemies are destroyed (the beast, the false prophet and Satan). What precisely is the significance of the systematic undoing of all the forces of opposition? How does this pave the way for the new heavens and new earth?

FOR STUDY 12: Read Revelation 21:1-22:5 and chapter 18 in the book.

STUDY 12: Revelation 21:1–22:5

AIM: To obtain a glimpse of what heaven will be like.

1. Can you imagine what the New Jerusalem will look like based on the description given in chapter 21? Consider how the closing chapters of Ezekiel influence Revelation 21. What will be the main differences between life as we know it now and life as it will be then?

2. Outline the use made in this chapter of the symbol of water, particularly as it draws from certain passages in the Old Testament

(in particular, why is the New Jerusalem described as having 'no sea'?). What does this signify about the nature of life in the New Jerusalem?

3. Outline how God's covenant with his people is brought to fulfillment in this chapter?

4. Are there similarities between the description of the New Jerusalem in chapter 21 and the description of Eden in Genesis 2? What do you think this signifies? To what can Christians look forward?

5. It was suggested that the absence of the sun and moon in the new heavens and new earth represented the truth that Christ dominates the landscape of this new existence. But what does that say about the realities of the new earth? Can you begin to describe what it will be like? Does this chapter give you some clues?

6. Would the author of the book agree or disagree with the statement, 'You can be so heavenly minded that you are no earthly good'? What do you think? What can we gain from thinking about heaven? How did this vision of heaven encourage the persecuted believers of the first century? Does the thought of heaven give solace to your soul?

FOR STUDY 13: Read Revelation 22:6-21 and chapter 19 in the book.

STUDY 13: Revelation 22:6–21

AIM: To bring together the teaching of the book of Revelation and consider how the nearness of Jesus' return should effect Christians.

1. What have you learned about the nearness of Jesus' second coming in your study of the book of Revelation? How did John understand the phrase, 'I am coming soon' (22:7, 12, 20)?

2. Revelation 21 pictures a new *city* whereas Revelation 22 pictures a new *garden*. What is the reason for the change? Is it significant? How do the two relate to each other?

3. How do the various interpretations of Revelation depend upon the date 70 AD? Can you begin to list the factors that now govern your own interpretation of this book? Has anything changed in your understanding of Revelation since you began this study?

4. What are main reasons why John came to write this book of Revelation? What do you think the first readers found whenever they heard it read in their local church?

5. The exhortation to obedience (22:7) was interpreted *covenantally*. What exactly does this mean? Are there any other passages in the New Testament that come to mind that suggest the same thing. How does this help us understand the relationship between the Old Testament and the New Testament?

6. The Bible ends with a look forward to the second coming. What part does it play in your daily life? How does an expectation that Jesus is coming again change the way you live your life? Are there factors that change due to the understanding that he is coming 'soon'?

FOR FURTHER READING

The following books are recommended for study of the book of Revelation:

VERN POYTHRESS, *The Returning King: A Guide to the Book of Revelation*, Philipsburg, NJ: Presbyterian and Reformed, 2000.

C. MARVIN PATE (ED), *Four Views on the Book of Revelation*, Grand Rapids, MI: Zondervan Publishing House, 1998.

DARRELL L. BOCK (ED), *Three Views on the Millennium and Beyond*, Grand Rapids, MI: Zondervan Publishing House, 1998.

WILLIAM HENDRIKSEN, *More Than Conquerors: An Interpretation of the Book of Revelation*, London: Tyndale House, 1960.

G. K. BEALE, *The Book of Revelation* (The New International Greek Testament Commentary), Grand Rapids, MI: Eerdmans Publishing Company, 1999.

JAMES B. RAMSEY, *Revelation, An Exposition of the First Eleven Chapters* [1873], reprinted Edinburgh: Banner of Truth, 1977.

CORNELIS P. VENEMA, *The Promise of the Future*, Edinburgh: Banner of Truth, 2000.

The LET'S STUDY Series

If you have enjoyed *Let's Study Revelation* and found it helpful, you will be interested in other titles from this series of books for personal and group Bible Study from the Banner of Truth Trust:

- LET'S STUDY MARK by Sinclair B. Ferguson
- LET'S STUDY LUKE by Douglas J. W. Milne
- LET'S STUDY JOHN by Mark Johnston
- LET'S STUDY ACTS by Dennis E. Johnson
- LET'S STUDY 1 CORINTHIANS by David Jackman
- LET'S STUDY 2 CORINTHIANS by Derek Prime
- LET'S STUDY GALATIANS by Derek Thomas
- LET'S STUDY EPHESIANS by Sinclair B. Ferguson
- LET'S STUDY PHILIPPIANS by Sinclair B. Ferguson
- LET'S STUDY 1 & 2 THESSALONIANS
  by Andrew W. Young
- LET'S STUDY HEBREWS by Hywel R. Jones
- LET'S STUDY 1 PETER by William W. Harrell
- LET'S STUDY 2 PETER & JUDE by Mark Johnston

The books in this series are written in a straightforward way to help ordinary Christians to understand and apply Scripture. They are ideal for personal use or for families and feature additional material for Bible study groups. Please order from your local Christian bookshop, or in case of difficulty from:

THE BANNER OF TRUTH TRUST

3 Murrayfield Road,
Edinburgh EH12 6EL

P O Box 621, Carlisle,
Philadelphia 17013,
USA